The Family CAREbook

A Comprehensive Guide for
Families of Older Adults

Dennis E. Kenny and Elizabeth N. Oettinger,
Editors

Contributors:

Mary Liz Chaffee, R.N.	Julie A. Miller,M.S.W., A.C.S.W.
Dixie Cole, R.N.	Ellen A. Minotti, M.S.W.
Beverly J. Crump, M.Ed.	Kathleen H. Moore, J.D.
Karan Dawson, R.Ph., M.S.	Elizabeth N. Oettinger, M. Div.
Barbara Isenhour, J.D.	Betty L. Pesznecker, R.N., M.N.
Dennis E. Kenny, J.D.	Marty Richards, A.C.S.W.
Diane D. Kenny, J.D.	William C. Severson, J.D.
Joan R. Lewis	Thomas J. Tubbesing, M.D.

Cover Design: Kris Morgan Design
Cover Illustration: Merle Nacht

Published by:

CAREsource Program Development, Inc.
505 Seattle Tower ◆ 1218 Third Avenue
Seattle, Washington 98101-3021
(206) 625-9128

ISBN 1-878866-12-5
Library of Congress Card Catalog Number: 91-72123

Acknowledgements

This book draws on the knowledge and experience of a wide variety of professionals. We wish to thank the book's sixteen contributors whose assistance and insights were critical in preparing the twenty-nine issue discussions that make up *Tabs 1* through *6* and the seventeen forms that comprise *Tab 9*. Biographical sketches for these contributors are found at the end of the index.

We also wish to acknowledge and thank the many other professionals who have read portions of the manuscript for this book and offered their helpful suggestions for its improvement: Lesley Althouse, M.D., geriatrician; T. Gary Connett, J.D., retirement community developer and consultant; Ruth F. Craven, Ed.D., R.N., Associate Professor and Assistant Dean, School of Nursing, University of Washington; Elizabeth Edwards, R.N., M.N., occupational and community medicine practitioner; David L. Glazer, M.H.A.; Sarah J. Goodlin, M.D., geriatrician; Karen Gwilym, R.N., hospital patient services coordinator; Richard A. Klobucher, J.D., fellow, American College of Probate Counsel; Thomas McCormick, D.Min., Department of Medical History and Ethics, School of Medicine, University of Washington; Joyce Prothero, Ph.D., Deputy Director, Northwest Geriatric Education Center,

University of Washington; Betsy R. Schneier, Publisher, Golden Horizons Retirement Housing Guides; and Barbara Wechsler, J.D.

One of the strengths of this second edition of *The Family CAREbook* is the addition to *Tab 7: Resources* of a complete, yet concise, *Directory of State Aging Information Sources.* This practical guide to the "point of entry" for aging issues and resources in each of the fifty states and the District of Columbia was generously provided by the National Association of State Units on Aging and is reprinted here with that organization's permission.

D. Kenny, E. Oettinger, Editors

Table of Contents

☐ TAB 3
Health Issues

☐ TAB 4
Legal Issues

☐ TAB 5
Financial Issues

☐ TAB 6
End of Life Issues

◻ TAB 7
Resources

◻ TAB 8
Glossary

◻ TAB 9
Forms and Family Notes

❏ **TAB 10**
Index

Introduction

When you were younger, members of an older generation took care of you. Mothers, fathers, aunts, uncles, grandparents—every family had its own particular family constellation, but within that context, the older assumed responsibility for the younger. They saw that your basic needs were provided for, that you had food, shelter, medical care, adequate clothing. Beyond that, they provided love and emotional support. They made important decisions on your behalf. They helped you make decisions for yourself. They were caregivers. You were the recipient of their caring.

Now, with the passage of time, those roles of giving and receiving care are changing. Increased longevity in our society means among other things that persons in their thirties, forties, fifties, and beyond are spending a significant proportion of their time and energy caring for those they love who are part of the generation before them.

For some, these new responsibilities lead to a role as primary caregiver—providing day-to-day nursing and personal care, financial management, and other necessary support. For others, responsibilities involve a mix of coordination and support—monitoring health care services, helping to select and manage a living situation suitable for current circumstances, arranging legal and financial affairs.

Being advocates and caregivers for your parents' generation is a challenging and often awkward task. There is no way to avoid the difficulty involved in changing the balance of authority and responsibility between parent and child. It pulls at the emotions of both parties on so many levels. Always the relationship will require sensitivity, love, patience, and a sense of humor. No amount of planning or information can substitute for those qualities of human interaction. But planning, information, and resources can be of help to you and your parents (or other person for whom you are acting as caregiver) as together you negotiate the changes that come with aging. Talking over ahead of time what might be done in various circumstances and what your parents' wishes are will help you and them to act with confidence and caring when the time for decision making arrives. Knowing where to go for help in the midst of changing needs and a complex network of services for older adults can save a lot of time and anxiety. Understanding the options makes for better decisions.

The Family CAREbook is a resource and guidebook for families and older adults as they work and live together and plan for the future. Since the majority of the relationships we address in this book involve adult children and an aging parent or parents, most issues are approached from that perspective and using that terminology. But almost all of the information in *The Family CAREbook* may also be used by those who are or will soon be acting as caregiver, advocate, or care manager for other older persons, such as a spouse, friends, patients, or clients.

The Family CAREbook can be most helpful to families if read and used for the first time when both generations are living independently and enjoying good health. In such situations, it can be a way into helpful conversation about financial or estate planning, what a person wishes done in case of medical emergency or physical or mental incapacity, or what arrangements would be most meaningful when death occurs. Often, family members are reluctant to initiate discussions about illness, loss of independence, and death when none of these circumstances seems imminent. It is almost as if by not talking about them, they can prevent these changes from taking place. But death is a fact of all life. Illness and loss of independence are often a part of growing old. By preparing for these eventualities in advance, family members feel calmer, more in control when a crisis or change of circumstance occurs. Both caregivers and those receiving care feel less vulnerable when they know each others' feelings and preferences, and have talked about a variety of options in advance.

Sometimes it is not possible to make plans in advance. A parent suffers a sudden change of health, and everything is left at loose ends. Something happens which you did not think of when you were planning. This book will also be of help to those who have not had the advantage of prior discussion of issues, those who are making decisions with and for an older person based on their best instincts and judgment in the present moment.

Whatever your particular circumstance, we hope that the resources and information gathered here will assist you to grow in confidence and skill as you assume a more active role as caregiver, advocate, advisor, or care manager for your parents, spouse, another family member, friend, patient, or client.

How to Use this Book

Learning to care for your parents or other older persons will introduce you to many of the issues that influence the lives of older Americans. This book is organized around these issues.

There are twenty-nine issue discussions in all, each suggesting practical steps for identifying and understanding the available options and for selecting what course to follow. Forms have also been included to help you organize your investigation, evaluation, and decision making. These forms are collected under *Tab 9: Forms and Family Notes*, where they may be filled out as you need them and kept together for future reference. *Forms and Family Notes* is also available as a large print, unbound supplement to the book. See *Tab 7: Resources*.

Under *Tab 7* you will find lists of additional resources available to help you. And *Tab 8* is a glossary of words and phrases commonly used in connection with issues affecting older Americans.

How you use this book is a matter of choice and need. Some will want to read it as a primer on caregiving and care management. Others will use it simply as a handy reference tool. Still others will find it a suitable means to prompt and give structure to discussions they may wish to have with parents, relatives, friends, patients, or clients.

Finally, developing the plans and skills covered in *The Family CAREbook* will almost certainly serve as a reminder that time and circumstance wait for none of us. The caring, planning, and awareness of issues that you apply for the benefit of those you care about will also help you lay a solid foundation for your own future.

The Family CAREbook is designed and written to help families understand and respond to the special needs of older adults. It is not intended and should not be used as a substitute for the advice and assistance of a qualified health care, legal, accounting, or financial management professional when such services are needed.

Issue 1

Taking Stock and Looking Ahead

One day you will notice that your parents are aging. You could be shopping with your mother and see that she walks more slowly or has less stamina than she used to have. Your father may stop and rest climbing up stairs because he has developed angina. If a period of months or years has passed since you last visited your parents, you may suddenly be struck with the fact that they look older, grayer, more tired. Such a realization usually occurs for the first time when parents are still living independently and still actively employed, not in need of your immediate help or concern. It is an important moment, however. For the first time you really understand that your parents are getting older, and in the future, instead of their taking care of you, you may need to help care for them.

This is an uncomfortable realization for many adult children. It may be equally uncomfortable for your parents. No one likes to face the fact that age is beginning to be a limitation on energy and activity. It is difficult for many people to adjust to the reality that more of their life is behind them than before them, or that it is time to begin preparing for possible disability or death. This transition time can be an anxious one for all members of a family. However, given good family communication and mutual support, it can also be a time of closeness and enhanced relationship for your parents and you.

This issue deals with the reality of your parents' aging, what it may mean for them, and what it may mean for you. Though we cannot remove the awkwardness of changing roles and expectations, we can offer information about resources and some basic guidelines for caregiving and advocacy which will make this new relationship as easy and untraumatic as possible for all parties.

Sometimes events will intervene which make careful advance preparation impossible. A sudden illness or disability can create a need for immediate response. That possibility is dealt with in other sections of this book. This section will be most helpful for those of you not thrust immediately into full scale caregiving by emergency situations. It assumes that you, your parents, and other significant family members are living independently, and you are looking toward the future together. It provides you with three general rules for helping your parents make the important decisions of their late adult life. For ease of remembering, these rules are titled:

- ✔ Sooner is better than later.
- ✔ Less is better than more.
- ✔ Together is better than alone.

❒ SOONER IS BETTER THAN LATER: THE IMPORTANCE OF PLANNING

Many people find the fact of aging unpleasant or uncomfortable. Because of that, they put off discussions about their preferences in various circumstances until a crisis is upon them. This is the most difficult way of dealing with the decisions aging may mandate. Often it makes for decisions which are hastily made and later regretted.

The best time to begin discussions about the medical, legal, and household aspects of aging is when your parents are in good health and approaching retirement. These discussions should start out being very general. What is your parents' retirement plan? Have they figured out what their post-retirement finances will be? If they are considering a move, what changes will that move necessitate?

Use conversations about your parents' friends' lives to ask some questions about their own preferences. For example, if your mother's best friend has just moved into a retirement home for retired teachers, and your mother says, "I could never live in one of those homes," ask her what alternatives she would prefer. Or if your father tells you about a colleague who has suffered a sudden stroke or heart attack, it may be a way into a discussion about his own preferences for medical treatment in case of emergency or disability.

As you talk with your parents, keep either mental or written notes. Written notes are generally more helpful over time than mental notes, though they obviously require more immediate effort. As you look around in your community, also keep notes on services you think might come in handy some day. You are in essence creating a "database" about both your parents' needs and desires and the options in the community that might help meet those needs and desires. *Tab 9: Forms and Family Notes* can serve as a convenient place to make and retain notes of this kind.

Finally, find some time to talk with siblings or other family members about their perception of your parents' health and well-being. Talk about some hypothetical futures together, and get a sense of the ways of sharing responsibilities that could occur if a need arose. If you do this kind of homework in advance, when the time for decision making comes, you will be better equipped to help.

Some parents will make it easy by initiating or willingly participating in such discussions. They feel more secure knowing that they have done their planning and talking in advance. If your parent is willing, there is some information that is best to have written down. Much of that information can be organized using *Form 1.1: Helpful Personal Information* found under *Tab 9*. Sharing the personal information form with your parents can be a beginning point for discussions about the future.

Other older adults are more reluctant to discuss personal issues. They may be embarrassed or uncomfortable. Such personal conversation may run counter to their sense of privacy and responsibility. They may not want to think about these important issues of aging themselves. Talking with such individuals will require great tact and sometimes painful honesty. Sometimes parents who would rather not discuss important matters for themselves are willing to do so if they realize that it is important to a child's peace of mind. Some will never be comfortable sharing, in which case you, as caregiver, do the best you can with whatever information you have.

In any case, the more information you have in advance, the more you are comfortable talking with your parents about what is happening in their lives, and the more you are in communication with other family members, the better chance there is of making decisions that are well-considered and positive. This holds true whether you are simply listening to and advising your parents or have become the primary decision-maker for them. In both cases, and in the range of possible situations between them, you and your parents will be more confident and comfortable if decisions are made on the basis of full knowledge about their needs and desires.

◻ LESS IS BETTER THAN MORE: RESPECTING YOUR PARENTS' AUTONOMY

Though you want to begin early having discussions with your parents about their changing needs and situation, you also must respect their autonomy as primary decision-makers for themselves and for each other. It is difficult to see your parents doing something which you consider to be a mistake—whether that be a major purchase, a move, or a decision regarding medical care. If your parents are legally competent, it is their privilege to make even bad decisions for themselves, just as it is your privilege to make your own decisions, be they foolish or wise, well considered or abrupt.

If you try to take over your parents' lives while they are still capable of managing for themselves, though perhaps differently and more slowly than you would, you run the risk of diminishing rather than enhancing family trust and cohesion.

Your role in your parents' lives will probably change only gradually. You begin as a person who loves them and who can be a valuable person with whom to talk over decisions. Later, you help collect and organize resources to help them make decisions. Gradually you become a partner in decision making. Only if they are clearly not capable, do you begin to act for them.

There will be times when you or other family members

may want to rush this process, and perhaps for good reasons, but the reality is that the more control your parents maintain over their affairs, the happier, healthier, and more in touch with life they will be. Your job is to be their friend and advocate, to do the things which are difficult or impossible for them, and let them do the rest. In most situations, you will be most effective as a caregiver and care manager if you act in a supporting role, rather than a controlling one.

❒ TOGETHER IS BETTER THAN ALONE: SHARING RESPONSIBILITY

Shared decision making

Involvement in your parents' affairs will usually be most effective if undertaken on a partnership basis. All of us, during our adult lives, depend on significant others when we make important decisions. Whether it be the decision to get married, the decision to change careers, or the decision to sell the family home and move to a retirement community in Florida, we all make better decisions—and feel more comfortable with our decisions—if those decisions are made with the advice and support of those we consider to be our closest family and friends. In significant ways, making decisions in old age is no different from making decisions at any time in adult life.

Your parents will make better decisions if they make those decisions after conversations with you and other close family and friends. If you are the primary decision-maker, you also will make better decisions if you are in conversation with family and friends. The opinions of others add perspective and support to the decision making process. One primary rule of caregiving is to use the resources available to help you, both personal and institutional resources. In that way, you will probably both reduce your anxiety and make better decisions.

Sharing the work

As you look ahead to increased involvement in your parents' lives, it will become increasingly important that you pay attention to three basic realities:

- *What are the limits of your ability to respond to the situation?* All of us are finite, with limited time and energy. Although you love your parents, you may not be able to meet all their needs and still pay adequate attention to your job, your family, your significant commitments and relationships. From the beginning, you need to understand and accept your own limits of involvement. Guilt is a pernicious emotion. It can be imposed from without or within. Before you let yourself feel guilty, consider realistically the limits of your time, your skills, your emotional energy. Do what you can, and feel good about that.

- *Who else can help and what can they do?* Earlier in this issue, we discussed having preliminary conversations with siblings and other relatives about how they might be able to help in a given situation. As your parents need more help, those conversations will become more frequent and less hypothetical. It is important as you move into a caregiving relationship to know who can share the work, and how it might be parceled out so that all of you feel supported and no one feels overwhelmed.

It will not always be possible to come to a completely equitable distribution of tasks, given the geographical and personal limitations of your particular family. If you or another family member takes on the primary caregiving role, organize as much back-up support as possible. Remember there are many agencies and service organizations which serve older adults. Don't be afraid to recruit support services from outside sources.

- *What do you need for yourself?* Taking care of one's parents can be very stressful work. In order to do it well over a period of time, you need to attend to your own needs. Family relationships break down, and sometimes abusive patterns of behavior emerge, when caregivers are overstressed. When you make a commitment to care for your parents, make sure you also commit yourself to getting adequate rest, good food, and time for relaxation. Not only will you stay healthier, but your parents will get better care.

As you look ahead to becoming more involved in your parents' lives, remember that planning, communication, mutual respect, and family support are the keys to loving and effective help. The chapters ahead will give you more specific information on some of the circumstances and resources which will be important to you. The advance preparation done by both your parents and you will help as you work through both the predictable changes and the crises of the future.

Issue 2

Community Overview:
Sources of Help

As the size of America's older population has increased, so have the number and variety of support services available to meet its needs. Some of these services are provided free of charge by public or private agencies, others can be purchased on a sliding fee scale, still others are available primarily on a traditional fee-for-service basis. The number of organizations serving older adults—and how they relate to one another—can be very confusing. This issue describes how the network of services for older adults is organized and how to make it work effectively and efficiently for your parents.

The service network for older Americans has grown quickly and without any overall plan or supervision. As needs have arisen or become widely recognized, organizations have stepped in to respond. Some of these are government agencies; others are private corporations, large and small, profit-making and not-for-profit. What they share is a primary focus on helping older persons live happier, healthier, and longer lives.

In some service areas, agencies compete aggressively with one another for the business of older adults. They advertise extensively in order to let the public know who they are and what services they offer. In some communities, home health care agencies, hospitals, or nursing facilities may be in this category. Other kinds of resources can be difficult to find; sources for them have to be intentionally sought out. Whether you and your parents are comparing agencies or individuals eager to provide a service, or searching for a service that is difficult to locate, understanding the formal and informal aging network will help you succeed in finding the services your parents need, when they need them. This is how the system works.

❐ THE FORMAL SYSTEM OF SERVICES FOR OLDER ADULTS

Senior information and referral

One program that is mandated by Congress and must be available in every area of the country is Senior Information and Referral. In some areas, this program is called "Senior Information and Assistance." The trained advocates who work for this program have information about all programs for older adults in the local area. They know eligibility requirements for the various programs and how to make contacts with services. If an older person is unable to make a contact with a social service program, the advocate at Senior Information and Referral will make the contact for him or her. The advocate also will follow up on all contacts made in order to be sure that the need has been met. If the advocate feels that there are needs that the older person or family has not considered, he or she will try to meet those needs as well. This resource is the best starting point in learning about and connecting with the services in your parents' community which would be appropriate for them.

If you need information or referrals for another part of the country, there is at least one agency in each state that can help you get started. Agency names, addresses, and phone numbers (many of which are toll-free) are listed under *Tab 7: Resources.*

Case management

Case management for older persons is a fairly new service which is becoming available in more and more communities. Case managers are social workers, nurses, and other trained persons who work with older persons and their families to assess services needed, and to make contact with and organize those services. For example, a case manager could work with a family where the parent just had hip surgery to find a suitable nursing home placement during the rehabilitation period, then to move the parent back into the home with appropriate help provided to regain maximum independence as quickly as possible. In another scenario, a case manager could come to your parent's home when he or she no longer feels able to live independently, do an assessment, and recommend suitable housing alternatives. Many older persons and their families are unfamiliar with both the range of alternatives available and the various eligibility requirements that may apply. In these situations, and when caring for a parent who lives a distance away, case managers can be invaluable.

Some state programs provide limited case management services at no charge. There are also private case management services available through either not-for-profit or for-profit agencies. All of these are usually listed with the Senior Information and Referral organization. Even when case management agencies charge for their services, it is often worth the expense if the case manager can match your parent with the appropriate level of care and monitor the situation as it changes.

Nutrition programs

There are three kinds of senior nutrition programs, all of which receive some federal subsidies:

- *Congregate nutrition sites.* These programs serve a balanced hot meal to older adults, usually at midday. Some sites serve meals five days a week, others only serve one or two days. Usually a small donation is requested at these sites. Some of these programs also deliver a hot meal to homebound individuals daily.

- *Home delivered meals.* Also known in many communities as "Meals on Wheels," this program delivers frozen meals once a week to the home of homebound or disabled older adults. Usually the program participant pays for the cost of these meals. If he or she is unable to pay, meals will still be provided.

- *Mobile Market.* Participants in this program may order basic, nonperishable foods and other household supplies at cost. They are ordered over the telephone and delivered to the home once a week.

In some areas, there are private businesses which will provide shopping services for older adults. These businesses ask that orders be called in to them, and delivery is within a day or two. A service fee is charged.

Transportation programs

Some communities have programs that provide transportation services to those who need assistance. These programs may include:

- van services for which a donation is asked or a standard fee-for-service is charged;

- reduced prices on taxi, bus, or rail tickets;

- escort services where a volunteer will pick up the older adult, stay with him or her while a visit to the doctor or dentist is completed, and then provide transportation back home.

Legal assistance

In addition to the private system for delivery of legal services, legal assistance programs for low-income persons typically are provided by nonprofit legal services groups, as well as state and local bar associations. Legal help can be obtained on a reduced fee basis by referral through the bar associations to attorneys participating in these programs. Some communities also sponsor free legal clinics. For more information, see *Tab 4: Legal Issues.*

Home care

Home health care agencies provide help in meeting a wide range of medical and physical care needs in the home. Their services can allow older adults to remain at home in circumstances where they might otherwise have to move into a more institutional setting. Home health care agencies may be either not-for-profit or for-profit businesses. Medicare will pay for some home care services, while others must be paid for by the individual in need of service. For a fuller discussion of home health care, see *Issue 14: Arranging Home Health Care.* Hospice services, which provide supportive medical care and other valuable services for patients and their families in the last few months of a terminal illness, are available in many communities through private agencies or hospital programs. Hospice services are discussed in depth under *Issue 27: Hospice Care.*

Assistance with household tasks, shopping, and other everyday functions may be obtained through chore programs. Some of these are funded through state or federal programs, while others are private agencies. The state will pay the cost of chore services for persons who meet certain income requirements, while those with higher incomes must pay all or a portion of the cost of services. For more information about chore services, see the discussion in *Issue 5: Arranging Support Services for Independent Living.*

Home repair

Some communities have programs which will assist older persons with home maintenance, seasonal weatherization, and needed repairs. Some of these programs are free of charge except for the cost of materials, while others involve a fee based on the older adult's ability to pay.

Housing options

Many family members know of only three options when concerned about housing for an older adult. These are: staying in the family home; moving in with an adult child; and placement in a skilled care nursing facility. Sometimes, none of these options is the best for the older adult or for the other family members.

Other living arrangements include:

- Home sharing,
- Retirement home or community,
- Senior or low-income housing,
- Group living in a boarding home or adult family home,

- Residence in a congregate care facility,

- Residence in an intermediate care facility.

These options become progressively more expensive as they provide the older adult with more individual or skilled care. All of these alternatives are discussed in some detail in *Tab 2: Household Issues*.

Respite programs

In many communities, programs are available to provide a primary caregiver with temporary relief from caregiving duties. These options include adult day programs, temporary beds in nursing homes, and in-home respite by a paid worker. Many adult day programs have a sliding fee scale, but the availability of other options will vary according to both the resources available in your parents' community and your parents' ability to pay for services.

Reassurance programs

Some communities have either public or private reassurance programs. In these programs, a call is made to the client each day to assure that he or she is all right. Some programs will call several times a day to remind an older adult to take medication at the appropriate time. The Lifeline program is also available in many communities. With this service, the subscriber wears a medallion that will send a signal to a central station when activated. By simply touching the medallion in the signal area, help is called. Most Lifeline programs are stationed in hospitals staffed twenty-four hours a day. There is a monthly fee for this service.

Support groups

Support groups are available both for older adults facing a variety of concerns and health problems and for caregivers and other family members. A support group can provide a place to share concerns and meet others who are coping with similar problems. These groups are particularly helpful to those who are experiencing stressful changes of life through disease or loss and those caring for family members who have impaired thinking or chronic debilitating diseases.

Information about any of the above programs may be obtained by calling Senior Information and Referral.

☐ THE INFORMAL SYSTEM OF SERVICES FOR OLDER ADULTS

The preceding sections have dealt with formal systems and services which can provide help to your parent and to you. However, there are resources outside of these formal agencies which can be very helpful. We call these resources the informal system. Families often forget to look to the informal system for help when an older family member needs assistance. The informal system includes peripheral family members—those whom you may not see too often such as nieces or nephews— neighbors, friends, or community organizations such as the church, the girl or boy scouts, or service clubs. A neighbor may check on your parent each day and pick up bread and milk at the grocery store. Someone from a community service organization may be willing to do yard work, or church members may provide some help with meals, transportation, or household chores.

People are often willing to help, but are afraid to offer for fear of offending. Many are busy and may not have

even noticed that there is a need. Sometimes it is helpful to have a family meeting to discuss care options. You
could also make an appointment to see your parents'
pastor or closest neighbors to see what services they
think the informal network can provide. The great
advantage of the informal network is that it is personal.
It can provide companionship and real personal caring
more easily than the formal system.

❐ MEETING THE CHALLENGE OF WORKING WITH LARGE AGENCIES

Older people or family members often are reluctant to
obtain needed services because of problems in coping
with large agencies. These agencies may seem bureau-
cratic and intimidating to some people. Here are a few
suggestions that may help:

- Before calling an agency, gather all of the information you think you will need. This usually will
  include your parents' Social Security and Medicare numbers (It is a good idea to keep those
  numbers in your wallet or datebook in case of
  emergencies).

- Your first call to the agency should be brief and
  to the point. Often, the first person with whom
  you speak will not be the one who can help you.
  This person only needs to know enough to direct
  your call. Sometimes, the person you want to
  speak with will have to call you back. When you
  reach the appropriate person, be as specific as
  possible about the services you are interested in.

- If you do not get the help you need immediately,
  don't become angry or give up. Explain your
  problem as many times as is necessary. Often,
  agencies have a number of departments, each one

with limited jurisdiction. It may take you a while to reach the spot where both you and the agency think there is a match between the services they offer and what you need.

- Be sure to write down the name of every person with whom you speak and what information was provided by that individual. Make note of the date and time of each call. You can use *Tab 9: Forms and Family Notes* to keep track of this information.

- Be patient. Large agencies move slowly at times. Be prepared to wait for services to be started. If your situation is an emergency, let the worker know this. Often temporary services can be put into place until regular arrangements are made.

- It is sometimes better to call on certain days or at certain times of the day. For example:

  ✻ if possible, avoid calling the Social Security office during the first week of the month;

  ✻ call agencies between 8 and 10 in the morning or right after lunch; many of the workers are out in the field much of the day;

  ✻ it is best to call in the middle of the week rather than trying to reach a worker on Monday or Friday.

- If you have not been able to get the response that you need from an agency, contact the agency supervisor or an advocacy service such as Senior Information and Referral.

- Never feel that you are asking for charity by approaching agencies to fill the needs of the older adult. Remember that taxes paid in past years have helped create the system of services provided now.

◻ GETTING YOUR PARENTS TO ACCEPT HELP

Some caregivers find that older family members resist any effort to bring in outside help. The aging person feels that the help received from the caregiver is all that is needed, even though the caregiver may feel greatly overburdened. Older people often feel very uncomfortable when strangers come into their home. Here are some hints to help reduce resistance to the introduction of new services:

- In the best of all cases, your parents will initiate the search for outside help. A neighbor or a trusted primary physician may be able to bring up the idea with a parent first, and thus make the idea seem more attractive.

- Learn all you can about the possible service before talking about it with your parent. Know what the costs are and how they might be paid.

- Introduce only one change at a time. Give the person you are helping time to adjust to a new service before another is added.

- Assure your parents that you still care about them. Try to help them understand that even though you can no longer provide all the care they need, you will be there and support them.

As you begin to work with the loose-knit web of services available in your particular community, you will meet people who are very helpful to you and others that you find not so helpful. Keep track of those who are helpful. They may be able to assist you in other areas. There is a lot of informal networking among senior service providers. Once you find good people in the system, it becomes easier to find additional help as it is needed.

Issue 3

Providing Support and Care Management at Long Distance

In previous decades, it was common for families to remain in the same community generation after generation. As children grew up, they married and found jobs in the same town, or at least in the same region where they grew up. It was not uncommon for the family home to remain in the family from one generation to the next and to house three or even four generations within it at any given time.

Shorter distances made it easier for families to remain close. Responsibilities such as child care and care for aging family members could be shared more easily. Families were also larger in those days, making it easier to spread responsibility for various tasks.

Today, we live in a more mobile society. Families are often spread out geographically because of employment, educational opportunities, marriage, and choice. Family members stay in touch by letter, phone, and occasional visits. When a loved one far away needs support or assistance, or when a crisis occurs, family members face a problem. They want to help, yet distance becomes an obstacle. This chapter addresses the issue of long distance support and care management for older parents. It discusses the essential elements of a strategy for overcoming distance and separation by carefully assessing the circumstances with which you are dealing and working together with friends, relatives, and professional service providers to coordinate appropriate care.

❐ ASSESSING THE SITUATION

Distance and physical separation are circumstances to be understood and accepted in your relationship with your parents. It is natural to feel overwhelmed or even guilty when a crisis occurs in the life of a parent far away. However, except in rare instances, the problem of distance is not going to change. A positive commitment to making the most of available skills and resources serves better than regrets or guilt over the limitations imposed by distance.

Being involved means first of all staying informed. Gathering and sharing information requires effective communication skills within the family. Candid discussions of changing circumstances and emerging concerns need to be supported and encouraged among all family members and specifically between close family members and your parents. As concerns arise, information on available resources should be collected, organized, shared, and used.

When shared information is limited to phone or letter contacts, it may not be readily apparent that parents need help. They may be reluctant to acknowledge personal problems, especially problems caring for each other, or may not want to worry the family. Obtaining more complete information will be the first task in determining when and what help is required.

While your parents may not request help directly, you may be alerted to existing or potential problems indirectly by changes in their living situation or in their behavior. For example, if your mother's regular Sunday phone calls become infrequent or irregular, you should check to find out why. Red flags which could signal the need for help include a major change in behavior patterns, recent death of a spouse, increased health problems or injuries, serious memory impairment, or loss of interest in previously enjoyed activities.

Information can come from many sources. If an older adult or couple seems to be experiencing serious difficulties, it is not unusual for friends, neighbors, apartment managers, or others concerned about their well-being to try to contact a family member. If your parents live in an apartment, find out who is the manager and contact that person every month or two. If you have reason to be concerned about a parent's memory, check to see if the rent is being paid on time. Discuss any concerns about safety. Give the apartment manager your phone number to call in case of emergency or if he or she thinks there is something you ought to know.

If your parent lives alone, keep up to date on the names and telephone numbers of some good neighbors, and have the name and telephone number of at least one person who sees your parent frequently. If you suspect a change in your parent's condition, call the friend or neighbor. These informal contacts can be a good supplement to family phone communication if handled sensitively. Generally, it makes sense to let your parents know you have these phone numbers available; ideally, you would get them to suggest who the best contacts might be. Most parents understand and appreciate that you would want the number of someone close at hand to call in case of a known or suspected emergency. It might make your parents feel more secure as well.

If you call the neighbors just to check on things, don't

suggest trouble unless you really are concerned about something. If you have a specific concern, be as concrete about it as possible. "I worry about whether taking care of my dad is becoming too much for Mom." Or "Mother seems depressed recently. Have you noticed anything?" In the absence of any specific observations on your part, listen to how the neighbors talk about your parents. Just casual conversation may bring to light circumstances needing attention. These same problems may be the ones which are most difficult for your parents to identify or discuss with you. Inadequate self-care, poor home management, or decreased ability to handle personal business are examples of these types of problems.

❒ ASSESSING YOUR FAMILY STRENGTHS AND WEAKNESSES

When parents need help, and other family members consult about it, there are often unresolved family agendas which get in the way of effective helping. Revisiting and reopening long-standing family issues of sibling rivalry, parental favoritism, and other family problems during the last months or years of a parent's life is a common trap into which adult children fall. The best way to minimize such problems is to be aware of their possibility and avoid them consciously. Work with your siblings and other involved family members to focus your interactions around your parents' needs, not other family business. If necessary, have a friend or professional counselor meet and talk with you to move the discussion along.

There are often good reasons why family disputes arise when trying to organize long distance care for parents. For example, the child who lives closest to home may not be the most capable child, and may not have the best relationship with the parents. Now that child feels responsible for major caregiving or care management responsibilities. Another sibling far away may be the one with whom the parents have had the most discussion; however, that child is less able to provide or organize care on a regular basis.

You probably are not going to change many of these basic dynamics in your family. However, you can be realistic in assessing who really is in a position—geographically, financially, and emotionally—to help. Try not to let caring for parents degenerate into an emotional battle between family members. It helps to recognize going into the caring role that some people are going to give more than others. Often, there is not much that can be done to correct this inequity of involvement. However, much can be done in terms of support and affirmation. Those carrying the major responsibility for managing or providing care need both help and appreciation. Do what you can do, and support those who are doing the rest. You want to avoid looking back on your parent's last months with regrets over tension, anger, or frustration within the family. At that point, there is nothing you can do—now, there is a lot you can do.

❐ DEVELOPING A FAMILY STRATEGY FOR HELPING

Pulling together when you can't be together is a significant challenge for any family, even when long-standing family issues are left out of it. Once a need for help develops, everyone should be part of the process of arranging care and dividing responsibilities. Strategies for sharing responsibilities are discussed in *Issue 1: Taking Stock and Looking Ahead*. For persons functioning at a distance, it is particularly important to communicate well and to share in problem solving. You may want to develop a written cooperative care plan. Then make copies of the plan and send them to all family members, so everyone remembers his or her role. Find ways to check in with each other and to support each other. Remember that your family, like all people, functions best when contributions to the common cause are affirmed and appreciated.

The need for help often will be uncovered by a family member who lives close enough to visit occasionally or who, in fact, has already assumed some responsibility for caregiving or care management within your family. Sometimes, there is the implicit expectation that that close-by family will provide all the necessary help. Such an expectation is unfair and may lead to resentment and conflict. If you are that local caregiver, ask for the help you need. If the local person is someone other than yourself, make sure that person is feeling all right about responsibilities taken on. At the very least, be supportive and appreciative. See if there are things which you can do to help. If outside professional help is needed, let the primary caregiver know that you support such an option.

Always keep in mind that it is important to include your parents in arranging for their care. It is easy for concerned family members to think they perceive a need and go about fixing it without asking those involved if they perceive the same need. In helping your parents with decisions about appropriate services and resources, you will want to encourage them to identify those friends and neighbors who can be counted on to help if needed. This may be especially productive if your parents have been long-time residents in their community. Perhaps they have ties with a local church, social club, or senior center. Residents of apartment buildings or a retirement community may have a network of neighbors who are able to check on one another, help with running errands, and provide some transportation.

If there is no family in the immediate area, it is particularly important to identify at least one emergency contact person in your parents' community. It helps to establish a regular relationship with this person in advance of a crisis. Such a relationship can both uncover important information about your parents' day-to-day circumstances and establish a line of communication in case of a crisis.

Once a need for a certain kind of help has been established and the key helpers identified, the next step is examining alternatives to meet the needs. There are some important points to remember when working with your parents to develop an appropriate care plan.

- *First,* include your parents in the decision-making process. The best laid plans are of no value if your parents do not accept them.

- *Second,* support your parents' maximum level of independence. Their sense of self-esteem and dignity is best maintained if they remain as active as possible.

- *Third,* establish priorities. It may not be possible to find solutions to every problem identified. Select those that warrant attention first.

- *Fourth,* set realistic goals. Despite your efforts, you may not always be rewarded with dramatic improvements in your parents' situation.

❏ FINDING AND DRAWING ON COMMUNITY SOURCES OF HELP

Gaining access to community services and resources for

older adults can be a formidable task for the out-of-town relative. Without knowledge of local agencies and programs, an individual is at a serious disadvantage in making connections. For this reason, referral agencies and case management services should be considered as a primary resource.

Creating Closeness in Spite of Distance

Sometimes, small things contribute to a sense of being in touch. For example:

* Old-fashioned letter writing is never out of style. Take the time to bring your parent up-to-date in this way. Encourage others in the family, including grandchildren, to write letters, make audio or video cassettes, or send photos to your parents.

* Make it easier for your parents to respond by pre-addressing and stamping envelopes to yourself and other members of the family. Provide your parents with a supply of greeting cards for all occasions and a calendar identifying major celebrations within the family.

* Anticipate that gift buying may be difficult and yet important. Call ahead with gift suggestions that respect your parents' financial situation. If you are aware of wedding and baby announcements you are both receiving, suggest a joint gift that you will take care of.

* Get in the habit of calling or having your parents call on a regular basis. If you can afford it, encourage your parents to call "collect"—make this an annual gift to your parents.

Senior information and referral services

Senior Information and Referral is a federally mandated information network of services for older adults. Telephone information services are available in most areas. The goal of this network is to establish a "single entry system," in which one agency serves as the point of access for all the available assistance programs in that particular area. You may call the Senior Information and Referral number in your own community for a referral to the counterpart agency in the community in which your parent lives.

Public case management programs for older adults

Case management programs have been developed nationally to coordinate diverse services and resources for frail, vulnerable older adults who are at risk of institutionalization. Although programs are administered differently in different regions, they all aim to provide services primarily to low-income adults over 60 years of age who have multiple service needs and limited family support. Case management services usually include: comprehensive assessment by a social worker; development of a service plan; implementation of this plan; and subsequent reassessment of the older person's situation after support services have started.

For the out-of-town relative seeking help, such case management services can be invaluable. Professionals with an extensive knowledge of the network of senior services can readily gain access to appropriate services and resources. Also, as a public program, there is no fee for these services. There are limitations, however, including financial and other restrictions on who is eligible for services and how much time can be allotted to work with each client.

Hospital discharge planning

If an older adult has been hospitalized, a hospital discharge planner, typically a social worker or a nurse, is usually available to assist the older patient and family in arranging for needed home support services or admission to a care center. The focus of this short-term assistance, however, will be on expediting discharge from the hospital. Long-range planning will remain the responsibility of the patient and the patient's family.

Private case management services

In addition to public programs and hospital discharge services, there are a growing number of private practitioners and businesses that provide care planning and service coordination to older adults and their families. The type of assistance provided can include service brokerage, care monitoring, guardianship, and other options. Fees are usually based on an hourly rate of between $40 and $60 per hour.

If your parents have purchased long-term care insurance policies, case management services may be a benefit included as part of the coverage. The insurance company will contract with a service provider or agency. Check your parents' coverage to see if this is an option.

If you are going to use case management services, you will want to consider the following factors in evaluating your choices:

- *Qualifications.* If you are contracting for services with a private case manager, be aware that there is no regulatory agency overseeing qualifications or competency. Ask about experience and education. Request references.

- *Affiliations.* Some service providers are affiliated with a particular company or group of services. In such cases, referrals may be directed to these associated services, even though other more attractive options exist.

- *Range of Services.* Be sure to check out the specifics of services to be provided. For example, will a case manager simply arrange support services with minimal follow-up, or will there be regular face-to-face meetings with your parents to monitor the situation after services are provided?

- *Cost.* Make sure you understand the fees charged and what they cover. Are the fees competitive with other case management services in your parents' area?

Use *Form 3.1: Checklist for Selecting a Private Case Management Professional* under *Tab 9* to help organize your selection efforts.

❒ MAKING THE MOST OF THE TIME YOU HAVE TO GIVE

Making the most of the time you devote to long distance support and care management for your parent or parents means structuring your efforts in ways that produce the most effective results. Here are some simple hints:

- Prepare ahead of time for your visits. Find out from family members, neighbors, or the private case management professional whether changes have occurred since your last visit and whether unaddressed needs exist. If there are tasks to be handled, allow enough time during your visit for them and arrange scheduling to coincide with the availability of resource persons with whom you will need to speak.

- Ask your parents before your visit if they have particular needs or goals in mind. This way you will not be surprised when you arrive to find an unexpected chore or need awaiting you.

- Be willing to say no. You can't do it all. It takes tact and objectivity to know when and how to refuse to become involved. Get in the habit of using your time and skills in ways that make sense and that lead to a positive contribution, but do so within the framework of a realistic care plan. Once responsibility for a task is accepted, it's important to fulfill that task.

Developing skill in long distance caring is one of the most important issues for many adult children of aging parents. Through planning, organization, effective communications, and family teamwork, the problems of physical separation can be overcome. Many community resources are available to assist those families who know when and how to ask.

2 Household Issues

Issue 4

Making the Home a Safer and More Convenient Place for Older Adults

This issue focuses on the importance of safety and convenience in a household in which there are older adults. It does not matter whose household. It could be your home if your parents live with you, or the family home in which you grew up and your parents still live. It could be an apartment or condominium to which your parents have just recently moved. Whatever the setting, there are four basic areas of concern relating to home safety and convenience:

✔ Has the home been made as safe as possible for older persons? Have precautions been taken to prevent accidental injury?

✔ Has the risk of fire been minimized? Would your parents be able to respond safely and quickly if a fire were to occur in the home?

✔ Have appropriate home security and crime prevention measures been taken? Do your parents feel secure in their home?

✔ Is their home a convenient, comfortable, and warm place for your parents to live?

☐ THE CONCERN FOR SAFETY

Most young and middle-aged adults tend to take for granted personal safety and convenience in their homes. When you were a child, your parents set up gates and railings to prevent you from falling. They covered electrical wall outlets and placed small objects out of your reach. By the time you were six or seven years old, you probably no longer needed special precautions. Now, as an adult, the details of your household surroundings are a matter of second nature. You don't think about them much. When a problem arises, you address it in time. If household security becomes an issue, there may be new locks or a security system to consider. If a walkway cracks and becomes unsafe, you repair it or arrange to have it repaired. Or you may even decide just to live with it for a while. Accident prevention is not a major preoccupation.

That sense of ease with things as they are often continues in a household with aging adults, though statistics tell us it should not. Each year more than 3 million Americans over the age of 65 are involved in accidents. The risk of death caused by accident is 3-1/2 times greater for persons over age 75 than it is for the population at large. In fact, accidents are the seventh leading cause of death among older adults in the United States.

Accidents in the home are most frequently caused by commonplace circumstances, conditions that are not usually viewed as creating a significant risk for young or middle-aged adults. Stairs without adequate lighting or handrails; showers or tubs without grab bars; worn carpeting and slippery or uneven floors—these are the common culprits in causing older adults to fall and injure themselves.

Accidents from these and similar causes are preventable. This is what is required.

> *First,* a conscious effort to understand the special needs of older adults due to changes in physical agility, sense of balance, strength, eyesight, and other physical limitations;

> *Second,* an evaluation of your parents' current living space, most effectively conducted by you and your parents together doing a thorough walk-through of the home and noting desirable changes;

> *Third,* follow up on the changes you noted during your evaluation. This could be as simple as you spending an afternoon in your parents' home with a few basic tools and supplies, or it might involve arranging for some professional assistance.

❏ PREVENTING ACCIDENTS

The efforts you and your parents put into home safety should be organized around three important principles:

1. *Don't ever take safety for granted.* Even after an initial evaluation and response, you will have to keep alert. Needs and conditions change. Your parents' physical condition will change over time, making them more susceptible to certain kinds of injury. They or other persons may unintentionally create unsafe conditions at home; for example, placing or temporarily storing items on walks or stairways, or leaving floors wet and slippery. You and your parents should therefore make *both* an initial home safety assessment *and* regular follow-up checks every twelve months or

more frequently in the years to come.

2. *Practicing safety should never be passive.* Working on safety in your parents' home should be something that you do *with* them, not *for* them. Everyone in the family, especially children who will be visiting or living in the same home with your parents, should know what the safety limits are and be sensitive to potential problems. For example, leaving small toys on the floor is inconvenient anywhere. However, it might create a real hazard at Grandmother's house.

Sometimes you will run up against conditions that cannot be corrected, or would be extremely difficult or expensive to correct. Discuss those conditions with your parents and work out with them a strategy for coping.

3. *The most common household accidents involving the elderly are falls in bathrooms and on stairways.* Start by identifying needs in those areas, then move on to the rest of the home.

Every home has its own structural and functional idiosyncracies. However, here are some of the major points to cover in any household safety assessment. These items are repeated in *Form 4.1: Household Safety and Convenience Checklist* under *Tab 9.*

Bathroom

✔ Horizontal and vertical grab bars are securely fastened to end and inside walls above tub or to walls of shower. Also consider installing a fixed or portable bench or seat in the tub or shower.

✔ Nonskid surfaces are applied to the bottom of the tub and shower.

✔ Water temperature in the hot water heater does not exceed 120 degrees.

✔ Floor surfaces are kept dry. Make sure that showers, sinks, and tubs do not leak water onto the floor.

Interior stairways and landings

✔ Handrails are installed on both sides of stairways.

✔ Lighting is adequate.

✔ Floor coverings are in good repair—no tears, bumps, wrinkles, or folds.

✔ All traffic areas are free of clutter and stored items.

Having checked these two most crucial areas, you are now ready to go on to the rest of the home.

Bedroom

✔ Nightlights provide low-level illumination of traffic areas.

✔ Unnecessary and awkwardly placed furniture is removed.

Kitchen

✔ The kitchen floor is kept dry. Sinks and appliances have been checked to see that they don't leak.

✔ Counters and appliances have been checked for sharp metal edges which could cause cuts or scrapes.

Other living spaces

✔ Throw rugs are removed or securely anchored.

✔ All floor coverings are kept in good repair.

✔ All traffic areas are adequately lighted.

Exterior walkways, stairs, and landings

✔ Lighting is adequate.

✔ Walking surfaces are kept free of moss, wet leaves, debris, snow, and ice.

❐ FIRE SAFETY

Fires are often caused by forgetfulness. A small appliance is left on and forgotten, or a cigarette or pipe is left somewhere where it can fall and ignite a rug or chair. Because forgetfulness is one of the predictable problems older adults face, fire is a significant risk to their health and safety. Any home safety assessment should therefore include items relating to fire prevention, warning, and escape. The following are basic fire safety precautions:

✔ The home should be equipped with an adequate number of well-placed smoke detectors/alarms. Batteries in these should be checked regularly.

✔ Hazardous materials (including combustible matter and flammable substances such as old paints and thinners) should be removed or stored safely.

✔ Fire safe extinguishers can be placed in kitchen and hallways. Like smoke alarm batteries, fire extinguishers need to te checked at regular intervals.

- ✔ Check for overloaded outlets or extension cords; see that electical wiring and appliance cords and connections are in good repair

- ✔ Electical appliances should be checked and in good working order; if safe use of appliances is a concern, look into the availability of appliances with automatic shut-off switches and other similar safety features

- ✔ Heavily used chimneys and flues need to be cleaned periodically.

- ✔ Escape routes from upper and lower floors in case of fire should exist and be periodically reviewed and understood.

❑ SECURITY AND CRIME PREVENTION

Unfortunately, older adults are an easy target for burglary and assault. Statistically, they are victimized more frequently than other age groups in the population. Because of that reality, many older persons living alone feel vulnerable. Here are several points to check:

- ✔ Doors and windows should be in good working order and capable of being securely locked.

- ✔ Exterior lighting should be ample. Shrubbery should be cut back or removed to improve visibility from the street and the neighbors.

- ✔ All exterior doors should have view holes.

- ✔ There should be a bedside phone for use in an emergency.

- ✔ Emergency numbers should be clearly written out and taped visibly to the side of the phone.

❏ IMPROVING CONVENIENCE AND
   LIVABILITY

Your parents' changing needs in the home relate to items of convenience and comfort, as well as safety and security. As you and your parents evaluate how to make the home safer and more secure, be on the lookout for conditions that, although perhaps not unsafe, are nevertheless awkward: a telephone with a cord that doesn't quite reach where it should; the main floor den or guest bedroom that your parent would find more convenient than the bedroom upstairs; a favorite sitting area that is inadequately heated or drafty in the winter.

Your parents themselves may not be fully conscious of these annoyances and discomforts. Even if they are aware of them, they may not bring them up in discussion for fear of bothering you. Be clear in your willingness to help. Here are some items to check for:

✔ The telephone should have a lighted face and be portable or conveniently located.

✔ Lighting should be adequate in all frequently used rooms.

✔ Weatherization should be adequate to prevent drafts.

✔ Beds and chairs should be firm and high enough to get into and out of with ease.

✔ Door handles and other knobs and pulls should be easy to grasp and operate.

One caution: modifying your parents' household for reasons of convenience—or even safety—should not be done without their permission and approval. It is *their* home. Make suggestions. Be concerned. Be willing to help. But remember, what seems inconvenient to you may be comfortable to your parent. Sometimes, familiarity is more important than convenience to an older person. There is a delicate balance between helping and taking over. Your parents, like you, need to be in charge of their surroundings as fully as possible. Work on safety and convenience together with your parents. In that way you will be improving their quality of life.

Issue 5

Arranging Support Services for Independent Living

If your parents are living independently, chances are they will prefer to continue doing so, even as the ordinary tasks of running a household become more difficult for them. There are significant advantages for your parents and for you, as one who is concerned about them, if they stay in their home. This issue covers the services and resources available to your parents to assist and support them as they continue to live in their own home.

❏ WHY STAY AT HOME?

Few people want to leave a home which is comfortable and familiar. Older adults in particular are usually emotionally tied to the place they call home. That home may be a large and now empty house, a downtown condominium, or a small apartment in a changing neighborhood. But if it feels like home, chances are your parents will not want to move unless they are incapable of functioning in that environment.

There are important plusses to remaining in the place called home. Usually, if parents have lived in a neighborhood for a significant period of time, they have friends there, people with whom they interact socially and who can be counted on to help in small or large ways in facilitating daily living. The neighbor who always brings the morning paper upstairs, the friend who stops in for coffee twice a week, the young family next door who enjoy having surrogate grandparents and who notice if your parents are out and around every day—all these people are part of a significant system of support difficult to duplicate. Such a web of relationships keeps your parents' lives interesting, provides necessary stimulation, and can be a help in monitoring your parents' safety and physical and emotional well-being.

Even though you may have anxieties about a parent or parents living alone, chances are they will be happier and healthier living at home as long as possible. The following sections provide information about the services available which will allow your parents to remain in their home as long as possible and enhance their quality of life there.

❏ KNOWING WHEN TO GET HELP

If you are like most children whose older parents are living on their own, you will both want to support them in living autonomously as long as possible, and worry about their well-being living alone. As persons grow older, the chores necessary for maintaining any size household become more difficult. You may notice a gradual change in how daily tasks of living—such as yard maintenance, housecleaning, food purchase and preparation, or personal hygiene—are being handled. An accident or illness may occur, and as a result you become concerned about your parent's ability to return to the routine of living independently. Often when a parent is living with a spouse or friend, one of the two becomes ill or disabled, and the extra burdens of that illness or disability make support services necessary.

No matter what the circumstances of observing that additional help is required, there is a simple three-step strategy for figuring out what services would be most helpful in your parents' particular situation.

1. *Make a needs list.* The first step involves sitting down with your parents and preparing a complete list of household upkeep and daily living needs. The best way to approach this is to look at all the things that need doing and then group them according to who can be responsible for each task (your parent, you, another family member, a friend, or an outside helper). This way you and your parents will be able to focus on specific needs and how they are or are not being met.

   Tasks to consider include:

   daily needs—
   - ✔ food preparation and clean-up
   - ✔ personal hygiene
   - ✔ straightening up

   weekly or periodic needs—
   - ✔ grocery shopping
   - ✔ housecleaning
   - ✔ washing and ironing clothes

   quality of life needs—
   - ✔ transportation to and from church, social events, hair appointments, etc.
   - ✔ purchasing clothes and other needed items

✔ visiting and entertaining friends

seasonal needs—

✔ yard maintenance

✔ weatherization

✔ snow and ice removal

Each family's needs assessment will be different, depending on the type of independent living situation involved and the capabilities and desires of the parent or parents involved.

In conducting your needs assessment, try to discern if your parents are being realistic in their evaluation of tasks which they can take on. Some parents, out of a sense of embarrassment or pride, will indicate their willingness and ability to perform tasks which are in fact difficult or impossible for them to do. Be sensitive to your parents' need to maintain self-respect even as they lose some degree of autonomy. Also, be aware that a realistic needs assessment is not a one-time process, but a continuing one.

At the other end of the spectrum is the parent who is depressed—unfortunately a common problem for older adults—and underestimates his or her ability to perform daily tasks. It is important for your parents to continue to do the household chores which they can do, in order to maintain physical strength and agility, as well as a sense of mental and emotional well-being.

2. *Establish an agreed set of goals and procedures.* Once your parents indicate areas of need, work with them to fill those needs. If it is realistic to get the necessary support from family and friends, and

your parents agree, you can offer to coordinate that help or assist your parents in doing so. Sometimes, a family conference or meeting is helpful under these circumstances, with all the involved parties present. That way everyone knows who is responsible for what, and you begin to build a feeling of cooperation and mutual support. In setting up family support, it is important to let your parents set the parameters—descriptions of tasks to be done and how frequently, what a convenient schedule might be, how each person might be involved.

If it looks like outside help will be desirable or necessary, encourage your parents to be involved in recruiting and supervising the service provider. Your continued involvement will be necessary, sometimes to do the "legwork" involved in arranging outside services, sometimes just to provide moral support and affirmation of your parent as he or she works the system. Sometimes, the circumstances may warrant your being the primary person to both arrange and supervise outside help.

3. *Be aware of the services offered in your parents' community.* As you and your parents address the issue of outside services, it is obviously important to know what kinds of help are available in their community and how much those services cost. Support services for older persons living independently will vary widely from community to community. The most important and most widely available forms of help are listed in the next section.

❏ SERVICES AVAILABLE TO SUPPORT INDEPENDENT LIVING

The following are helpful services available in most communities, which may allow your parents to remain in their home with outside assistance.

- ✔ *Home delivery of groceries and prescriptions* is often available, if getting out to shop is a problem.

- ✔ *Meals on wheels and hot lunch programs* can help to assure good nutrition and reduce or eliminate the burden of food preparation.

- ✔ *Senior vans and cabulance transportation programs* may be available to provide low cost transportation to medical appointments, church services, or community centers.

- ✔ *Adult day care and senior center programs* offer opportunities to mix socially with other people outside the home.

- ✔ *Yard upkeep and major housecleaning* are often available on an as needed or continuing maintenance basis. These services are typically provided in blocks of two to eight hours at a cost of from $5 to $10 per hour.

- ✔ *Housekeeping/escort service* usually does cleaning, laundry, and shopping and transports the older person on errands or to appointments. Costs run to an average of $6 to $12 per hour, with services typically provided during scheduled visits lasting from two to four hours.

- ✔ *Personal care aides* will provide light housekeeping and errand service, and will help with safe bathing, meal preparation, and supervision of medications. Personal care aides can be found for full

Personal and Household "Adaptations"

Many tasks of daily living can be simplified by using tools, articles of clothing, and other items adapted to meet the special needs of older persons. Examples include:

✔ stove knobs, cabinet pulls, and door knobs and latches shaped for use by someone with arthritis or poor eyesight;

✔ eating utensils that are weighted or have large handles for better control and comfort;

✔ items of clothing with snaps or zippers in place of buttons; shoes that slip on or have velcro in place of laces;

✔ convenience tools such as "reachers" for picking up things and reducing the need to bend over and stoop.

Sources for items such as these are listed under *Tab 7: Resources.*

or part-time help; compensation is generally between $8 and $16 per hour.

✔ *Attendant care service* means a live-in helper who does all that a personal care aide does, but on a 24-hour basis. Live-in help can be difficult to find, and there is usually a need to hire a relief person as well, unless family members or friends are available to cover during the attendant aide's time off. Attendant care ranges from $50 to $100 per day in cost and brings with it the adjustment of having someone else living in the house. However, a well-matched aide whose company your parent enjoys can be a source of support and companionship for your parent as well as personal care.

❏ FINDING SATISFACTORY HELP

The best place to start a search for these kinds of help is your parents' local Senior Information and Referral number. The yellow pages of the telephone book will also contain listings under "housekeeping," "home health services," and other similar headings.

If your search brings you in touch with a for-profit or not-for-profit home care/chore service agency, remember that your parents will be establishing a service relationship with both the agency and the person or persons it places in the home. *Be as specific as you can about your parents' needs and desires.* Especially if your parents value having a consistent person providing services, make sure you make that known to the agency or else you may end up with different helpers every day.

You should be aware that agencies often charge up to twice what they pay the person actually providing the service, the markup covering the administrative overhead of running the agency. It may not be important to you to know the details of the agency's financial relationship with its personnel, but you will want to be sure the agency has done a thorough job screening and training (or at least orienting) its people. Chore service jobs often pay at or only slightly above minimum wage. There is also a risk of turnover and burnout you will want to minimize in order to maintain a sense of stability and order in your parents' home.

If you have the time and energy to place ads and check references, you might want to try to recruit a helper yourself, without going through an agency. If you wish to do this, it is important to be extremely clear about the scope of services expected when you interview candidates, to check references scrupulously, and to insist on some sort of trial arrangement to see if the person is satisfactory for your parent.

Be wary of any person who uses a helping position to gain your parents' confidence for personal reasons such as asking for loans or other forms of monetary assistance. Older people are often vulnerable to this kind of pressure. Whoever is hired for support services, the relationship will have to be carefully monitored over time to see if that person is fulfilling his or her contracted for services and developing an appropriate relationship with your parents.

As you and your parents go about hiring help, you will find it helpful to follow these simple steps:

✔ Write out your needs ahead of time—what you are looking for in a service relationship;

✔ Ask questions that will help you evaluate the experience, training, performance standards, and expectations of the person and/or agency; a recommended checklist of questions follows under *Tab 9* as *Form 5.1: Questions to Ask a Chore Service Provider;*

✔ Ask for references—and make a few calls to see how the person is regarded by other families served currently or in the past;

✔ Make clear your own expectations and those of your parents. Don't be afraid to say that you are looking for someone who will bring a sense of professionalism to the job, someone willing to offer caring help to your parent the same way a family member or close friend would.

◻ INTEGRATING HOUSEHOLD HELP INTO YOUR PARENTS' SUPPORT SYSTEM

As in the case of any service relationship, there are steps you and your parents can take to help get the most out of the arrangement. Start with a clear understanding of what is expected; then follow up with regular, informal evaluations, taking care to insure that just one person within the family has this responsibility. Negative feedback should be given promptly, candidly, and in a con-

---

Enhancing the Quality of Life at Home

Many times there are special services available that go beyond the "essentials" of independent living:

✔ home library service;

✔ large print books and books on tape;

✔ massage and relaxation therapy;

✔ music tapes and records from the library;

✔ fresh flowers or fruit.

Neighbors and friends from work, church, or clubs can be a valuable part of the social aspects of independent living for your parents. By making a few calls to mobilize this network of personal support, you may be able to avoid a growing sense of isolation or unhappiness. Also see *Tab 7: Resources* for recommended large print book and audio tape titles.

---

structive spirit. Any serious difficulty with service providers should be reported to the agency without delay. Positive feedback and expressions of appreciation—given promptly when earned—are equally important. Other tips include:

- ✔ Give the helper your name, address, and phone number and those of other involved family members, and ask for a phone call if problems or needs come up.

- ✔ Give the helper's full name and work schedule to other family members so that when they call your parent and the helper answers, they will be able to carry on a short conversation and not seem out of touch with the household support being provided to your parents;

- ✔ Make it a point to ask your parents regularly how the relationship is going; find out whether they are comfortable or uncomfortable with the arrangement; if they are uncomfortable, find out why and what can be done to put things on a better footing.

Choosing to live independently as one grows older and more dependent is, like so much of life, a trade-off. So is the process of providing or arranging the kinds of support services that make independent living a viable alternative for older persons whose illnesses or disabilities would otherwise require that they move to an assisted living situation.

Some older persons readily accept help in any form; others would prefer an increase in personal inconvenience and risk to the reduced sense of independence that accepting help sometimes seems to bring. Some persons who accept help do so with active participation and enthusiasm, while others become passive, resentful, or increasingly demanding. Each family's circumstances are unique. Your situation, if you are involved in arranging support services for your parents' independent living, is unique. Your best resources are your own good judgment and sense of timing and your willingness to share in your parents' experience and needs.

An organized approach to assessing your parents' needs and finding people to meet those particular needs will help all of you get the most out of the service relationships your parents establish.

Issue 6

Other Retirement Living Alternatives

Many people have a limited view of the retirement living alternatives open to older adults. They think of only three options: staying at home, moving in with a child or other relative, or going into a nursing home. All of these are in fact options. In recent years, however, in response to the growing needs of older adults, a variety of new housing alternatives have become available. These offer a full range of choices, from self-sufficiency to various levels of assisted living. The suitability of any one of these housing options in a particular case depends on many considerations, the most important of which are discussed in this section.

The decision to move into retirement housing may come about in different ways. Active, independent parents may decide to move to a retirement community in the Sunbelt. A family may suddenly be forced to assist a parent in finding alternative housing because of a disabling injury or illness. A widowed spouse might want to give up the burden of housekeeping and home maintenance now that she is alone. Each situation is different, and the role of adult children in helping a parent or parents choose among housing options will also be different in each case. This section provides a guide for identifying and evaluating housing alternatives. The information will be helpful whether you are a primary decision-maker, or merely an advisor and advocate for your parents.

❐ THE DECISION TO LEAVE HOME

The decision to leave home is often a difficult and emotional one. Most older persons prefer to maintain their independence for as long as possible. Usually, staying in the family home is a key aspect of this independence for parents, even when other family members feel a move would be desirable. When parents have a strong desire to stay at home, children and family members should do what they can to facilitate that desire. The preceding issue discussion, *Issue 5: Arranging Support Services for Independent Living,* outlines resources available for providing such support. However, conditions may arise that make parents feel it is time to leave the family home. These can include:

- ✔ increasing difficulty in getting around, climbing steps, cooking meals, bathing, and other daily activities;

- ✔ the loss of nearby friends and family;

- ✔ the death of a spouse;

- ✔ the burden of maintaining a house and yard;

- ✔ a sense of isolation or lack of personal security;

- ✔ financial needs.

When moving becomes necessary or desirable, sensitive family support can be crucial. Be positive about the move. Help make the move as easy as possible, both emotionally and logistically. Set aside extra time to help your parents get comfortable in their new home when the move is complete. All changes in life require adjustment. Your parents' adjustment process can be made easier with your help.

❐ PLANNING AHEAD

It is an excellent idea to consider retirement housing alternatives before a need for immediate change occurs—while your parents are still active and independent. Some housing options such as life care or continuing care communities only accept new residents who are in generally good health. Other facilities may have long waiting lists. If your parents delay too long in addressing the issue of what to do when they give up their home, the alternatives open to them will likely be narrowed.

Once your parents decide to consider a move, they should begin an evaluation process including these five basic questions:

1. What are their short and long term needs and preferences?

2. What kinds of options will their finances permit?

3. What are the specific housing opportunities in the geographical area of their choice?

4. Having looked at the available options, what are their best options from the point of view of needs, preferences, and finances?

5. What steps need to be undertaken, and on what timeline, to secure their preferred option?

❐ HELPING TO ASSESS NEEDS AND PREFERENCES

The first step in choosing among housing options is to

identify the kinds of facilities and assisted living services your parents want and need. They (and you) will want to consider these factors:

- Can your parents bathe, prepare meals, and take medications without assistance?

- Are they able to shop and run errands on their own?

- Do they require assistance in transportation? Do their interests require regular traveling about?

- What geographic location makes the most sense in terms of their interests and closeness to family and friends?

- Do they want this to be their last move, or is this a move that is good for now, but may have to be modified later?   For example, a move to a retirement community condominium may have to be reconsidered later if your parent comes to need skilled nursing care.

Your parents should carefully consider these and other similar questions in evaluating needs and desires. This will help to narrow the field of options they will want to pursue.

❐ PREPARING A BUDGET FOR LIVING EXPENSES

Housing costs are always a major part of any household budget. The costs of various levels of assisted living are likely to be higher than what your parents are accustomed to paying—and these costs seem likely to rise further in the years to come. It will therefore be important for your parents to determine carefully what they can afford. Preparing a household budget is discussed in *Issue 22: Financial Planning for Older Adults*, and *Form 22.2 Household Budget* under *Tab 9* will help facilitate this part of the evaluation process.

Remember, as a plan for household financial management, a budget is only as valid as the assumptions and information that go into it. Be sure the estimates of income and expenses are as realistic as possible. Extend income and cost projections as far into the future as possible, with a generous allowance for health care, in order to know what level of housing expenditure your parents can comfortably sustain. Recognize that costs generally increase over time and that health care costs have risen much faster than any other category of expense in recent years. If your parents have an accountant or financial advisor, it might be a good idea to involve that person in the process of creating a useful household budget.

❐ UNDERSTANDING HOUSING OPTIONS

There now exists a broad range of housing options that runs the spectrum from complete self-sufficiency to assisted living environments to 24-hour attendant care facilities. These options can be grouped into the following categories:

Apartments, condominiums, and manufactured (mobile) homes

These forms of housing provide independent living alternatives to the single family home. The choice of one of these forms of housing will be your parents' decision. Each has advantages and disadvantages. A rental apartment frees the tenant from the concerns of home ownership, but eliminates the potential to gain from property value appreciation. Condominiums may be somewhat less burdensome than single family homes, but joint ownership creates the possibility of disputes among the condominium owners. Manufactured housing provides a low-cost alternative, but you must be careful in purchasing and locating the home. Also, be aware that manufactured homes tend not to appreciate in value as much as other forms of housing (if at all), and they may be more difficult to resell.

Homesharing

This option involves an agreement between two or more people to share the same residence. Each person usually has a separate room or floor of a house, while the kitchen, dining room and other common areas are used jointly. In exchange for board and meals, a resident pays monthly rent or in some cases performs chores and other services as part or in lieu of rent. Homesharing can create a homelike atmosphere, furnish companionship, and reduce housekeeping responsibilities and expense. In recent years, nonprofit programs to match seniors with homesharing opportunities have been launched in many communities. Housemate agencies have also become popular, as have advertisements in newspapers.

Adult family homes

These are private homes licensed by the state to provide room, board, and assisted living services, usually for up to four elderly or disabled people. For those who have been recently released from a hospital and do not need round-the-clock supervision or skilled nursing care, this option may be an attractive and practical temporary alternative to a nursing home. It can also be an option for long-term care. Major benefits of adult family homes include individualized attention, a family atmosphere, and low cost.

Congregate care homes

This category encompasses a variety of facilities, and may also be referred to as board and care homes or domiciliary housing. Congregate care facilities provide lodging, three meals a day, and at least some assistance with personal care, such as dressing, arranging transportation, and taking medication. Congregate care is geared towards older adults in generally good health who need minimal assistance in order to live independently.

Retirement homes

Like board and care homes, these are geared to independent older people in generally good health. They may be distinguished from board and care facilities by an entrance fee charged in addition to monthly rent. They usually provide less than full meal service. Popular variations include apartment high-rises in urban areas and retirement villages in suburbs.

The chief advantage of retirement homes and congregate care facilities is that they eliminate many if not all the tasks associated with household upkeep—housekeeping, laundry, and meal preparation. Other advantages include the potential for an active social life and reduced concerns about security and crime. Retirement facilities located near (or developed in partnership with) a skilled nursing facility or an acute care hospital may be able to offer the important advantage of assured access to a higher level of care, should it ever be needed.

Low-income senior housing

These are units constructed by private developers using public funds or mortgage guarantees from federally sponsored housing programs. Prospective residents must meet a minimum age requirement, usually 62, and their incomes may not exceed a specified maximum. Many of these buildings are situated in pleasant surroundings with security and some amenities. In fact, some retirement homes set aside a specified number of units for those qualifying under low-income programs.

Life care communities

These facilities provide living units and specified health care coverage for the life of the resident in exchange for a sizeable entry fee and monthly charges. The major advantage of a life care investment is that it combines an opportunity for continued independent living with the security of knowing that nursing care will be available when needed in the same building or complex of buildings, and at little or no extra cost.

Integrated care communities

The most recent and comprehensive development in housing options for older adults is a variation often referred to as integrated care communities. These communities provide an array of housing alternatives within the facility: boarding homes, retirement apartments, low income units, a skilled nursing facility. Residents may elect to enter any of the facilities, depending on the level of care required at the time. As their needs for skilled care increases, they may move to another facility within the cluster without uprooting themselves from their familiar surroundings. Because of the comprehensive nature of these communities, they are usually located away from urban areas.

Each of these types of housing has particular advantages and disadvantages that should be matched against your parents' needs, desires, and financial means. A good place to start in investigating these options is to obtain a copy of a register or listing of senior housing options for the geographical areas in which your parents are interested. These may be found at local bookstores and libraries. The local Senior Information and Referral office should also be able to help get your parents started.

☐ MAKING THE DECISION

Before making any final decision, your parents—possibly with your assistance or with the participation of another family member—will want to visit the facilities under consideration. During the visit, they and you will have an opportunity to verify a variety of important facts about the facility, its costs, and the people who own and operate it. Points to cover include:

- *Building design and function.* Is the space clean, comfortable, and attractive? Have adequate safety features (for example: handrails, call buttons, emergency exits, and curb cuts) been provided? Is the space easy to navigate? Are maintenance and security adequate?

- *Location.* Is the location convenient and desirable? Are transportation needs met?

- *Staffing.* What are the credentials and experience of the staff? What is the staff-to-resident ratio? Has there been much staff turnover? Do employees seem to have a positive, upbeat attitude? How do the staff treat the residents?

- *Financial.* Do you understand completely all of the charges? Do you know what is included in the regular fees, and what services require extra payments? What is the procedure for refunding deposits? How often are rates adjusted? When was the last significant rate increase?

- *Terms of occupancy.* What rights of ownership or occupancy does a resident have? Under what circumstances can your parent or parents be required to leave? Will the room or apartment be held in the event of a prolonged absence, for example, in case of hospitalization? If so, what are the charges during a period of absence? What services and facilities are promised by the contract, and under what conditions might those service levels change?

- *Other residents.* Your parents should meet with some of the other residents (all of them, if the facility is an adult family home or a homesharing situation) to make sure there is a strong likelihood of compatibility.

- *Management and ownership.* Find out who owns and manages the facility. Are they a profit or a nonprofit organization? What is their experience, operating philosophy, and reputation? Is this the only facility they own in the area, or do they have others? Ask residents and other visiting family members how they feel about the management.

- *Access to health care services.* How far away is the nearest hospital? Will your parents have to change primary physicians? Will your parents be comfortable with the health care providers in the vicinity?

- *Social and other support programs.* What social and recreational programs are available, and do they correspond to your parents' needs and interests?

Don't hesitate to visit a facility more than once. Your parents are making a major commitment for the future, just like the selection of any living situation, and they should take their time in deciding what is best both for the present and for the future. Visits should be made at such times as will allow observation of typical activities. Visits should include a meal at the facility and an opportunity for informal discussions with residents, visitors, and employees.

Form 6.1: Checklist for Choosing a Retirement Living Facility follows under *Tab 9.* You and your parents will find this form useful in organizing an investigation and evaluation of available options.

❏ FAMILY SUPPORT FOR PARENTS IN TRANSITION

Moving is always a chore. For older adults, moving may be a particularly difficult experience because it has the potential of ending or changing some of life's accustomed patterns. Friendships and other sources of security and comfort may be threatened. This is a time for family members to be available, actively involved, and emotionally supportive. Some of the ways to help include:

- Try to make the move itself as smooth and non-disruptive as possible. Careful planning and organization will help.

- Be sensitive to your parents' need to retain memorabilia and possessions. As we all get older, our possessions are invested with a sense of history.

- Try to be available to help your parents adjust to their new home. Visits will help provide continuity and security. Watch for things in the new environment that your parents may find inconvenient or troublesome. Try to come up with changes or adjustments that will help them overcome their problems.

- Accept your parents' new residence as a place in which they rightly take pride. Reinforce a sense of positive decision making. This is a difficult task. When it is completed, both you and your parents deserve some pats on the back.

Housing is a crucial aspect of daily living, and moving is always stressful. Careful planning will help smooth this transition and avoid rushed decisions under crisis conditions. Remember, if they are able, your parents are the right people to decide what is in their own best interests. Yet the prospects for making good decisions will likely increase if you participate with them in a supportive, informed way.

Issue 7

Sharing Your Home with an Older Adult

As your parents get older, you may become concerned about their ability to continue to live on their own. Safety hazards in the home, inability to drive, a changing neighborhood, declining health, loneliness, or other factors may cause them, and you, to consider other options. As one of those options, you may want to offer to share your own family home with your parent or parents.

Sharing your home with a parent can be a delightful, enriching experience for everyone involved, or it can become a very difficult situation, with everyone diminished by the experience. This issue discusses the most important aspects of a decision for or against having a parent move in with you and your family. It emphasizes that living in a multigenerational household can be wonderful, but is not for everyone. It is better to say "no" and work with your parent toward another more satisfactory living alternative than to struggle with a situation that simply doesn't fit your parent's or your needs and limitations. For those already in a homesharing situation or making the decision to have a parent move in, this chapter includes practical suggestions for making the arrangement succeed for everyone's benefit.

❐ MAKING THE DECISION TO HAVE A PARENT LIVE WITH YOU

Sharing your home will have an impact on everyone in the household—you, a spouse, children, other persons living in the household, and, of course, your parent. Everyone will have to make adjustments and be a part of making the newly configured household work smoothly. Therefore, everyone needs to be a part of the decision-making process. Together, the family must determine whether this will be a good idea or not, and in this instance the word "family" includes all living with you now whose lives will be affected by this decision, as well as your parent.

If your family currently has its own significant problems with health, family relations, or other stressful situations, adding another person to the household may make things harder, no matter how much you and your family love that person. You need to decide as a group whether or not you have the emotional energy to take in another person. Of course you will not be able to anticipate all that the future may hold, but careful thinking and planning before you commit yourself and your parent to living together may help you to avoid an awkward or unworkable situation.

As you check out your ability and willingness to have your parent, parents, or parents-in-law live with you, they should be going through a similar evaluation process. This is not a decision to be made in haste. Both you and your parent should understand and be able to articulate in advance why you think this would be a mutually beneficial arrangement, what you expect from each other, and what you expect from yourselves. In that way, if you decide to live together, each of you knows the other's feelings.

Here are some of the more important factors to keep in mind as you make this decision.

Family stability and attitude

A primary reason for an older parent to live with his or her family rather than in an apartment, a retirement home, or a home shared with strangers, is that he or she is looking forward to a feeling of warmth, of closeness, of familiarity. If your immediate family, for whatever reason, is having major problems and you cannot provide that closeness, you may not be offering your parent an alternative better than the others available. You will not have the ability to share much of yourself. Likewise, a parent cannot be expected to move in and solve all your problems, regardless of how much he or she loves you and your family. Ask yourself and other family members these questions:

✔ Is your spouse (or other adult living in the home) willing to have your parent or parent-in-law living in your home?

✔ How healthy is your marriage or other primary relationship?

✔ If you have children living at home, how are they doing generally? Do they enjoy their grandparent? What accommodations will they be expected to make in a homesharing arrangement? What benefits will they gain?

✔ How well do you get along with your parent? Is the prospect of having him or her in your home for several years a pleasant and realistic one?

✔ Have you resolved any old family grievances and disagreements, or will they resurface and have to be dealt with?

✔ Can you talk with your parent about problems that come up between you without undue tension? Can your parent talk to you easily?

✔ What kinds of things do you disagree about? Will those disagreements be a source of tension in the household?

✔ Do you enjoy spending time with your parent? Does your parent enjoy time spent with you and your family?

✔ Do you or your parent have any habits that are unacceptable to each other, such as smoking or drinking?

✔ How strongly does your parent *want* to come to live with you? Is this option a last resort or a first choice?

✔ How much work will having a new household member add to the household tasks? Who will do that additional work? How do other family members feel about sharing the extra work load?

✔ What kinds of personal care needs (for example, assistance in dressing, bathing, or grooming) does your parent have? How do you and other family members feel about performing those needed services? How does your parent feel about receiving that kind of personal help from family?

✔ What is your reason for inviting your parent to live with you? What is your unique mix of personal, family, historical, and financial reasons?

These are difficult questions to answer, both for you and for your parent. There are no standard right answers which will assure you all of a successful match. Be aware also that there are no ideal solutions. In answering the above questions, one or more of them will normally seem problematic. The purpose of such questions is not to scare you off, but to help you anticipate problems in advance of a difficult situation.

Your home and neighborhood

One of the major considerations in having a parent move in with you is the size and layout of your home. Issues of safety, privacy, and convenience need to be examined. The neighborhood in which your home is located is also important in assessing how disruptive the move would be to your parent's current pattern of life. Availability of transportation and ease in maintaining friendships and other social relationships will be important to your parent and to you.

✔ Is there a private bedroom for your parent in your home? If not, how will a parent's privacy, and yours, be maintained?

✔ Is the bedroom your parent would use easily accessible? Can you get to it without climbing stairs? Is there an outside entrance?

✔ What will you do with your parent's furniture and belongings? Can all of them, or some of them, be incorporated into your household to add a sense of familiarity for your parent? What arrangements for storage or sale of unnecessary household goods can be made?

✔ Is your home safe for your parent? (See *Issue 4: Making the Home a Safer and More Convenient Place for Older Adults*)

✔ Even if your parent has no mobility problems now, is your home adaptable to canes, walkers, or wheelchairs if the need should arise in the future?

✔ Is the house in a relatively safe neighborhood, so

that your parent can take walks, get to the bus stop, or visit neighbors without fear?

A feeling of independence is important to both the family and the older parent sharing a home. Physical arrangements that allow for everyone's privacy promote well-being. Too much togetherness can be grating. But remember that even if you don't have lots of space, you can create the feeling of privacy by scheduling times for certain rooms and activities, so that everyone, including your parent, can have a sense of peace and quiet now and then.

Some neighborhoods may limit what your parent can do or where he or she can go independently. For example, living where public transportation is not easily accessible may increase your parent's dependence on you if he or she does not drive. You can get around this by arranging rides for your parent when it is not convenient for you to drive. Friends, other family members, churches and senior organizations can often help with transportation needs.

Finances and household chores

Money issues are often the most awkward to talk about. You may start to share your home with no thought of the cost, and gradually realize that you and your parent had very different assumptions about the situation. You assumed that Grandma would love to take care of the kids, while she assumed that having raised you, she has done enough child rearing. It is better to agree on mutual expectations before you and your parent begin living together, so that resentment about financial concerns and household chore responsibilities does not develop later on. These are some of the questions to ask:

✔ What do you expect from your parent in return for sharing your home? Will he or she have regular household chores or services to be performed as part of the household responsibilities?

✔ Do you expect your parent to pay room and board? To pay for some expenses? Can you afford to have your parent as a permanent guest?

✔ Will any of your brothers or sisters, or other family members, help out financially?

Claiming your parent as a dependent

If you provide more than half the financial support for your parent, you may be able to claim an additional personal exemption on your federal and state income tax returns. To do so, you will have to qualify under this five-part test:

1. *Support:* Did you provide more than half of your parent's support during the taxable year; this includes food, household expenses, clothing, medical/dental expenses and transportation;

2. *Member of household or family relationship:* Was the person you claim as a personal exemption a resident in your home or a qualifying relative (this includes parents, parents-in-law, step-parents, and grandparents);

3. *Gross income:* You may not claim the personal exemption for your parent if he or she has gross income for the year that equals or exceeds the amount of the personal exemption ($2,050 in 1990); income from tax-exempt bonds, some kinds of social security benefits, and certain other sources of income are not included in determining the amount of your parent's gross income;

4. *Citizenship:* To qualify, your parent must be a U.S. citizen, resident, or national, or be a resident of Canada or Mexico; and

5. *No joint return:* You may not claim the personal exemption if your parent files a joint return with another person.

Two other tax tips are worth keeping in mind:

First, if two or more persons each contribute more than 10% of the support of a dependent, but each contributes less than 50%, they may decide between themselves who will take the personal exemption; those not taking the exemption must sign a written Multiple Support Declaration (IRS form 2120) in which they agree not to claim the exemption that year.

Second, remember that the IRS considers a person to be a dependent for the entire year, even if he or she dies during the year. If the other conditions are met, you may be able to claim your parent as a personal exemption, even if he or she died on January 1.

Family lifestyle

The way your family lives its common life is an important consideration in deciding whether to share your home. Day to day activities and the whirl of family life—work, school activities, clubs, sports, vacations—are important to many individuals and families. To your parent, your household may seem too busy or disjointed to suit his or her needs or preferences. Consider questions like these:

✔ What effect will having your parent living with you have on your social life?

✔ Does your parent have friends near where you live? Will your parent expect to entertain friends in your home? How will you negotiate time and help for your parent's entertaining?

✔ Will you include your parent in all your outings? Which ones will be suitable? Will you expect your parent to include you in activities that you would be interested in; for example, if he or she is thinking of going to see a play you would like to see?

✔ Is your parent accustomed to a schedule like your household's? Is he or she willing and able to adapt to the family schedule for mealtimes and other important routine household events, or will changes need to be made?

✔ Is your parent willing and able to cook on occasion? Does he or she have any special dietary needs or restrictions that would affect the household?

✔ Does your parent drive? Have a car? Is he or she willing and able to use public transportation? If not, will your parent depend on you for transportation to the doctor, the store, to see friends? Is that compatible with your schedule?

Having a parent live with your family can be a joy and a time of enhanced family life. It can also turn out to be a painful experience. Talking openly about all these practical considerations can help everyone involved to examine the day-to-day reality of homesharing, a reality which will involve give and take and mutual consideration on all sides in order to succeed.

❐ THE FUTURE

It is a very different thing to share a home with a parent who is active and independent, than it is to live with your parent when he or she is quite confused and his or her needs for personal and nursing care are extensive. As you and your parent move into deciding to live together, these are some of the questions you should be thinking about:

✔ How long are you envisioning your parent living with you? Does your parent share that assumption? From the beginning, is this understood to be a limited or open-ended arrangement?

✔ What will you do if your parent becomes ill or disabled and needs more of your time and care? How will you and your parent decide if your parent needs more care than you can provide at home? What if you and your parent disagree about this?

✔ What will happen if one or more members of your household is unhappy with the homesharing arrangement?

✔ If you have children living in your home, what effect will their growing up and leaving home have on your arrangement with your parent? Will having your parent living with you significantly affect your plans?

✔ If you become ill, or need a break, what resources are available to you and your parent for respite care?

These are not the easiest questions to ask of your parent or of yourself, and it is not necessary to have all the details worked out before your parent comes to live with you, but once you are comfortable living together, you should discuss how you will go about making difficult decisions if the need arises.

Seven Rules of Successful Homesharing

Rule 1: It is okay to say "no."

Rule 2: Develop a creative, flexible plan for making the arrangement work.

Rule 3: Make sure expectations of yourself and others are realistic.

Rule 4: Deal with problems and concerns early and openly.

Rule 5: Challenge everyone in the household to get behind the effort.

Rule 6: Incorporate reasonable financial arrangements and trade-offs.

Rule 7: Help your parent stay active and involved in the family and community.

❐ HOW TO MAKE IT WORK

There is no magic formula for making a home run smoothly with two, three, or four generations under its roof. There are, however, several strategies that can help.

❋ *Identify and follow a set of rules.* Decide how members of the family will share household chores, limited bathroom facilities, limited transportation resources, and time. Trades and rotations may be appropriate. When you work out reasonable allocations or schedules, put them in writing and post them. Press everyone to get in the habit of respecting what's been agreed to.

❋ *Establish a family habit of effective communication.* Letting people know what is coming up is always important. If your mother has scheduled minor out-patient surgery and is looking forward to a quiet weekend to recover, your teenage son will appreciate knowing this ahead of time—before he invites friends over. If you and your spouse are hosting a party that will last late into the evening and perhaps disturb your parent's rest, he or she might want to spend the night with a friend.

Two simple approaches to insuring good communication are periodic family meetings and a common family calendar posted in a conspicuous place. If yours is a particularly large or active family, you may want to go to the extreme of copying the family calendar for each family member each week, and having regular weekly family meetings.

❋ *Work out appropriate financial trade-offs.* Having a parent live with you can both save your parent money and increase the costs of running your household. Specific trade-offs aimed at balancing these costs and benefits can help everyone see the benefit side. It might be reasonable, for example, to ask siblings who would otherwise be helping to pay for a parent's care to contribute to your household expenses.

You might also work out an arrangement whereby a portion of your parent's income every month is paid either directly to you or into a trust or bank account for your children's college education. If this is discussed in a caring way, your children and your parent will have another bond which makes the homesharing arrangement special.

❋ *Develop and follow a plan.* It is reasonable to adopt and follow a plan that places limitations on the commitment by both sides. For example, you, your parent, and your family may agree to a six-month trial period. Or you, your parent, and your siblings may work out a rotation system that meets everyone's needs and limitations. Knowing ahead of time that there are limits to what you and your parent are willing or able to do, and realizing what those limits are, can and should be a part of your planning.

❋ *Help your parent stay active and involved.* Perhaps the most important commitment you can make is the resolve to make it possible for your parent to remain active and involved in a wide spectrum of activities and relationships for as long as possible. This means making arrangements for transportation so that he or she can participate in church or social events. It also means actively encouraging your parent to invite friends into your home for meals or visits. In addition, it involves intentionally engaging your parent in family discussions of current events and issues or concerns that affect the family.

Success in sharing your home with an older adult requires a multifaceted commitment on the part of you, the other members of your immediate household, and your parent. Each affected member of the family needs to be a part of both the decision to have your parent move in and the process of making the arrangement work out smoothly for all.

Issue 8

The Family Car

The ultimate sign of American independence—driving a car! Getting a driver's license is the first rite of passage to adulthood. Losing the ability to drive can be one of the more painful losses of growing older. We Americans invest a lot of emotion in our cars. They have become in many senses a symbol of the culture at large—representing power, control, individualism, independence, and mobility. It is no wonder that older adults often want to hang on to their cars, and their ability to drive them, longer than is prudent or safe. In many people's minds, not having a car means being trapped, being dependent on others, losing a significant element of freedom and spontaneity in life.

The normal physical changes of aging make driving unwise beyond a certain point. Hearing loss, vision problems, decreased reaction time, memory loss, and limited manual dexterity are all normal in older adults; however, they all are impediments to safe driving. A person losing depth perception, peripheral vision, and reaction time creates a hazard on today's crowded streets and highways. That person risks not only damaging his or her own car or another vehicle, but also injuring him- or herself or another person. This section offers strategies for helping your parents assess and improve their driving skills as they grow older. It also addresses how to help a parent cut down on or stop driving if that seems wise for reasons of safety.

❏ ASSESSING AND IMPROVING DRIVING SKILLS IN OLDER ADULTS

There are several steps which your parents can take to extend their capability as safe drivers. Some of these steps—like additional driver's training or special modifications to the car—may be difficult for your parents to accept. After all, they may have been driving for over fifty years. Some tact and preparation may be necessary. Often it is easier for an older person to sign up for a driving course if he or she doesn't have to do it alone. If you can get a spouse or friend to initiate a discussion about car safety, or sign up for a class with the parent you are worried about, that may be the easiest way to address your concern. Some steps which can be taken include:

- The American Association of Retired Persons (AARP) offers special classes on defensive driving for drivers age 55 and over. Portions of this class focus on the impact of the aging process on the ability to drive safely, and specific strategies for safer driving are offered. Contact your local AARP office for more information. Local automobile clubs such as the American Automobile Association (AAA) also offer safe driving courses for older adults.

- Encourage your parents to keep their car in good repair. Many local AAA offices will conduct periodic free safety checks. Watch for carpet and pedal wear that may cause an accelerator or brake to stick or a foot to slip off.

- Have your parents explore modifications which might be made to their car to enhance driving safety: e.g., installation of different types of side and rear-view mirrors, a rear window brake light, a back up warning buzzer, steering wheel grips, and pedal adjustments.

- If your parents' car is large and difficult to maneuver, suggest trading it in for a smaller car which might be easier to handle and park.

- Remind your parents to check to see if their driver's licenses and license plate tabs are current. As part of their driver's license renewal, they will have to pass a vision test. If their licenses are allowed to lapse, they will have to take a road test to get a new license.

- Check with your parents to see that their automobile insurance is adequate and current. Often an insurance agent will reinforce the hazards of keeping a car too long while explaining rising insurance premiums.

- If your parents are becoming nervous about driving, suggest route and time of day adjustments to make driving easier. Many people give up night driving while continuing to drive during the day. Busy highways and rush hour traffic can often be avoided with some advance planning and allowance for additional travel time. Use of Park and Ride lots allows combining auto and bus travel.

- If there has been any kind of questionable incident concerning a parent's driving, as an alternative to giving up the car immediately, you might suggest taking a refresher driving course which includes driving with an instructor. Such impartial professional assessment and comment about your parent's driving skills may be more acceptable than family pressure.

☐ WHEN A PERSON SHOULD NO LONGER DRIVE

There comes a point when it is clear that your parent or parents should no longer be driving. Usually it is clear to your parent as well. Many older drivers realize their decreasing ability and grow increasingly nervous about their own driving. The problem is how to make the transition from being a driver and owning a car to *not* being a driver and *not* owning a car with as little emotional trauma and decreased mobility as is possible. There are ways to make this transition easier.

- While your parent is still driving, suggest that you drive more and more often. Or explore taking a bus to the doctor's office to save the inconvenience of parking. Create or take note of opportunities where your parent is not driving, but still mobile and independent. The *reality* of being a nondriver is usually less confining than the *thought* of not driving. Help your parent to see that her life will go on pretty much as usual without the car.

- Sometimes after a serious illness or hospitalization, you or your parent's health care provider can suggest that your parent not drive for "a while." If during that time, your parent does not miss driving, he or she might give up the car voluntarily.

- There are advantages as well as disadvantages to not driving. One major advantage is the expense. Many older persons are reluctant to give up their cars because they believe the expense of taxis to be prohibitive. Yet they rarely calculate the cost of owning and operating their cars. You might want to sit down with your parents and add up their expenses for car payments, gasoline, car maintenance, parking, insurance, and any other applicable expenses. If your parents gave up the car, how much money would that free up for other activities or other forms of transportation?

- Research the alternative methods of transportation that are available to your parents. What are your parents' routine needs for transportation? Is there a bus that can take them to church or to the senior center? Are there cab companies in your parents' community which will take standing assignments for a daily, weekly, or monthly ride, and even provide the same driver? What are the public bus routes that will be most helpful to your parents? Are there friends and neighbors still driving who might enjoy companionship on a shopping trip or a movie downtown?

- If your parent is wavering about giving up the car, you might talk with some of his or her friends who have either given up their cars and are happy and well-adjusted to the change or who can be counted on to offer rides or companionable adventures on the bus to your parent. One of the real resources for older people is their network of friends. Don't be afraid to tap that resource to help solve this difficult problem.

Despite your creative use of the strategies outlined above and other approaches, often giving up the car keys comes down to someone having a difficult conversation with your parent saying in a direct way that he or she is no longer a safe driver. There is no way to make that conversation easy. However, sometimes it must occur.

The question comes up of who should initiate the conversation. If your parent is married, and the marriage is strong and comfortable, often the spouse can be the best person to address the issue. Other times the best person might be an old friend, a health care provider, insurance advisor, clergy person, social worker, or other outside person. The most important qualities of this person will be: a positive relationship with your parent, an ability to be direct, and an understanding of and sensitivity towards the difficulty of this issue for an older person.

The location of the conversation might also be important. Some people will be most comfortable having this discussed on their turf—in their home. For others, talking about giving up the car might best happen out of the home—in an office or coffee shop—so that the topic is broached as a business matter for consideration, not a control issue within the family.

There are ways to lessen the impact of giving up the car. One is to have your parent agree to keep the car—in case it is needed—but to try not to use it for a trial period. Another can be to suggest that your parent give the car to a favorite grandchild starting college, or a niece who is recently divorced and has limited finances. Such a gift allows your parent to save face, and to turn this loss into an opportunity for giving and being appreciated for that gift.

Once your parent gives up the car, it is important that you do all you can to see that life goes on as before. There will probably be an adjustment period of several months. During that time, it is crucial that your parent remain active and get out. Once the transition is behind them, many older adults experience a sense of freedom and relief in not having to deal with a car or the pressure of driving. Being a user of public transportation or a more frequent pedestrian can become a source of pride and self esteem, as well as a good source of exercise.

Handled with sensitivity and good planning, giving up the family car can merely be a change in older life, and not a serious loss.

Issue 9

Traveling in Safety and Comfort

Most people enjoy traveling. One of the pluses of grow-ing older is that many older adults have the time and freedom to travel extensively. Because seniors represent a significant slice of the travel market, there are now a variety of vacation packages, services, and discounts available specifically for them.

❏ PLANNING A TRIP

Some trips require little in the way of planning. For ex-ample, if your mother in Cleveland wants to come see you in your home in San Antonio, more than likely she will check some dates with you, make arrangements to leave her home secure, buy a plane ticket, and her trip is arranged. Planning has played a minor role in her travel experience.

More challenging from the planning perspective is the act of combining the urge to travel with both the avail-able budget and the most interesting possibilities. Say your parents have $8000 put aside in a travel fund and want to use that money in the next year to fulfill some of their travel dreams. Their goal is to get the greatest satisfaction possible out of their travel dollars. To achieve that goal will often involve extensive planning—which can be almost as much fun as the trip itself!

When trying to decide among various travel destinations, there are a number of factors to consider which may be helpful in focusing the best possibilities. They include:

✔ *climate*— What kind of climate does the traveler wish to experience? Is he or she extremely uncomfortable if the climate is too hot, cold, humid, or dry?

✔ *activities*— What kinds of activities does the traveler enjoy? Does he or she wish to focus the trip around one particular activity such as fishing, shopping, or museum visiting, or would it be preferable to include a variety of activities?

✔ *season*— What is the best time of year to travel to a desired destination? How far in advance should arrangements be made? Interesting travel spots often offer significant discounts to those willing to travel in the "off season." However, such discounts should be weighed against other factors such as weather, range of activities available during the off season, and personal scheduling preferences.

✔ *companions*— Does the traveler have friends/family to travel with? What are the interests and special needs of the traveling companions? Is one of the goals of travel to meet others, or to spend time alone? Would the traveler prefer to travel in a group of persons of similar age, or with a mixed age group?

✔ *special needs*— What is the physical condition of the traveler? Are there health factors that should influence a choice of destination? Will a desired destination be able to meet special dietary needs, allow the traveler to move about with a sense of security, have adequate medical facilities nearby in case of emergency?

❏ THE TRAVEL AGENT

In answering all of the above questions and others, there are several sources of available information. Friends and family members who have traveled to a possible destination can be a valuable source of first hand impressions. Travel books and guides can offer a wealth of information from sightseeing possibilities to visa and health regulations. However, there is no substitute for a good travel agent.

Experienced travel agents are travel professionals. Most agents and agencies specialize in certain regions or certain kinds of travel experiences. Some are well-versed in cruises, and will be able to give you or your parent specific and accurate information about varying levels of service, food, and accommodation on different cruise lines and ships. Others are more knowledgeable about package tours, exotic locations, or special focus travel— such a golfing tours, or bed and breakfast accommodations in foreign countries. Often, agents have traveled extensively in the area of their specialty.

In looking for a travel agent, your parents should not be afraid to shop around and talk to several before making a selection. Ask others who have traveled extensively what agent they use. The goal is to find someone who is knowledgeable about the kind of travel your parents are interested in and who is willing to do some research to make their trip as interesting and affordable as possible.

There are agents, groups, and travel companies that specialize in senior travel. They offer options that range from educational packages such as elderhostel, to cruises, to "senior only" tours designed to provide comfort and a leisurely pace for older travelers. Some of these organizations require membership; others simply cater to an older clientele. For persons with physical disabilities, the Society for the Advancement of Travel for the Handicapped (SATH) can recommend agents who specialize in travel arrangements for the disabled. (For more information about this agency, see *Tab 7: Resources*.)

☐ TRAVELING ALONE

Many people enjoy setting off on a trip alone. It adds to their sense of adventure and independence. And they perceive it as an opportunity to meet and interact with persons they encounter along the way. Solo travelers usually are comfortable seeking out others when they want company, striking up conversations, making friends quickly.

Other people find themselves traveling alone not because they want to, but because they do not have a traveling companion. Often, family members are concerned when an older parent sets off alone on an extended trip. The following suggestions may help your parent line up a suitable traveling companion who will make his or her trip both safer and more enjoyable.

- Let it be known that your parent is interested in traveling to a certain destination and would enjoy company. A friend or acquaintance might be able to suggest a possible match.

- Look for a "travel-partner club." The purpose of these organizations is to match up single persons who are looking for the social and financial benefits of traveling with a compatible companion.

Your travel agency should be able to suggest such a club in your parent's area.

- If finances permit, your parent might consider a paid companion. This could be anyone from a granddaughter who could not afford such a trip alone and would be excited to go along, to a trained nurse or personal care attendant who could help with personal or medical needs during the trip.

Whatever your parent's budget, special needs, and circumstances, careful planning can be the key to positive, memorable travel experiences.

❐ BUDGET

Once an older traveler has decided on a destination, companions, and a general dollar amount available for a trip, it is a good idea to work out a more specific budget. If the travel option selected is a package tour, budgeting may be fairly simple, depending on what the package covers. When buying into package trips, it is important to make sure what the basic rate includes. Does it include:

- ✔ all meals?

- ✔ sightseeing tours or side trips?

- ✔ all transportation and accommodations?

- ✔ tips, baggage handling, and other miscellaneous expenses?

- ✔ activity fees, such as golf green fees or museum admission fees?

- ✔ the services of a guide or tour director?

When putting together a trip independently, budgeting is more complicated, but the traveler has more flexibility. For example, a person might choose to travel between destinations by train rather than by air, both for financial savings and for the sightseeing possibilities. Another person might choose to travel economy class for part of a trip in order to save for better accommodations or an expensive side trip later on. A realistic budget will help the traveler work most creatively with the financial resources available. Any travel budget should include:

- ✔ Transportation expenses, including air, train, bus, boat, or other.

- ✔ Lodging costs at all destinations

- ✔ Local travel, including bus, taxi, rental car, hotel transfers

- ✔ Meals, including tips and beverages

- ✔ Admissions/tickets

- ✔ Local tours/sightseeing

- ✔ Entertainment/activities, including nightlife, green fees, side trips

- ✔ Gifts

- ✔ Spending money

- ✔ Other incidentals

These budget items also appear under *Tab 9* as *Form 9.1: Senior Travel Planner.*

If you have questions about any of these costs or others, speak with your travel agent or tour director. Establishing and sticking to a realistic travel budget can be a satisfying and creative part of travel planning.

☐ SPECIAL TRAVEL SERVICES FOR SENIORS

Discounts

One of the "perks" of becoming an older adult is the range of discounts available to them. Travel is an area where such discounts are almost universal. Depending on the travel service involved, the minimum age requirement varies from 50 to 65, and the amount of the discount covers a wide range as well. The older traveler is well advised to ask about senior rates when inquiring about any travel option. Some typical discounts worth checking include:

- ✔ *Airline Fares*— Most major American airlines offer a senior discount of 10% or more, both for seniors and for a companion traveling with an older adult. In addition, some airlines offer senior coupon books that include significant savings if the traveler plans to fly several times during the course of a year.

- ✔ *Amtrak*— Amtrak offers a discount of 25% off full fares for individuals over age 65.

- ✔ *National Parks*— The National Park system offers a Golden Age Pass for persons 62 and over entitling them to free admission and half-price camping in all national parks.

Whenever judging discount travel, it is important to understand two things: whether the discounted fare is the lowest fare available; and what limitations apply. Sometimes, there will be a better option than the senior discount off a full-price fare, or your parent might want more flexibility to reschedule or cancel than a discounted ticket allows.

Special assistance

Some older persons are reluctant to travel because they feel insecure negotiating the crowded service desks and corridors of busy airports and other transportation terminals. A person with hearing difficulty often has the hardest time hearing when there is significant background noise. Someone suffering from dizziness, limited vision, or mobility problems may fear falling or being jostled by crowds. If your parent is basically able to travel, but just needs a little extra assistance, it is important to know about these services available to all travelers:

✔ *boarding assistance*— Most airlines and rail lines have both wheelchairs available for those unable to walk long distances, and formal "meet and assist" programs. These programs assure that a traveler in need of assistance will be met at the check-in counter and given assistance getting to the point of departure, onto the plane or train, and off safely at the other end. It is best to confirm when booking tickets that your parent will need either wheelchair transportation or meet and assist service.

✔ *special meals*— When flying, it is also usually possible for travelers on restricted diets to order special meals. Most major airlines regularly offer vegetarian plates, kosher meals, and special meal service for persons on bland, low cholesterol, or low salt diets. The airline should be told of your parent's need at the time the trip is booked.

✔ *oxygen required*— Persons with medical conditions requiring the use of an oxygen tank can travel safely on most kinds of public transport. Airlines have strict requirements about oxygen use. These usually include a letter from a physician explaining the person's oxygen requirement and a statement certifying that the oxygen provided by the airline is acceptable. If your parent is a supplemental oxygen user, make sure that he or she understands the regulations regarding oxygen use on whatever mode of transport is chosen.

✔ *handicapped accessibility*— Most aircraft are wheelchair accessible, though some small commuter planes are not. Trains and ships generally have a limited number of handicapped accessible cabins or compartments. Many resorts offer specially designed rooms and suites for use by persons in wheelchairs. When planning a trip, these options can be researched and reservations for special facilities confirmed in writing before the trip begins.

Though frailty or physical disability may make travel more of a challenge for your parent, many obstacles and potential problems can be easily overcome with a little advance planning. It is also important, if your parents have any significant medical problems, that they carry a medical history and a complete list of current medications with them when they travel. Their primary care physician should be able to provide all the necessary information, so that if one of them needs medical assistance away from home, the doctors there will have enough information to provide prompt, effective treatment.

Your parents should also be sure to travel with adequate supplies of their medications. These should normally be kept on them, or in carry-on luggage, and *not* in checked baggage. If for any reason medications are lost, your parent should be in touch with a physician. Most hotels and airlines can help someone find a doctor in an emergency.

Finally, every traveller should carry adequate personal identification. An older adult should have his or her Medicare or other health insurance information and phone numbers of family members or friends to be contacted in case of emergency.

Planning and preparing for a successful trip requires effort. However, the pay-off comes when a long awaited vacation or extended adventure lives up to its potential for relaxation, excitement, and enrichment.

3 Health Issues

Issue 10

Staying Healthy

There are many physical changes that occur as a person grows older. Some of these changes begin at age twenty and others not until the fifties or sixties. At whatever age a normal change may begin to occur, there are simple steps that can be taken which will help delay or minimize that change if it is negative. The five basic components in maintaining the best possible health in older age are:

- ✔ exercise,
- ✔ diet,
- ✔ sleep,
- ✔ maintaining activities and interests,
- ✔ attitude.

Of course, along with these, it is important to see a health care provider for regular check-ups and avoid smoking, social drug use, and excessive use of alcohol.

❐ EXERCISE

One of the most important things a person can do to stay healthy at any age is to maintain a regular program of exercise. This program may consist of taking a walk three or four times a week, going for a swim, or working out in the gym. A regular exercise regimen will help to maintain joint flexibility as well as maintain or increase muscle strength. Flexibility and muscle strength will allow for greater freedom of movement for the older person.

Even if a person has not been exercising regularly in the past, it is never too late to begin. If your parent begins a regular program now, he or she will see positive effects in general health, appetite, sleeping, and state of mind. It is important to begin any exercise program slowly. Your parent should not begin a vigorous exercise program without first checking with his or her health care provider.

Exercise and the cardiovascular system

Exercise works to maintain and improve health in several ways. First, it can improve the condition of the cardiovascular system (the heart and blood vessels). If, for example, a person walks at a moderate to rapid pace—fast enough to raise the heart beat—for twenty minutes three to four times a week, that exercise will strengthen the heart muscle, improve the blood cholesterol level, and may improve the general state of that person's cardiovascular health. Many diseases of the heart and blood vessels are caused, in part, by improper diet, lack of exercise, and smoking. Beginning an exercise program late in life may not undo changes in the heart or blood vessels from a previously sedentary life; however, a carefully planned exercise program with gradual increase in degree can improve one's sense of well-being and overall cardiovascular fitness.

Tips for exercising

- Choose an activity that you enjoy.
- Be sure to wear comfortable clothing and shoes.

- Use the proper equipment for your activity.

- Find a regular time of the day to exercise.

- Exercise with a friend or family member.

- Begin slowly and increase length of exercise gradually.

- Establish a positive image of yourself as healthy and relaxed, and work toward that goal.

Exercise and osteoporosis

Osteoporosis is a loss of mineral from the bones, causing the bones to be less dense and likely to fracture easily. Post-menopausal women are most a risk for developing osteoporosis. By their eighties, all people are affected. Exercise can prevent osteoporosis if a program is begun early and continued regularly. Exercise can slow the progression of osteoporosis at any point in the disease, and can be an effective way to treat some of the pain and discomfort caused by osteoporosis.

A common problem from osteoporosis is a "kyphotic" spine. The building block shaped bones in the spine can fracture in a wedge shape, causing a forward curvature of the spine. These fractures may cause a lot of pain and discomfort for a month or two after they occur, and they may occur relatively painlessly. Many individuals who have a badly curved spine have muscle aches and pains as a result of the curvature in the spine and the change in the shape of the thoracic (chest) cage. Exercise is effective in reducing the muscle aches which are present with osteoporosis and often can reduce the acute pain from an osteoporotic fracture. Individuals should consult with their physician or with a physical therapist for an appropriate exercise program.

Exercise and the lungs

Exercise is of great benefit to the lungs. With age, there is some decrease in the amount of functioning lung tissue in all persons. Also the thoracic cage and muscles which control respiration can become stiffer. The lungs and chest muscles may become less efficient, and breathing may become more difficult with exertion or if compromised by an infection or another illness. In some individuals, the lungs also suffer from the affects of air pollutaion and smoking. As with the heart, exercise can benefit the lungs by improving endurance and the efficiency of the respiratory system.

◻ DIET

In growing older, changes occur in the way the body uses food and other substances taken into it. As a general rule, an older person's body becomes less efficient in absorbing vitamins and minerals from food. With increased age and decreased activity, an individual may require fewer calories in order to maintain a constant weight, but the nutritional requirements stay the same as for a younger adult. Therefore, older adults need to plan meals more carefully to include all of the essential nutrients without consuming too many calories. They will have fewer calories available for desserts, "junk food," or alcoholic or carbonated drinks. Many older people lose their appetite and may also find it difficult to sit down and eat regular meals if they live alone. It is important for older adults to continue to have regularly planned, well-balanced meals.

If you are worried about your parents' diet and they are willing to cooperate—or humor you—have your parents list everything they eat for a day or two. Then take the list and place each item into the proper food group. An older person should eat daily:

- two 3 oz. servings from the meat, fish and chicken group
- two servings from the milk group
- four servings from the bread and cereal group
- four servings from the fruit and vegetable group

If you are not sure which foods fit into which food group, or have further concerns about your parents' diet, you might look at a nutrition text, call your local county health department, or talk with your parents' health care provider. Some older adults find the need to take one good multiple vitamin a day. An excess intake of vitamin pills will not help more, and may, in fact, cause problems.

◻ SLEEP

Getting adequate amounts of sleep is important. Most body systems can rest while one is awake, but the brain and nervous system are in constant action during waking hours. It is only during sleep that these important systems can rest and rebuild. Without enough sleep, an individual may be unable to cope with the normal demands of a day. Fatigue will increase feelings of discouragement and depression and will accentuate emotional problems. Prolonged loss of sleep may cause personality changes.

Many older persons sleep fewer hours at night. This is a normal part of the aging process. Older persons tend to have less dream sleep, less deep sleep, and may wake up feeling like they have not slept at all. Even though your parent may sleep fewer hours and wake feeling less rested, this should not cause you or your parent to worry. A time of relaxation or a nap during the day can adequately compensate for the sleep loss at night. Sleep can often be improved by maintaining an adequate exercise program.

Sleep and the mentally disabled adult

Sleep may become a major problem for caregivers of severely mentally disabled adults, such as those who have Alzheimer's disease. The person with Alzheimer's disease will often sleep for only very short periods, and may spend much of the night wandering the house. These individuals develop a "sleep-wake" disturbance and often sleep during the day. This creates a problem for the caregiver. Here are a few suggestions to help deal with this problem:

- ✔ Strictly schedule the day for the impaired adult for activity periods, meals, short daytime naps, and bedtime.

- ✔ If possible, try to eliminate daytime naps and increase daytime activity. A walk in the evening is often helpful. The evening should be a relaxing time.

- ✔ Be sure that your parent's sleeping arrangements are as comfortable as possible. Night clothes should be comfortable; the room warm enough, but not too hot.

- ✔ Use nightlights in the bedroom, hall, and bathroom to increase orientation if your parent should get out of bed and wander about.

- ✔ Place a bell on your parent's bedroom door. This will allow you to rest without worrying as much about your parent leaving his or her room to wander about the house.

✔ Other helpful suggestions for this situation can be found in the book *The Thirty-Six Hour Day* by Mace and Rabins. See *Tab 7: Resources.*

❏ MAINTAINING ACTIVITIES AND INTERESTS

In order to maintain a proper state of good mental health, it is important for an older adult to continue to take an interest in, or participate in, a variety of pursuits. These may be activities enjoyed in the past, but which he or she never had enough time for, or new interests developed only recently. Activities, whether they be playing golf, shopping, volunteer work, or reading books, help maintain perspective and balance in life. They also provide the opportunity to develop relationships with persons other than family and old friends. Adult day care and social programs at senior centers in the community can be especially helpful. New relationships add complexity and depth to an older person's life, just as they do to yours.

Preparing for retirement

Preparing for retirement is very important in maintaining good mental health. Many people leave their working life without having adequately prepared for the many hours of the day that must be filled up by other activities. Encourage your parents to make specific plans about activities they wish to undertake in retirement, trips they would like to make, hobbies they would like to pursue, volunteer work in which they have an interest. Older adults, especially in the early years of their retirement, have much to offer to the communities in which they live. Such activities help to ease the transition between active work life and retirement and also help maintain self-esteem and identity, a problem for many retired adults.

❐ ATTITUDES

With increasing years, many persons begin to think of themselves as being old or disabled in some way. Some of the ways in which our society is insensitive to the needs and experiences of older adults only make this problem worse. One's mental perspective often influences the way one lives. One of the things your parent needs from you is continuing support and positive reinforcement. Just as you needed encouragement from your parents to think highly of yourself when you were young, so your parent can use your support in maintaining self-esteem and a positive self-image in old age.

This is especially true with adults who are suffering from physical and mental limitations. Be careful how you talk with your parent. Try not to be patronizing. Never laugh at a parent because of an impairment; however, the two of you may laugh together over some of the awkward incidents that occur if there is a bond of love and support (and a shared sense of humor) between you.

There are some who believe that the second fifty years of life are the most exciting and rewarding. That is a healthy attitude for an older person to have. If negative feelings are a problem, help your parent find ways to affirm the positive aspects of his or her life. Such a positive outlook will be a help to both your parent and to you.

When professional counseling is needed

If your parent suffers from chronic depression or is otherwise unable to cope emotionally, you should look into the availability of professional counseling. In many areas there are excellent community mental health programs operated with full or partial government support and geared to the special needs of older adults. Referrals are available by calling the Senior Information and Assistance number.

❐ STAYING HEALTHY YOURSELF

All of this advice about maintaining good health in your parent is also applicable to you. As an active adult, you need to be concerned about regular exercise, a proper diet, adequate sleep, maintaining interests and activities, and keeping up a positive attitude. Especially if you are engaged in a demanding caregiving situation, you need to pay attention to the things you need to do to stay healthy. If you are under stress, remember the following rules:

- Set realistic expectations of yourself. Decide what is important to *you* and learn to let go of the details and tasks that are not important to you.

- Simplify your life. Learn to say *NO* or to leave undone those things unimportant to you.

- Plan for short term attainable goals.

- Focus on the small problems, or manageable parts of large problems. This will allow you to see when progress is being made.

- Talk with a counselor when problems feel overwhelming, or join a support group where you can share concerns with others whose situations are similar.

- Ask for help. Don't try to be a superperson. Get help from family, neighbors, friends, social service agencies, or your health care provider.

Take care of yourself. If you are reading this book, the chances are that at least one other person counts on you to be healthy and able to help. You can't give that help if you don't help yourself first.

Issue 11

Health Concerns of Older Adults

One of the realities of the aging process is that it affects both physical and mental health. The longer a person lives, the more likely that he or she will encounter serious health problems, many of them chronic health problems for which there is no cure, only more or less successful methods of control. By the time they reach age 65, most adults have developed at least one chronic health problem. By age 80, the majority of adults have two or more such problems. These conditions require careful monitoring by a health professional, and may involve certain adjustments or lifestyle changes. However, it is possible to live a full and rewarding life despite the diseases and disabilities of aging.

If you or your parents have serious medical questions, those questions should be discussed with your parents' primary care physician or another health professional. This chapter is not a substitute for such discussions. Instead, our purpose here is to identify many of the major physical and mental health concerns commonly faced by older adults, to alert you to symptoms to be aware of, and, when possible, to point out ways to prevent these problems or minimize their impact on your parent's life and sense of well-being. It is not possible within the scope of this book to give an exhaustive listing of all the medical problems which may occur with your parent. A number of helpful references are listed in *Tab 7: Resources.*

Again, for more information contact a physician or other health care professional.

For convenience, the health concerns of older adults listed have been grouped in the categories below. These categories include:

- diseases of the cardiovascular system (the heart and the blood vessels),

- diseases and problems of the bones and joints,

- elimination problems,

- cancers,

- diseases and disabilities affecting the mind and personality,

- problems with the eyes,

- hearing problems,

- miscellaneous (including: diabetes; hypothyroidism; Parkinson's Disease; and care of teeth and mouth).

❏ DISEASES OF THE CARDIOVASCULAR SYSTEM

The cardiovascular system includes the heart and the system of blood vessels which circulate blood throughout your body. Your heart is a muscle. Its pumping action causes the blood to move through the circulatory system. Like all muscles and other body parts, your heart needs to receive oxygen and other essential nutrients from your blood in order to function properly. Blood is carried around the body in arteries and veins. If those arteries and veins become clogged, blocked, or otherwise impaired, the blood can not adequately circulate and a number of problems can result.

As adults grow older, many things may occur which impair the functioning of the cardiovascular system. This section will list first the most common types of vascular disease (diseases of the blood vessels), then diseases of the heart. Strokes are covered separately, followed by a discussion of diet and lifestyle change to prevent and limit cardiovascular disease.

High blood pressure

Your heart pumps blood through your blood vessels under pressure. At times, this pressure builds up until excessive pressure is present. This is called hypertension or high blood pressure. There are often no signs or symptoms to tell if your blood pressure is too high until damage has already been done to your vessels. In most cases, the cause of high blood pressure is unknown. There is no cure, but treatment can be very effective and prevent the development of other problems. All adults—both your parents and you—should have their blood pressure checked regularly. Failure to treat high blood pressure may lead to heart attack, congestive heart failure, strokes, blood vessel damage, and kidney failure. Those most at risk for high blood pressure are those with a family history of this disease, persons who are overweight, those who eat a high sodium (salt) diet, and persons under high stress. If your physician diagnoses your parent as having high blood pressure and prescribes medication to control it, it is extremely important that your parent continue to have his or her blood pressure and the effects of the medication monitored, as long as treatment for this condition continues. Many blood pressure medications have side effects. Your parent should be aware of the most common side effects of the particular medications prescribed. Because there are no visible symptoms of high blood pressure, patients often neglect to continue taking their medication. They forget to refill prescriptions, or just let it go. This can be a very dangerous problem.

High cholesterol

Cholesterol is a substance which is both produced in the body and taken in with the food you eat. Some cholesterol is needed for body functioning, but scientific studies have shown that excessive amounts of cholesterol in the blood stream may cause, or complicate, cardiovascular diseases. Excess cholesterol attaches to the walls of the blood vessels, causing narrowing of the arteries and limitation of the amount of blood which can pass through them. Some people are genetically inclined to manufacture more cholesterol than is needed and may have great difficulty lowering blood levels of this substance. High cholesterol can often be controlled by diet alone, but sometimes a physician may prescribe medication. As in the case of high blood pressure, it is important to continue the medication for as long as the physician indicates.

Atherosclerosis

Atherosclerosis is a slow, progressive disease involving the thickening of the walls of the arteries and the deposit of fatty cholesterol plaque there. These deposits narrow the passageway through the arteries and thus limit the amount of blood able to pass through. Blood carries oxygen to the tissues. As less blood is available to the various organs of the body, those organs may not have adequate oxygen for their continued functioning. This is true particularly under stress or when exercising, when tissues need more oxygen. Decreased blood and oxygen supply can lead to angina, heart attacks, strokes, or blood clots in the legs. Progression of atherosclerosis can be slowed by diet, cessation of smoking, and control of diseases which accelerate atherosclerosis, such as diabetes and high blood pressure.

Angina pectoris

Angina pectoris or angina is chest pain, pressure, or heaviness which occurs due to insufficient blood flow to the heart muscle. Shortness of breath may also be a symptom of angina. Angina pain may spread to the neck, jaw, or arms when severe. It is often associated with exercise or stress which increases the work done by the heart muscle. Angina may go away with rest alone. Medications are often prescribed to treat it. These medications improve circulation to the heart muscle or decrease the work of the muscle.

Heart attack

A heart attack occurs after a prolonged episode of angina or decreased blood flow to the heart muscle. Inadequate blood flow causes muscle damage, which, if severe enough, may impair heart function. Symptoms of a heart attack include: angina, shortness of breath, dizziness, sweating, and nausea.

People who suffer a heart attack are usually hospitalized and their hearts monitored for disturbances in heart rhythm. A heart attack is confirmed by changes on an electrocardiogram (heart rhythm tracing) and laboratory tests. Some patients who display symptoms or are at risk of a heart attack may have a test called an angiogram. This study uses dye and x-rays to look at the arteries in the heart. If your parent suspects that he or she is experiencing a heart attack, 911 should be called immediately.

Peripheral arterial disease

Peripheral arterial disease refers to atherosclerosis in the arteries which leave the heart to supply the limbs and rest of the body. Symptoms include blood clots, pain or cramping in the calves with exercise which goes away with rest. As the disease advances, it can result in damage to tissue due to inadequate oxygen supply.

Congestive heart failure

Congestive heart failure occurs when the pumping action of the heart is impaired, usually due to damage to the heart muscle from coronary artery disease or some other source. This failure of the heart to pump adequate amounts of blood through the body is caused by the weakness of the heart muscle. Because of the extra work it must do, the heart becomes enlarged and is even less able to pump efficiently. There is decreased strength to the beat, and blood flow is slowed. Blood may back up in the veins and lungs. The ability of the kidneys to dispose of salt and excess water is impaired, and excess fluid accumulates in the tissues.

This is a slow and progressive disease. Its symptoms may include tiredness or a feeling of weakness, shortness of breath as fluids accumulate in the lungs, and swelling in the legs and abdomen. This condition must be treated by a physician.

Strokes

A stroke occurs when the blood supply to any part of the brain is reduced or cut off entirely. Strokes may be caused by blood clots blocking an artery, progression of atherosclerosis, or by bleeding into the brain through a ruptured artery. Strokes can be minor or severe. They can cause temporary or permanent problems. The sever-

Communicating with a Stroke Patient

The following tips are often helpful in communicating with someone whose ability to communicate has been seriously diminished by a stroke:

- ✔ Get the person's attention before beginning to speak.

- ✔ Keep messages short enough to fit the person's attention span.

- ✔ Speak slowly and distinctly, but don't shout.

- ✔ Use simple sentences; repeat your thought if it is not fully understood the first time.

- ✔ Use gestures and more expression.

- ✔ Pose questions that require only "yes" or "no" answers.

- ✔ Give the person plenty of time to respond.

- ✔ Give constant reassurance—touch the person.

- ✔ Help the individual who can speak, but has difficulty coming up with the correct word—provide the word.

- ✔ Some individuals can write words and thoughts that they are unable to speak.

- ✔ Point to pictures, objects, or words written on a chart.

ity of the stroke depends on the extent and location of the blockage of blood flow in the brain. Strokes can affect sensation or strength in the limbs, memory, ability to think and process information, or speech and communication.

At times, a "transient schematic attack" or "TIA" can occur as a warning sign of an impending stroke. Symptoms of a TIA include: temporary dizziness or unsteadiness; recent changes in personality or mental ability; loss of vision or double vision. If your parent shows any of these symptoms, contact a physician immediately.

The rehabilitation process may be difficult and frustrating for a recovering stroke patient. Learning to reuse affected parts of the body can take a long period of time. Some function may never be regained. Physical therapy, though often tiring and even painful, is an essential part of the rehabilitation process. Stroke patients, especially those who have suffered a severe stroke, need encouragement and support. Remind your parent of the progress he or she has made. Modify the home environment to make functioning easier. Use memory aids such as an appointment book and written notes. Plan extra time for completing tasks to reduce frustration about being slow.

Dealing with a recovering stroke patient can be physically and emotionally taxing for the primary caregiver, whether that be you, another family member, friend, or other. Stroke patients often experience frustration, discouragement, anxiety, or depression. Because of changes within the brain, you may notice that your parent has trouble controlling emotions, especially anger or tears. He or she may become inflexible, impatient, or irritable.

Many recovering stroke patients have difficulty in social interaction. They can seem insensitive to others or may misinterpret other people's behaviors and motives. If you are having difficulty dealing with your parent after a stroke, the following strategies may help:

* First, learn as much as possible about strokes. Your parent's physician or your own health care provider may be helpful in this. You can also contact your local Stroke Association or the American Heart Association for information. Several helpful resources are listed in *Tab 7: Resources*. Information will help you put your parent's behavior in context. Usually, it helps to understand that the patient is not being deliberately difficult; he or she simply can not control behavior at this point.

* Second, get help for yourself. Talk to a friend. Go take a walk. Join a support group. However you deal with stress, take the time to take care of yourself. Especially if you are the primary caregiver in the situation, you need to give yourself frequent breaks and time for restoration of your perspective. Taking care of yourself is an essential part of being able to take good care of your parents.

Thrombo-phlebitis (deep vein)

Deep vein thrombo-phlebitis is a condition where clots and inflammation form in the veins. These clots occur because of slowed movement of blood through the veins.

Symptoms of this condition include tenderness or pain in the leg, lower leg discomfort or swelling, or an area in the lower leg that feels hot to the touch. If untreated, thrombo-phlebitis can be dangerous. If your parent experiences the above symptoms, make sure he or she contacts a physician immediately.

Prevention or minimization of thrombo-phlebitis depends on several factors. The most important of these is to maintain adequate exercise. Even if your parent is bed-ridden or forced into a period of inactivity, a limited exercise program can minimize the risk of developing clots. Cessation of smoking is another important factor. Finally, it is important for older persons, especially those with a history of clots, to not wear garters or other constricting bands around the legs.

❏ DIET AND LIFESTYLE MODIFICATION FOR THE PREVENTION AND MINIMIZATION OF CARDIOVASCULAR DISEASE

The diseases and conditions discussed above can be serious, potentially fatal health problems. Some of the risk factors which contribute to them are outside of individual control—such as a family history of disease. However, other risk factors are largely a matter of personal choice. Smoking is a good example of such a factor. The decision to cut down or quit smoking is a positive step towards improved cardiovascular health.

Along with quitting smoking, the three other lifestyle changes over which persons have most control are diet, exercise, and stress reduction. In this section we will talk about these three contributors to prevention and minimization of cardiovascular dysfunction.

Diet

In *Issue 10: Staying Healthy*, we talked in general terms about the importance of good dietary habits in older adults. Older persons need fewer calories, but need as much in the way of vitamins and other nutrients; therefore an older person's diet needs to be more carefully planned than a younger person's. There are several ways to be aware of how diet interacts with cardiovascular disease. First, being overweight increases the risk of many of the diseases and conditions discussed above. A carefully planned diet will get rid of excess weight or maintain a reasonable target weight, thus reducing that particular risk factor.

Second, most adults are becoming increasingly aware of simple diet modifications which promote cardiovascular health. Even restaurants are now beginning to understand that healthy eating habits are important to people, and offer "happy heart cuisine" or other such sections on their menus. Simple but significant modifications of diet include:

✔ low or no salt preparation of foods; the use of other spices, herbs, or a salt substitute to flavor foods;

✔ restriction of fats, especially saturated fats, in the diet;

✔ use of low-or non-fat dairy products;

✔ avoidance of high cholesterol foods;

✔ inclusion of increased fiber in the diet.

There are many cookbooks in circulation today which specialize in tasty foods for those whose diet is restricted because of cardiovascular disease. See *Tab 7: Resources* for references. Look through some of these. Buy one for your parent. Once the habits are changed, many people find they prefer their new style of eating.

Exercise

Exercise, especially aerobic exercise which conditions the heart muscle and cardiovascular system, is an important component in cardiovascular fitness. All older adults should be encouraged to exercise regularly. Before beginning an exercise program, however, your parent should consult his or her physician. Overdoing it, especially after a heart attack or some other forms of heart problem, can be dangerous. Outside of special exercise programs prescribed by your parent's physician, the section on exercise in *Issue 10: Staying Healthy* should help your parent decide on a suitable exercise program for his or her particular circumstances.

Stress reduction

One of the factors that health care professionals are learning more about in regards to health is stress: how we handle the variety of challenges our living environment creates. No one can avoid stress entirely. Living is stressful. However, it is possible both to reduce the causes of stress encountered in daily living and to learn to cope better with those that can not be avoided.

Cardiovascular difficulties often push a person to evaluate his or her life. This should be a positive undertaking. It can be beneficial at a number of levels to take the time to look at one's life, decide what is really important, and what can be given up. When illness forces such an assessment, often the shift in priorities, the giving up of unnecessary causes of stress, gives the patient a sense of greater control over his or her life and increased well-being.

For stresses that can not be eliminated, there are strategies which reduce the impact of stress on the body. Exercise for many people is such a reducer. A valued hobby or favorite activity might also decrease the stress level. Talking with a friend, mental health professional, or other counselor can also be helpful. Every person develops individual ways of adapting and coping best.

If your parent suffers from cardiovascular problems, it might be helpful for you or a health care professional to explicitly help to name the stresses of his or her life, evaluate which ones are important and which ones can be given up, and strategize the best ways of dealing with the stress that remains. Such an evaluation can both reduce your parent's risk of subsequent problems, and contribute to an enhanced sense of well being.

◻ DISEASES AND PROBLEMS OF THE BONES AND JOINTS

As persons grow older, there is inevitable wear and tear on the joints of the body. Coupled with that, older people's bones often grow more brittle, and healing of bones and other tissues occurs more slowly than in younger persons. Over 90% of persons over 60 have some degree of problem with their bones and joints. These problems can be caused by heredity, by general wear and tear, by poor diet, or by falls—a major problem for older adults. In this section, we will discuss four major problems older persons encounter involving bones and joints:

- arthritis,
- osteoporosis,
- falls,
- foot care.

Arthritis

There are many types of arthritis. The type that usually affects older adults is osteoarthritis. This is a degenerative disease of the joints caused both by heredity and by years of use and stress on the elastic tissues (cartilage) of the joints. A person with osteoarthritis feels stiffness and pain in the affected joints. The joints become inflamed and can become swollen.

Your parent's health care provider can help to treat arthritis with specific exercises and anti-inflammatory drugs. Sometimes, physical therapy or joint replacement is necessary. Other things which can help include keeping as active as possible, maintaining a balanced schedule of rest and activity, applying heat to painful areas, and maintaining a healthy weight to reduce stress on affected joints.

Osteoporosis

Osteoporosis is a bone disease which affects twenty million Americans, about 75% of them women. Approximately one quarter of all women over the age of 60 may be affected by this disease. Osteoporosis is a major cause of back pain, hip, wrist, and spinal fractures, and Dowager's Hump. In some cases, the bones may become so brittle that an older adult can break a vertebra simply by sneezing, or fracture a hip by turning over in bed.

Osteoporosis is caused by a loss of minerals from the bones. There are many factors which contribute to the development of osteoporosis. Women are three times more prone to it than men, especially small-boned and underweight women, or women who experienced early menopause or the removal of their ovaries. Family history, smoking, excess intake of alcohol, thyroid problems and lack of exercise are all potential contributing factors. Intake of dietary calcium is also important while bones are developing.

A physician can diagnose osteoporosis through a physical examination. Once at least 30% of bone mass has been lost, osteoporosis can be detected on an X-ray. Treatment usually includes increasing exercise, and sometimes giving estrogen or other medications to post-menopausal women. Bones become stronger and denser when doing weight bearing exercise such as walking, running, weight lifting, or bicycling. Exercise can also help decrease the pain due to osteoporotic fractures.

Falls

Falls are not, strictly speaking, either a disease or a disability. However, they are a major health problem for older adults. One third of all people over age 65 will fall this year. Falls are the leading cause of accidental death for persons over 75 years of age. Approximately 30% of nursing home admissions are due to falls. They are a major preventable health problem for older adults.

Falls are especially dangerous to older persons because their bones are slow in healing. Broken hips are the most common fracture caused by falls. They carry with them a high death rate. Falls can also result in head injuries which can lead to neurological damage.

The reasons older adults fall are many. Often, falls occur because of some physical problem which has come on so gradually that it is not recognized as a problem. Failing eyesight, increasing dizziness, and slow reactions are examples of this kind of problem. Heart and blood pressure problems can also lead to falls. As your parent gets older, it is important that you watch for the subtle signs of increasing physical handicap. It is also important that your parent live in as safe an environment as possible without removing the comfort and ambiance of home. *Issue 4* in this book deals with home safety, including how to reduce the risk of falls.

Foot care

In order to maintain adequate mobility with increased age, foot care becomes very important. Eighty percent of persons over 65 have foot problems. Yet foot care may be neglected because the older adult can no longer lean over comfortably to reach the feet or see to care for their feet. The skin becomes more sensitive; therefore, it needs more care in order to prevent sores and discomfort while walking. The toenails thicken and become harder to cut.

Basic Foot Care for an Older Adult.

Sit on a low stool. The feet should be soaked in warm water for about ten minutes. The water softens the toenails and makes them easier to cut. One foot is left in the water while you are working on the other.

Take one foot out of the water and pat it dry, taking special care to dry between the toes. Inspect the foot for any signs of problems such as redness, cracking, cuts, corns, ingrown toenails, or edema.

Clip the nails straight across, taking little nips rather than trying to cut across the width of the nail. Do not clip shorter than the end of the toe. A pumice stone or emery board may be used to remove dry skin from the heels and the sides of the feet or to smooth down any calluses. Never attempt to cut away a callus. Complete the process by massaging the foot and nails with cream or lotion, but do not use cream between the toes.

Problems of the feet include bunions, hammer toe, joint deformities, arthritis, calluses, corns, ingrown toenails, fungus of the nails, athlete's foot, and edema. Athlete's foot and other fungal infections may have been present in the older adult for many years. They are not harmful and are usually treated only if the individual is uncomfortable from them. Corns, calluses, and bunions are most often caused by repeated pressure on an area from years of wearing improperly fitted or poorly designed shoes, or from deformities of the joint. Edema is the gathering of fluids in the tissues of the feet and legs often caused by poor circulation. Elevation of the feet and legs will reduce edema. Well fitted, supportive shoes can increase walking ease. In order to walk with comfort, the problems mentioned above need to be treated by your health care provider or a podiatrist (foot specialist).

Expert care of the feet is particularly important for those who have diabetes or circulatory problems.

❐ ELIMINATION PROBLEMS

One of the realities of the aging process is that often it has an effect on the body's elimination system. The two most common problems encountered by older adults in this area are constipation and incontinence. In this section, we discuss these two problems and ways that you can help your parent minimize or live with them.

Constipation

Constipation is a common problem for older people. When a person becomes constipated, the waste matter of the bowel becomes too hard to pass easily, or bowel movements become so infrequent that they are uncomfortable. There are several causes of constipation. They include lack of exercise, a diet low in fiber or fluids, many diseases, and use of certain drugs. The symptoms are easy to spot, primarily no or infrequent bowel movements, or a feeling of discomfort in the rectum or intestines. Often these primary symptoms are accompanied by other gastro-intestinal symptoms and urinary incontinence or infection.

Constipation is something that should be noted by, and talked about with, a physician in a regular check-up if your parent is open with the physician about the problem. There are several things which your parent can do on his or her own to relieve this problem. They include increasing the amount of daily exercise, increasing dietary fiber and fluids, and taking bulk fiber supplements, such as Metamucil, if needed. A combination of these three strategies may take care of the problem. A regular time of the day for bowel movements, usually after breakfast, and spending adequate time on the toilet help reestablish a regular bowel pattern.

Enemas or laxatives should be reserved for severe constipation. A glycerin suppository is often helpful in stimulating bowel movements and is very safe. If an enema is used, a prepackaged enema bottle or tap water enema is safest.

If all of the above suggestions do not produce relief for your parent, it is important for him or her to talk with a physician or other health care professional.

Incontinence

Incontinence is the inability to maintain control over the release of urine from the bladder or of feces from the bowel. The causes of incontinence vary widely, as does the degree of the problem. Incontinence may be brought on by illness, fatigue, confusion, or a hospital admission.

It also may be caused by weakening of the sphincters (muscles which control bladder outflow), disorders of the central nervous system, obstruction to the bladder, or the after-effects of childbearing.

It is helpful to be able to distinguish between the different types of incontinence:

✔ *Urge incontinence.* This type of incontinence occurs often in the elderly and can be the result of neurological damage, strokes, or the aftermath of bladder infections or kidney stones. In this circumstance, the individual does not receive a signal in time to reach the bathroom before the bladder begins to empty itself. This kind of incontinence often can be controlled by learning to empty the bladder every two hours, even when the need is not felt. If your parent has trouble moving quickly to the bathroom, a commode chair may be placed in a convenient place.

✔ *Overflow incontinence.* Overflow incontinence occurs where there is obstruction to the flow of urine; for example, in men, due to enlarged prostate. This type of incontinence is characterized by a swollen or distended bladder, often without pain.

✔ *Stress Incontinence.* Stress incontinence has to do with the involuntary passing of urine during any increase in abdominal pressure, such as coughing, sneezing, or laughing. It is often seen in women who have had relaxation of the muscles of the pelvic floor, usually due to childbirth.

When incontinence is experienced, it is important to consult a physician to determine its cause and type. A physician will be able to treat any disease that is present, check and reevaluate medications that might cause or increase incontinence, and evaluate the severity of the problem. Surgery is sometimes effective, especially in treatment of stress incontinence and incontinence due to prostate enlargement. Only a physician can tell if such treatment would be effective for any particular case.

There are several things your parent can do on his or her own to help live with incontinence. There are exercises called "Kegal exercises" which can be done to strengthen the bladder muscles and the muscles of the pelvic floor. Ask your health care provider to recommend some. Sometimes biofeedback is helpful to help an older person become more sensitive to and control the body's signals. Reduce intake of caffeine and alcohol. Both caffeine and alcohol increase incontinence by irritating the bladder. Stop smoking—cigarette, cigar, and pipe tobacco also irritate the bladder. Drink 6-8 cups of liquid daily; concentrated urine is another bladder irritant.

Your parent may feel more secure wearing disposable undergarments designed for persons with problems with incontinence. One of the achievements of modern technology is the production of what are essentially adult diapers that are inconspicuous and quite effective in masking the incontinence. These undergarments are sold in drug stores and supermarkets, and though they don't "solve" the problem, they may bring a sense of peace of mind and dignity to your parent.

When dealing with an incontinent adult, tact and sensitivity are always necessary. Try not to overreact if your parent has an accident around you. Dignity is a fragile thing in all of us, and it is something we all need to maintain. This is one of those occasions in which you need to be particularly careful in your caring.

◻ CANCERS

With increased age, there is a greater likelihood of developing cancer. Just the word "cancer" is frightening to many people. They associate it with sure and painful death. It is true that some cancers cannot be effectively controlled or cured. But with the advances made by medical science in the past 25 years, given early detection and treatment, many cancers can in fact be cured.

There are seven danger signs for cancer. If a person has one of these signs, it does not necessarily mean that cancer is present, but it does mean that it is crucial to see a physician immediately to have the problem properly diagnosed and treated. The seven danger signs are:

- unusual bleeding or discharge,
- a lump or thickening in the breast or elsewhere,
- a sore that does not heal,
- a change in bowel or bladder habits,
- continual hoarseness or cough,
- difficulty in swallowing,
- a change in a wart or mole.

Many people are afraid to consult their doctor when they see one of these signs. They think that if they do not know about the problem it won't really be there. Many persons convince themselves that if it were really cancer, they would feel sick or would be experiencing pain. It is important to note that pain is not an early sign of cancer. Usually by the time there is pain, the disease is far advanced, and there is less chance for effective treatment.

As you care for your parents, it is important that both you and they are familiar with these seven signs of cancer. If your parent shows any of these signs, he or she should

Patient and Family Support Groups

When you or someone you love is diagnosed with a serious disease or disability, it can be a cause of considerable stress. There is usually much new information to learn, as well as the uncertainty of exactly how this new development will affect life both for the patient and for the patient's family.

Physicians and therapists have found that it is often helpful for patients and/or their families to participate in support groups specially geared for persons coping with this particular disease or disability. Support groups can be organized by hospitals, physician groups, nursing homes, or community service providers. They usually provide both education about the disease and an opportunity to share experiences. Participation can help a person to overcome feelings of isolation, fear, and powerlessness. It helps to see others coping with the same problems you have, to laugh, and cry together, and find friends who really understand what is going on in your life.

Senior Information and Referral and most clinics, hospitals, home health agencies, and nursing homes are able to help you locate a support group that fits your needs or the needs of your parent. Early contact can significantly reduce the stress of coping with serious illness or disability.

consult a physician. It could make a significant difference in outcome.

Also, it is important to have regular screening evaluations for common types of cancer. These include breast exams, mammograms, pelvic exams, prostate exams, and tests for blood in the stool.

Cancers have many causes, some that we understand, and others that we don't. There are some standard things a person can do to minimize the risk of some cancers. These include:

- do not smoke;

- avoid overexposure to the sun and needless x-rays;

- avoid exposure to car fumes, factory exhausts, household cleaners, solvents, and garden and lawn chemicals;

- decrease the quantity of smoked and fatty foods in your diet;

- avoid excess caloric intake; if overweight, lose weight;

- eat a high fiber diet.

Cancer is not a disease but a class of diseases where abnormal cells multiply and invade normal tissue. There are many different kinds of cancers, and they affect different parts of the body. It is not possible in our space here to list all the various cancers, their signs, causes, and treatments. However, that information is readily available in local communities through the American Cancer Society and other local resources.

If your parent is diagnosed as having a particular type of cancer, there are several things you can do which will help. First, find out as much about that particular type of cancer as possible. Learn what the treatment options are. Often a physician will have a preferred mode of treatment, and because of time or training will present that as the only appropriate course of treatment. Press for alternatives. If the treatment suggested is extensive, it is perfectly all right to ask for and get a second opinion.

Because most people experience some degree of shock or denial or both when given a diagnosis of cancer, it may easily fall to you or some other close relative to ask questions of the physician. Your parent may just not be up to it. It is important to remember, however, that the treatment decision is your parent's to make. If he or she wants to take on aggressive treatment to extend life, support that decision. If he or she would prefer palliative care—that is, care directed at comfort, rather than cure—support that as well. It is your parent's decision to make. Your job is to help understand options, listen to questions and concerns, try to get the information he or she needs, and to love and support your parent as he or she carries out the preferred treatment plan.

❐ DISEASES AND DISABILITIES AFFECTING THE MIND AND PERSONALITY

The brain is an organ of the body like any other, and with advancing age, it is more likely to be struck by disease or disability which can cause impaired functioning. Beyond that physical reality, old age is often a time of mental and emotional stress. Older adults suffer many losses: loss of friends and partners, loss of a job and the self-esteem work brings, of secure income, of independence, of good health, and more. These are not easy to face for persons of any age. And when many losses come at once or one after the other, as often happens with older persons, the burden of stress and grief is significantly increased.

In this section, we discuss a number of conditions which cause noticeable behavior change in older adults. This behavior change can be evidenced as confusion, depression, irrational anger or swift mood changes, or other more subtle changes in spirit or personality. The sources of such common behavior changes in older adults are many. Some are caused by disease or emotional stress; others are caused by medications. Below, we discuss the most common problems involving older adults which cause change in mental status. They are:

- memory loss,
- dementia, including Alzheimer's Disease,
- depression,
- alcohol abuse.

Memory loss or confusion

Some people, even health professionals, consider memory loss or confusion to be a normal part of the aging process. This is not true. Only 20% of persons over age 80 are confused. A large percentage of the older population lives into their 80s, 90s, or even to 100 with no signs of any confusion.

There are many reversible causes of confusion in older adults. They include:

- ✔ toxic reaction to medications—this is the most common cause of reversible confusion,
- ✔ conflicting drugs added to existing ones,
- ✔ nutritional deficiencies,
- ✔ illness—sudden onset of confusion may be the first sign of a heart attack, fever, infection, or other illness in an older adult,
- ✔ head injuries,
- ✔ Transient Ischemic Attack,

- ✔ thyroid problems,
- ✔ depression,
- ✔ alcoholism,
- ✔ lack of sleep,
- ✔ sensory (visual and auditory) impairment.

If your parent shows signs of becoming confused, a complete physical examination should be done by a physician familiar with the problems of older persons. Even in those who have some irreversible confusion, a treatable cause may coexist. This could be complicating the irreversible confusion. Always look for and treat reversible causes of confusion.

Dementia and Alzheimer's disease

Dementia is the progressive loss of the ability to process information, memory, language, or spatial discrimination. There are many causes of dementia, including multi-infarct disease (loss of brain function from many strokes), Alzheimer's disease, chronic alcohol abuse, vitamin deficiencies, Parkinson's disease and other rarer causes. Some changes in brain tissue occur in all aging persons. In the Alzheimer's disease sufferer, those changes occur in large numbers of cells and in specific areas of the brain. Alzheimer's patients develop neurofibrillary tangles—nerve cells which become tangled and dysfunctional. Certain chemicals in the brain responsible for transmitting nerve impulses are reduced.

There are many changes in behavior noted with the onset of Alzheimer's disease. At first, you may notice a progressive deterioration of memory, and difficulty learning new information. Gradually the person develops problems in carrying out familiar tasks, understanding concepts, and taking care of grooming or work. Perceptual disturbances, spatial disorientation, and restlessness might also occur.

As the disease progresses, there is more disorientation, and a decreased ability to understand concepts, to perform daily tasks, and to sleep. In its final stages, Alzheimer's disease is characterized by a total lack of concern for appearance or body function, significant sleep disturbance, extreme irritability, and loss of ability to talk. Alzheimer's is a terminal illness. Gradually the person stops eating or drinking regularly and may die from an infection which the body's defenses can't fight, or from dehydration.

Alzheimer's disease must be diagnosed by a physician who is experienced in testing and diagnosis of this disease. At this time, there is no treatment for the disease. Several drugs are currently being tested; they may in the future offer a more concrete hope to patients and families. In the absence of effective treatment, some things can be done to help. They include treating all coexisting diseases, using medications to help control anxiety or other symptoms, evaluating medications to see if they are making confusion worse, and making changes in the home to reduce confusion there.

The adjustment of both patient and family to a diagnosis of Alzheimer's may be very difficult. If your parent receives such a diagnosis, there are some strategies for successful coping. Learn all you can about the disease. Mace and Rabin's *The Thirty-Six Hour Day* or Powell's *Alzheimer's Disease* are excellent references. Talk with others who are living or have lived with a family member with Alzheimer's. Join a support group. Make sure your parent does necessary legal, financial, and medical planning while he or she is still competent. This will make life easier later. Make sure that the primary caregiver has good respite care.

Consider placing your parent's name on the waiting list of a good nursing home equipped to handle Alzheimer's patients. Many facilities have waiting lists of several years, and if the time arrives when your family cannot care for your parent, you will be grateful to have already begun the wait.

Alzheimer's disease can be an exhausting, emotional, and isolating illness to deal with. Get all the support you can for both you and your parent. Make sure that you understand what is going on, and are not unrealistic in your expectation of your parent's behavior. Often, counseling or regular contact with someone who has been a caregiver for a family member with Alzheimer's can be a source of practical ideas and support. This is a difficult and emotional disease. Take care of yourself as you take care of your parent.

Depression

Depression is a serious problem with older adults. It can have many causes. Among these are health problems that limit life and mobility, a variety of illnesses, drug interactions, medications (some drugs cause depression), nutritional deficiencies, deafness and other sensory changes, and chronic pain. One adds to these potential problems the predictable losses of old age: loss of friends, loss of self-worth, loss of social status and social support, loss of financial security, loss of spouse and other intimate relationships. Not every older person experiences all of these losses, but all older persons experience some of them. Often, the accumulation of things adds up to serious depression.

Some of the symptoms of depression follow. They must usually be present in the older adult for at least two weeks, with no other major health problem present before a diagnosis of depression may be made. They are:

- a persistent sad mood;
- the inability to find meaning or pleasure in life;
- unusual lack of interest or ambition; hopelessness;
- disturbances in eating or sleeping patterns;
- feelings of being alone, rejected, no good;
- lack of energy, deliberate isolation;
- withdrawal from previously enjoyed activities;
- changes in gait or speed of movement;
- neglect of personal appearance.

Often depression is transitory and easily explainable. Your parent experiences a major loss. That loss is followed by a period of depression. Other times, the cause of the depression is not evident. You merely notice its signs in your parent. Your parent may not even know what is causing the depression.

There are several important steps in dealing with depression in older adults. The first is to get your parent to talk about it and to accept treatment for it. Often older adults are resistant to talking about or being treated for depression. They grew up at a time when the conventional wisdom was just to "tough it out," and not accept treatment for mental health problems. Your hardest problem may be convincing your parent that it is okay to accept help.

Begin the helping process with a visit to the doctor. That is a type of help your parent is accustomed to receiving, and it may be that the depression is a side effect of illness or medication. If so, your parent's physician will be able to help. Also, in many older individuals, depression can be treated effectively with medication. Be positive with your parent. Find ways to increase his or her self-esteem.

Reinforce opportunities for success and affirmation. Many times a depressed person feels out of control of life. Help your parent establish control over as many areas of life as possible. Focus on short-term goals and keeping life simple. Encourage your parent to stay active and involved in life.

In all of this, be as matter of fact and positive as possible. Avoid patronizing your parent or treating him or her as a child. If it seems necessary, you may want to get professional help for your parent. There are more and more therapists who specialize in working with older adults. Ask your doctor or Senior Information and Referral for referrals.

Remember that the hardest part about depression is that the sufferer is depressed. At first, that may seem like an absurd statement, but one of the problems associated with depression is lack of motivation and inability to picture the depression getting better. It may be a long and frustrating process to get your parent to acknowledge that he or she needs help, to accept the help needed, and to exercise the necessary initiative to get well. Remember that this slowness is at least in part connected with the disease. It will take a great deal of patience and supportiveness for you to help. However, in most cases depression can be reversed or controlled. Your help will make a difference.

Alcohol abuse

It may be that as many as 10% of those over age sixty have a problem with alcohol. With the numerous losses that occur with the aging process, many people who did not drink heavily in earlier days may begin to use alcohol for company and comfort. At the same time, these people's bodies react to alcohol differently. With age, major changes occur in the body's ability to absorb and dispose of alcohol. Less drinking is required to produce an effect.

Alcohol abuse is often difficult to diagnose in older people. Alcohol abusers of any age experience denial, but denial is particularly intense among older adults. Along with denial, the symptoms of abuse may be masked as normal aging, depression, or drug side effects. Signs of possible alcohol abuse include: inappropriate behavior; odor of alcohol on the breath or the clothing; altered appearance; a bloated, red look around the face; bruises from falls which the person tries to cover up or make light of; blackouts; little or no appetite; frequent hand tremors; refusal to answer the door; a large number of bottles in the trash or refrigerator.

If you suspect your parent of alcohol abuse, the first rule is to get help. This is not something you can fix alone. Do not confront your parent if you find him or her drunk. Instead, call Alcoholics Anonymous—they have a special "Golden Years" program for older adults—or one of the many alcohol abuse treatment centers in your area, and find out how best to stage an intervention. Much has been learned about alcoholism and treatment for alcohol abusers over the past two decades. There is a lot of good professional help available in most communities. Draw on that help. It will both give you support in the process, and maximize the chances of successful treatment for your parent.

As your parent is receiving help, or if your parent refuses help, there are a large number of resources available to support family members of alcohol abusers. This is a family concern. Though only one person may be a problem drinker, other family members may have problems due to that person's drinking. Al-Anon is the parallel organization to Alcoholics Anonymous for family members and friends. It has been helpful to many people and may have a local program that can help you.

Finally, you have to accept that there is only so much you can do to help a parent with this problem; he or she must want to recover. Do what you can, then let go of any feelings of guilt or anger you have about the situation. That is, of course, easier said than done. That is one of the reasons why support is so necessary with this problem. However, it is important for families of alcohol abusers to know the limits of their ability and responsibility for their loved one's life.

❐ EYES

With increasing age, several diseases and conditions of the eye can impair eyesight or even cause blindness. The most common of these are described here.

Cataracts

A cataract is a cloudy spot on the lens of the eye. Persons of all ages develop cataracts, but they are especially common among older people—one of the normal processes of aging which cannot be prevented. Because the lens of the eye works like the lens of a camera to focus images on the retina, when the lens becomes clouded by a cataract, the images a person sees become hazy and blurred. The more severe the cataract, the more significant the loss of vision.

The only way to treat a cataract is to remove it and implant a clear lens in its place. Cataract surgery is the most common surgical procedure in this country; over a million are performed each year with a very high success rate. Because it is a relatively simple and short operation, it is usually performed as a day surgery procedure.

There is no magic point at which it becomes advisable or necessary to operate to remove a cataract. That is a decision each patient must make on the basis of a physician's recommendation. Timing will depend on the person's health and how much vision loss is being caused by the cataract. Some people would rather live with diminished vision than undergo surgery; others want to have surgery early, at a point of relatively minor vision loss. It is a matter of personal choice, and the success of the operation does not depend on the severity of the cataract or how early or late the problem is addressed.

Glaucoma

Glaucoma is the leading cause of blindness in persons over age 40. It is a condition in which the fluid in the eye either increases or does not drain adequately. The pressure from the additional fluid can cause damage to the structure of the eye. There is no way to prevent glaucoma; however, early detection and treatment can help control it. Because glaucoma has no symptoms in its early stages, it can only be detected through a regular and complete eye examination by an eye care professional. Once diagnosed, glaucoma patients should take care to use their medications as prescribed. It can make the difference between sight and blindness.

Macular degeneration

Macular degeneration is the process of wear and tear in the macula, the part of the eye responsible for sharp central vision and color. It usually affects both eyes and can result in either gradual or sudden loss of vision. Because the macula is not responsible for side vision, macular degeneration rarely results in total blindness. Depending on the type and severity, some macular degeneration responds to treatment. Only consultation with a qualified eye care professional can determine the extent of such degeneration and the appropriate options.

Diabetes

Blindness can be a major effect of diabetes in older adults. All persons with a history of diabetes should have their eyes examined annually by an eye care professional. Vision loss can be prevented with laser treatment, but such treatment is often necessary before there are any noticeable symptoms.

Routine eye care

Because eyesight is so important, all older adults should have their eyes examined regularly. They should also see an eye doctor immediately if they experience any of the following symptoms:

- ✔ sudden severe pain in the eye;
- ✔ acute vision loss or significant blurriness;
- ✔ recent onset of double vision;
- ✔ recent onset of flashing lights, floaters, or veils across vision.

Adapting to vision changes

As a person's eyesight changes with advancing age, it may necessitate some changes in daily routine. However, there are a variety of aids available to persons with impaired vision to help them use their remaining eyesight effectively, and to compensate for vision loss. These include magnifiers, large print books, audio tapes, large print attachments for telephones and clocks, talking calculators, and more. These aids, though they cannot return lost sight, can make an important difference in a person's quality of daily life.

◻ HEARING PROBLEMS

As persons grow older, many develop problems with hearing. Hearing problems can range in severity from being a minor annoyance to a significant disability. In this section, we deal with the two most common problems with hearing in older adults: hearing loss due to otosclerosis, and tinnitus.

Hearing loss

There are many factors which can influence hearing: childhood disease, occupational noise or injury, family history. However, when hearing loss comes on gradually in older adults, its most common cause is otosclerosis, a kind of arthritis of the small bones in the inner ear. Persons with hearing loss from otosclerosis may first notice that they have trouble hearing in noisy environments, where there are large groups of people present or a lot of background noise. Even hearing at the dinner table when there are several people present may be a problem. As hearing loss continues, a person may have trouble hearing the ends of sentences when persons drop their voices or miss words if the person talking looks away.

Hearing loss due to otosclerosis cannot be prevented or cured, but it can be helped by using a hearing aid. There is no set rule about when a person should get a hearing aid. A hearing aid will not slow or stop hearing loss; it merely amplifies sound so that persons with hearing problems can hear better. Many physicians recommend that persons should look into getting hearing aids when hearing loss becomes embarrassing or frustrating to them, when they feel they are missing out on important information or have to ask speakers to repeat themselves over and over again.

Getting a hearing aid

If your parent is having trouble hearing and feels that he or she should look into getting a hearing aid, the first stop should be his or her primary physician. The physician can do a preliminary evaluation of your parent's hearing, and make sure there are no other physical causes for hearing loss. If your parent experiences a sudden loss of hearing, or hearing loss is accompanied by other symptoms such as vertigo, ringing in the ears, or nausea, he or she should see a physician immediately.

The physician will recommend that your parent see a licensed audiologist who will then do a more complete test of your parent's hearing and prescribe an appropriate hearing aid. It is important to make sure the business which sells you the hearing aid is one which employs a licensed audiologist to do the testing. It is also generally in your parent's best interest to do business with an audiologist who represents more than one brand of hearing aid. Such a person will have a wider range of products available, and is not captive to any one maker. If your parent has problems with the hearing aid prescribed, he or she should not be afraid to say so. Sometimes, hearing loss is not entirely replaceable, but other times it just takes some work to get the hearing aid functioning most effectively.

If your parent develops problems with hearing loss, then he or she should be very careful taking aspirin. Aspirin overdose can cause increased hearing loss without a person being aware of the problem. Your parent's physician can provide more information on how to avoid this problem and what safe limits for aspirin consumption might be.

For some people, hearing loss is embarassing. They don't want to admit that it is happening to them, and so they avoid for as long as possible facing the problem and getting help. Your support and help in treating the problems caused by hearing loss sensitively and matter of factly will be important.

Tinnitus

Tinnitus is a head noise disorder. It affects approximately thirty-six million Americans. Of those, about 20% are so severely affected that it is a significant limitation. The noises of tinnitus may be heard in one or both ears. It may be experienced as ringing, buzzing, or some other sound. In most cases, head noises are accompanied by some hearing loss.

There are many possible causes of tinnitus. Wax pressing against the eardrum, deafness, medications, tumors in the ear or brain, Meniere's disease, or exposure to loud noises can all cause this disorder. Another common cause is the sclerosis of the tiny bones in the ear. In this condition, the bones grow together instead of vibrating freely with the passage of sound waves.

Tinnitus can be a very stressful problem. The first step towards solving it is to see an ear specialist (otologist or otolaryngologist) in order to determine whether the problem can be treated to reduce or eliminate the noise. There are some general guidelines for persons who suffer from tinnitus. They should stay away from loud noises, reduce salt and alcohol intake, and avoid stimulants such as caffeine and nicotine. Adequate rest and exercise are important. So is trying to ignore the sounds. If the sounds are impossible to ignore, then your parent can try to mask them by playing music, or by purchasing a masker which merely substitutes a more pleasant sound for the disturbing one. There are also support groups for sufferers of tinnitus.

❒ MISCELLANEOUS PROBLEMS: DIABETES MELLITUS, HYPOTHYROIDISM, PARKINSON'S DISEASE, AND CARE OF THE MOUTH

Diabetes mellitus

Diabetes is a disorder caused by a disturbance in the action of the hormone insulin in the body. Because of this disturbance, the body is unable to digest carbohydrates, fat, and protein efficiently. Diabetes is detected by elevated blood sugar levels, and treatment is directed at controlling blood sugar. Severe health problems such as infection, blindness, kidney failure, heart disease, nerve damage, stroke, or gangrene may occur with uncontrolled diabetes. These may be lessened by controlling the diabetes.

There are two types of diabetes. Type I is found most often in children. Type II diabetes, noninsulin dependent, is most common in older people. Type II diabetes may be prevented or controlled by the maintenance of proper weight, diet, and exercise. Risk factors for this disease include family history, increased age, obesity, and gender (women are three times more likely than men to develop diabetes). Diabetes is diagnosed by a physician through blood and urine tests.

Signs of diabetes include fatigue and general weakness, excessive or frequent urination, increased thirst, increased appetite without weight gain, infections, pain or numbness in the legs or feet, slow healing of cuts or bruises, blurred vision, and inability to recover from minor illnesses. If your parent shows any of these signs, he or she should see a physician. The physician will recommend a diet. It is very important to adhere to this diet. Exercise is also important as it helps the body burn off excess sugar. Medication may be prescribed, usually pills, which help control blood sugar. Diabetics should monitor their blood sugar as directed by their physician. Because diabetes affects blood circulation, special attention may be needed in care of feet and skin.

Special Hints for Management of Diabetes

The following can be particularly helpful in maintaining health and comfort in someone with Type II diabetes.

✔ Avoid hot water baths, heating pads, or electric blankets, because burns can occur without being felt.

✔ Bathe feet every day in warm water. Dry well. Test water with elbow, not toes. Inspect feet regularly for cuts, bruises, or infection. Always wear properly fitted shoes that are in good condition. Cut toenails straight across. If your parent has trouble cutting nails, obtain professional foot care.

✔ Avoid smoking.

✔ Have an eye examination once a year.

Hypothyroidism

After diabetes, hypothyroidism is the most common endocrine disorder in older adults. The thyroid gland ceases to produce adequate levels of thyroid hormone. Thyroid hormone stimulates the body's metabolism and contributes to the energy level. Five to fifteen percent of persons over age 65 are affected by this disorder. It can be detected by a physician by administering a simple thyroid test.

The symptoms of this disorder are as follows: apathy, constipation, a feeling of weakness, muscle pain, cramps, weight gain, hoarse voice, and sometimes depression and confusion. Once the disorder is diagnosed, it is easily treated with thyroid replacement therapy.

Parkinson's disease

Parkinson's disease is a progressive disorder of the brain that occurs most often in later life. It is characterized by tremor and stiffness of the muscles. In particular, Parkinson's sufferers have difficulty initiating movements. A large proportion of individuals with Parkinson's disease suffer from depression and/or dementia. This dementia is different from that suffered by persons with Alzheimer's disease.

The cause of this disease is unknown. It's symptoms include: cramping or tremor of the hand, foot, or leg; nodding of the head; movements that are slower and more difficult; loss of mobility in the face; a shuffling gait; muscle stiffness; a stooped stance. There is medication to treat Parkinson's Disease. Physical therapy and light massage are also helpful. Increased fluids and roughage are necessary for good bowel function.

Support groups for patients and caregivers can be found

in most communities. This disease can be both physically and emotionally demanding. Look for and find help for your parent and for yourself.

Care of the mouth

The need for care of the mouth continues to be important as we grow older. Many people feel that with age, it is no longer important to see the dentist. This is far from true.

In older persons, the gums normally recede, exposing the sensitive and prone-to-decay tooth surfaces which are normally protected. The internal surfaces of the mouth become thinner and more fragile; thus, they are more susceptible to injury from hard foods or the hard bristles of a toothbrush.

Problems with receding gums are complicated by the fact that many older adults lose fine muscle control and have trouble adequately brushing their teeth. If your parent has difficulty brushing, ask a dentist for a recommendation about brushing aids. There is some new technology available which can help your parent restore proper dental hygiene.

Lack of good mouth care can affect other things such as facial appearance, clarity of speech, and the ability to chew. These changes limit choices and enjoyment of food, social interaction, and freedom from pain.

If teeth are lost and not replaced, the bony structures of the mouth may deteriorate. This will cause an increase in other mouth problems and make it difficult to eat and maintain adequate nutrition. Modern dentures can be quite comfortable. Proper care of these is important in order to increase their life span and reduce mouth odors.

Care of the mouth and regular visits to the dentist are important throughout life regardless of age.

This issue discussion has been a quick trip through the major health concerns of older adults. In it, we have tried to highlight symptoms to watch for, and things which you and your parent can do to help manage disease and disability. Your best ally in helping both you and your parent can be a supportive and caring primary physician who monitors your parent's care over time, who is available for questions, and who will connect you with other important resources available in your community. For more information on physicians and developing a good relationship with them, see *Issue 13: The Role of Physicians.*

One final thing to remember. Some patients do abuse physicians' time with recurrent trivial complaints. However, most patients are more prone to wait too long to call a physician because they don't want to be a bother. It's better to be safe than sorry. If you or your parent suspects the presence of a serious illness or condition, seek help promptly.

Issue 12

Making Appropriate Care Decisions

The past twenty years have seen an explosion in new health care technologies, many of them directed toward extending and improving the quality of life of older people. Appropriately applied, these new technologies can add years of productivity and meaning to life. Many argue, however, that inappropriate application of such advances only extends dying rather than living; it can decrease, rather than increase, the quality of a life lived by an older adult.

❒ WHAT IS APPROPRIATE HEALTH CARE?

Different stages of life bring with them different priorities. Appropriate health care is care that serves the goals of the patient at a given stage of life. For example, a thirty-year-old mother might choose painful chemotherapy for cancer to have the chance to see her children grow up. An eighty-year-old woman might elect to forego chemotherapy and concentrate instead on making the most of the limited time left to her. Neither of these decisions is necessarily "the right decision" for all persons. They are examples of differing decisions which might appropriately be made by patients at different points in their lives.

Our health care system is geared to high technology curative medicine, and it functions best when the goal of medical treatment is clear and achievable: to restore the patient to a state of good health and function. However, sometimes this goal is not possible due to the nature of the patient's medical problem or problems and the limits of available therapies. In such circumstances, there can be several different goals of medical treatment depending on the point of view of the one looking at the case. As examples of such circumstances, consider the following:

> *Scenario 1*—A seventy-year-old woman, recently widowed, in general good health, finds out that she has cancer of the liver which has spread to other areas. There are chemotherapy and radiation treatments available which might slow the cancer and extend her life, but the treatments have significant unpleasant side effects. What is appropriate medical care in this case?

> *Scenario 2*—An eighty-two-year-old man is being discharged from the hospital having suffered a moderately severe heart attack. It would be best medically for him to go to a nursing home, but he does not want to go, and becomes very agitated whenever the subject comes up. He wants to return home, where he can see his garden, and talk with his neighbors. He lives alone, but has good friends and a son who comes to visit him on the weekends. What is appropriate medical care for this man?

> *Scenario 3*—The man in Scenario 2 above goes home. Before this recent hospitalization, he had a long talk with his son, saying that he was ready to die and wanted no extraordinary measures taken to keep him alive. He has a signed Living Will which he previously has shown his son. He has said to the son over and over again, "If you ever see me have a heart attack, don't call 911. Just

leave me alone." The son comes to visit his father on a Saturday afternoon and finds his father collapsed on the floor, barely breathing. His father says to him feebly, "Don't call." What should the son do?

In the above examples, the medical "good" of the patient is in conflict with other "goods" in the patient's life. When such situations occur, they always are difficult to sort out. Patients, families, and health care providers can have very different opinions as to the proper course to take. Whenever possible, the patient's preferences should prevail, whether or not they are shared by either the health care professionals or other family members. Your job as an advocate is to know your parent's preferences and help see that they are carried out as fully as possible.

❏ WHAT CAN BE DONE IN ADVANCE?

Difficult choices in health care are becoming more common as medical advances provide more and more treatment alternatives. Circumstances like the above three scenarios occur all the time. As an advocate for your parent, your job is to see that he or she gets the kind of health care that *he or she* feels is appropriate given the circumstances. This can be easier for everyone if certain things are done in advance of a medical crisis. The things which you and your parent can do ahead of time include the following:

1. *Talk with your parent about what he or she wants.* Most people, especially older people, have some idea about what they would like done in case of a medical emergency. Some people want all possible treatments tried. Others are uncomfortable with certain life-sustaining and life-prolonging

procedures. If you and your parent talk seriously about these matters in advance of an illness or emergency, then both of you can have more peace of mind when a problem comes up. Your parent will have a stronger advocate in you because you are sure of his or her position, and you will feel more confident in acting because of your previous knowledge. Your job will be made easier if your parent has discussed these issues with his or her physician and other family members, as well as you. Good communication ahead of time is essential if your parent's desires concerning care choices are to be carried out.

2. *Take the necessary legal steps to give effect to your parent's health care decisions.* Often, when a serious medical problem occurs, the patient is not in a good position to make his or her feelings known. The patient is too sick to talk, or a medical problem makes verbal communication impossible. There are two ways your parent can protect himself or herself from being voiceless in such circumstances. One is to execute a living will while still healthy. Although each state's law regarding living wills is slightly different, a typical form is included as *Form 19.1: Living Will Form.* Forms may also be available from health care providers. Living Wills are discussed in *Issue 19: Estate Planning Considerations.*

The second legal step which can be taken is for your parent to sign a durable power of attorney for health care by which he or she gives someone else (an "agent" or "attorney-in-fact") the power to make health care decisions on behalf of your parent if he or she becomes incapacitated. Durable powers of attorney can be useful, especially in making sure a person's wishes are respected in circumstances that fall outside those covered by a living will. Durable powers of attorney are discussed in more detail in *Issue 19: Estate Planning Considerations*.

3. *Make others aware of your parent's wishes.* If your parent has told you his or her thoughts about appropriate care and taken legal steps to secure those wishes, you should let other involved parties know your parent's wishes. Those other involved parties might be his or her physician or physicians, the treating nurses if your parent is hospitalized, the staff of the nursing home where your parent lives, and other family members. The more specific your parent is about his or her desires and the more people there are who understand those desires, the more likely it is that his or her desires will be honored and acted upon.

Conversations about health care choices may be uncomfortable. You may disagree with your parent's wishes; your parent's physician or other family members may disagree with his or her wishes. No matter how difficult these encounters may be, when a crisis occurs, your parent will be better served if such conversations have been held in advance. They mean that you, the family, and significant others will have time to get used to your parent's wishes before such wishes are put into effect.

❑ WHEN A CHANGE OF CIRCUMSTANCE OCCURS

As your parent's advocate in making health care decisions, there are certain guidelines that are helpful to follow when his or her health status changes. Often patients and families feel vulnerable and under stress in the health care setting. They are afraid to ask for more information or to admit that they do not fully understand the information given. In all health care encounters, the following guidelines should be followed:

- *Make sure you understand the information given to you.* If you are uncertain about what the doctor is saying, repeat what you *think* is being said. If your version is not correct, have the physician try again, and then you repeat it again. If you really don't understand what the physician is saying and seem to be getting nowhere, you have two other options. If your parent is hospitalized, talk with the nurses involved in your parent's care. Frequently, nurses have more contact with patients and families, and may be more skilled in communicating medical information in lay terms. If there is not a nurse to speak with, consider having your own physician contact your parent's doctor and translate for you. In any event, it is crucial that your parent (and you, if you are acting for your parent) understand the pertinent medical information concerning diagnosis, treatment, and prognosis.

- *Make sure you have heard and understood all the treatment alternatives.* Usually a physician has a preferred course of treatment. This judgment results from the physician's training, talent, personality, and experience. This preferred treatment may be the only treatment alternative that your parent is offered. Always make sure you ask about alternatives, even alternatives that the physician considers less attractive. Have the physician explain the reason for the recommended treatment. What would happen if a more conservative treatment were chosen? What would happen if no treatment occurred? Understanding all the alternatives, along with the attendant risks and possible benefits, is a fundamental right of patients (and those making decisions for patients unable to decide for themselves).

- *Help your parent sort out his or her decision.* When people are sick, they have limited energy available for making decisions, even important health care decisions. You can help in these situations. Listen to your parent's concerns. Help him or her organize thoughts. As much as possible, keep your own opinions out of the discussion. Focus on helping your parent clarify what is important and appropriate for him or her. When your parent makes a decision, support that decision.

- *Communicate the decision.* When your parent has made a decision and seems at peace with it, stay with him or her while your parent communicates the decision to the physician and others. You may be needed for support if others question your parent's preferences and decision. Listen to the information others present, but give support to your parent if he or she has made a firm decision. If the conversation becomes distressing for your parent, you may end it, either to be continued at a later date or not to be continued at all, if that is your parent's wish.

Usually when there is disagreement about appropriate care decisions, it is because people either do not understand the medical information in the same way, or because they have different values or goals. You can be the best advocate for your parent when you know that he or she understands the medical information, including the various treatment alternatives, and has made a decision based on his or her most fundamental values, fully understanding both the risks and possible benefits of the chosen alternative.

❑ WHEN YOUR PARENT IS UNABLE TO MAKE DECISIONS

When your parent is competent to make decisions, he or she has the right to make the decisions he or she deems best. When your parent has lost the capacity to make decisions, the situation is more difficult. If your parent has a durable power of attorney for health care, the person designated as agent is charged to be your parent's surrogate—that is, to make the decision he or she believes your parent would have made if able. If you are that representative, consider your decisions carefully. It is difficult to make life and death decisions for another person, but sometimes it has to be done. Remember your previous conversations and what you know of his or her wishes, and then make the best decision you can.

If your parent has executed neither a durable power of attorney for health care nor a living will, and if there is disagreement among family members or between the family and the physicians or other health care professionals, there are a variety of things which can be done to help resolve the dispute:

* You can call for a conference with all interested parties, including family, advisors, and health care professionals. Often, in sharing information and explaining the reasoning used, a consensus can be developed.

* If your parent is institutionalized in a hospital or nursing home, the institution may have an ethics committee or other institutional review process to help your parent, the family, and members of the caregiving team sort through and resolve differences of opinion.

* If differences cannot be resolved any other way,

a guardianship or other court action may become a necessary last resort. This alternative is discussed in *Issue 20: Guardianships.*

Because of the possible complications in decision making when a person is not competent to judge for him or herself, we strongly urge families to talk about preferences in advance, and to prepare the necessary legal documents to establish both treatment preferences and surrogate decision making authority while a parent is still in good health. Such advance planning makes it easier for everyone to work together to deliver appropriate health care when it is needed.

Issue 13

The Role of Physicians

Physicians play an important role in the lives of older adults. In today's environment of medical specialization, it is not uncommon for an older person to be under the care of several physicians at one time. This issue looks at the doctor/patient/family relationship and what can be done to strengthen it, and allow you and your parents to feel more confident in the medical care they receive.

☐ THE PRIMARY CARE PHYSICIAN

Why does my parent need a primary care physician?

In negotiating the medical system, especially as parents become older and require more medical attention, there can be no better friend than a helpful and supportive primary care physician. Primary care physicians—usually internists or family practice physicians (what used to be called general practitioners)—provide important routine medical care and can be consulted on short notice for both major and minor problems. They represent an important aspect of continuity of care and of the caring relationship which can become crucial if a parent is suddenly gravely ill and a variety of specialists are trying to decide what treatment option is in your parent's "best interests." Should that situation arise, a physician with a history of relationship with the patient and the patient's family often has the best understanding of what the patient—your parent—would want done under the circumstances, and can be an important advocate for appropriate care. A primary care physician also helps by coordinating care if your parent develops a medical condition which requires complex or extended care. Finally, the primary care physician can play an important role in channeling important information between members of the health care team, the patient, and the patient's family, resulting in higher quality care and a greater sense of cooperation and satisfaction among all involved.

Many older adults already have a primary care physician whom they have known over a period of time and with whom they feel comfortable. If your parent has such an existing relationship, you should support that relationship. Get to know your parent's physician, and begin the process of becoming acquainted with how he or she customarily practices medicine, so that as you become more involved in your parent's medical needs, your parent, you, and the physician are comfortable with the relationship.

If your parent does not have a primary care physician, you should find a way to help him or her find one. Talk with your parent about the advantages of developing that kind of a health care relationship. Often a parent simply does not know where to start in finding a suitable physician. You can help by connecting him or her with available referral sources and by discussing with your parent his or her needs and preferences. However, unless your parent is in a situation where he or she is no longer able to make decisions, your parent should make the final decision of a primary care physician.

How to find a primary care physician

Information about physicians is more accessible now than in the past. Some sources of referral information include:

- ✔ local medical societies and the physician referral services they operate;

- ✔ local hospitals, many of which also provide a physician referral service (usually limited to the doctors on their medical staffs); and

- ✔ yellow page listings organized by medical specialty.

Identifying your parent's needs and preferences

Physician practice styles, attitudes, and skills vary widely. It is a good idea to discuss with your parent ahead of time what he or she is looking for in a personal doctor.

Is a relaxed atmosphere with ample opportunity to ask questions important? If so, look for a physician who has made a conscious commitment to that style of practice. Is your parent more comfortable with a doctor who aggressively prescribes treatment for all conditions "just in case," or would he or she prefer a physician with a more "wait and see" attitude? Does your parent want a physician to share information with you and other family members? If so, your parent should make that clear, and choose a physician who welcomes a family approach to care.

Doctors are busy people. However, their ability to practice medicine depends on their relationships with their patients. When looking for a new physician, have your parent call the doctor's office and ask to speak to her or him on the phone before making an appointment. Have your parent write down any preferences and the questions he or she wishes to ask the physician. If the physician is unwilling to spend the time to answer your parent's questions, or if your parent feels as if he or she is being rushed or is intruding on the doctor, that is significant information. There is nothing wrong with "doctor-shopping," except that it takes time and energy. The choice of a primary physician is an important one. Support your parent in looking until he or she finds a good match.

When your parent's physician no longer practices medicine

A common occurrence with older adults is that a trusted personal physician retires or dies, and that physician's practice is sold or transferred to another physician. This is often quite upsetting to those who have come to depend on a close personal bond and sense of history with a single physician. At that point, your parent has no choice but to make some change. It is important, however, for your parent to know that he or she is under no obligation to receive care from the new physician recommended. If that relationship proves unsatisfactory, your parent should shop around for a better match, and request that his or her records be transferred when a new physician is found who better suits his or her needs.

❏ BUILDING A SUCCESSFUL RELATIONSHIP

For a patient to have trust and confidence in his or her doctor requires good communication. The importance of your parent feeling comfortable in talking freely with a physician and asking questions of that physician can not be overstressed. As your parent grows older and medical needs increase, you also need to feel comfortable with your parent's physician and how he or she relates to you. Here are some basic suggestions and things to think about in building a successful physician/patient/family relationship.

- Encourage your parent to write down a list of questions before going in for a physician visit, so he or she won't forget those questions in the awkwardness of the examination process. Have your parent write down the answers to questions if memory is a problem or there are questions about the doctor's explanations and recommendations. Encourage your parent to be clear and specific in reporting medical information to the doctor.

- Reach an understanding with your parent as to your role in helping attain good health care. The relationship might start out simply as you driving your parent to physician appointments and waiting there in case a situation arises where he or she feels your being present while talking with the doctor would be helpful. If your parent is forgetful or hard of hearing, it is important that someone be present when a physician is talking with your parent. Be sensitive to your parent's sense of modesty and desire for privacy—how many people do you want standing around while you are seeing the doctor?—but also stress how much help it can be if you hear what the doctor has to say in explaining a diagnosis or treatment plan. Such discussion usually takes place after the examination part of the visit is over. This would be a good time for you to be included in the conversation.

- It is always important that someone be empowered to make medical decisions in case of incapacity. Your parent's physician should be informed who that person is. The empowerment should take the form of a durable power of attorney for health care. For a fuller discussion of powers of attorney, see *Issue 19: Estate Planning Considerations*. It is also important to let your parent's physician know if he or she has signed a living will specifying treatment preferences under various circumstances. Such open communication and sharing of information up front goes a long way toward promoting a healthy and constructive medical relationship.

- If your parent has a significant health problem, it is important that *someone*—perhaps you, perhaps a friend or other family member—be familiar with the condition and in contact with the appropriate physician or physicians. If that person is you, ask your parent if you may talk directly with the doctor. Let the doctor know the role you are playing and that you have your parent's permission to discuss confidential issues with the doctor. Again, it is best to establish the relationship with the doctor *before* a crisis occurs. Let him or her know that you are a resource both for your parent and for those providing medical treatment.

- It is generally helpful to get to know the personnel in the doctor's office. Often, office personnel can be helpful in providing information and in getting the doctor's attention in an emergency.

- As you become involved in a flow of information on medical conditions, options for care, opinions, and outcomes, try to keep some basic notes on the things you learn. *Tab 9: Forms and Family Notes* provides a convenient space for such notes. These should cover items you learn from the doctor or his/her nurse or colleague and may wish to pass along to other members of the family, as well as questions you, your parent, or other family members have for the doctor.

- If your parent suffers from a severe medical problem and information becomes important to the entire family, make sure there is *one* person within the family who will be responsible for obtaining status reports and passing this information along. It is a reasonable expectation that a physician will keep in communication with the family, but not that he or she will communicate the same information several times for various family members.

- Don't be reluctant to ask your parent's doctor if he or she has any questions of you or other family members. This may prompt a discussion of fears, concerns, or expectations within the family that may help the doctor better understand your parent's situation and needs. It may also help avoid future misunderstandings.

- Finally, don't forget the value of positive reinforcement. If your parent's doctor is doing a wonderful job, send a note from the family expressing appreciation and offering continued support. We all like to be thanked. If communication and responsiveness are good, say so.

Dealing with multiple physicians

In this era of medical specialties, most persons with complex medical problems find themselves under the care of more than one physician. If handled well, this arrangement can result in high-quality specialized care. However, there is always the risk that if many physicians are involved, care will be uncoordinated and information difficult for either you or your parent to obtain. There are things which you can do to cut down on the confusion and possible risk involved when many physicians are taking care of your parent.

First, understand who the physicians think is in charge of the case. Is it the primary care physician? Or the surgeon? The oncologist or cardiologist? Ask your parent's nurse who he or she would go to for specific information. Or ask your parent's primary care physician to look into it for you. Once you have ascertained who is in charge, channel both your requests for information and your input through that person. Physicians often communicate better among themselves than with lay people. Try to use that to your advantage.

Second, nurses can be a wonderful source of information and support, especially when your parent is hospitalized. If there is something you don't understand or something you wish to communicate that you think is important, try the nurse as your first line of communication. Often the nurse can either deal with your concern directly or refer it to the appropriate physician.

Third, it is important for all persons who are on a regular schedule of medications to keep a list of those medications, their dosages, and the schedule of taking them. One of the growing reasons for hospitalization among the elderly is adverse drug reactions brought about by the interaction of drugs with each other in the patient's body. Any time your parent sees a doctor, he or she should have the medications list at hand and show it to the prescribing physician. For more information on this topic and a form for organizing and retaining this information, see *Issue 17: Medications* and *Form 17.1: List of Current Medications.*

Selecting Physicians that
"Accept Assignment"

Receiving care from a doctor who "accepts assignment" of Medicare payments can save your parents money. Medicare pays only 80% of the charges it approves. Doctors must charge their patients the 20% co-payment (the difference between 80% and 100% of the amount Medicare approves). In addition, if the doctor's actual fee is higher than what Medicare approves, the doctor may bill the patient for the excess. This is optional, however. If the doctor foregoes billing the excess, he or she "accepts assignment." Some physicians routinely waive billing the balance due, and many others participate in local programs under which patients may qualify for assignment based on ability to pay.

If your parents' finances are limited, it is a good idea to encourage them to inquire whether their doctors are willing to accept assignment, especially if they are in the process of finding a new doctor or are being referred to a specialist for additional medical services.

Fourth, in managing complex care for your parent, one of your primary jobs will be making sure that everyone is working with the same understanding of the medically relevant data in the case. Often it seems that one doctor says one thing, and another doctor's information is contradictory. Or your parent thinks one thing and the nurse says something else. Sometimes it is helpful to leave written questions for physicians, and ask them to phone you with their response and recommendations. If you or your parent feel like you are confused, and none of the strategies mentioned thus far resolves that confusion, you can ask for a conference to sort out the reasons for confusion. Some physicians are more amenable to this than others; however, sometimes it is the only way to straighten out what is going on.

❐ DISAGREEMENT AMONG PHYSICIANS

Though we would prefer otherwise, medicine is at its most predictable an inexact science. There are circumstances in which physicians might look at exactly the same data and have differing or even opposing points of view on what should be done. When such significant disagreement occurs, or if the disagreement involved is between the physician and the patient or the physician and the patient's family, there are several steps which can be taken to reach a resolution. They include:

- calling a care conference;
- talking with the hospital ethics committee;
- determining who has the legal authority to make a decision—or having the courts appoint a guardian to act for your parent.

There is a wonderful sense of satisfaction in seeing a health care team composed of many members delivering high-quality, compassionate, efficient care to your parent. This is modern medicine at its finest. However, sometimes the system breaks down and you will need to become an advocate—the primary person to see that care is delivered in a coordinated and appropriate manner. That can be difficult and frustrating work, but as the population ages, it will become a more and more significant and commonplace part of providing care and care management to the older members of one's family.

Issue 14

Arranging Home Health Care

This issue focuses on selecting, using, and evaluating health services received in the home. There has been a marked increase in the demand for home health services in recent years, and a corresponding increase in the types of home health care services available. Older adults, particularly, may find the option of receiving health services at home more comfortable and satisfactory than care in a hospital or nursing home. There are four basic concerns that need to be addressed in considering home health care options:

✔ When is home health care appropriate? Can it replace going to the hospital or being in a nursing home? Is the patient living alone, and if so, are there friends or family who can supplement professional home health care services?

✔ What kinds of home health care are available in your parent's community and how should your parent go about selecting a home health agency or independent professional?

✔ Who will pay for home health services?

✔ How do you evaluate the home care provider and the service?

❒ WHEN IS HOME HEALTH CARE APPROPRIATE?

Many people would prefer to receive health services at home, rather than in a hospital or nursing home. However, personal preference is not the only factor to be considered. Both health care providers and patients share a concern these days for carrying out a plan of treatment in the least restrictive, most cost effective environment. Often, that leads to providing services at home. The decision whether or not to use home health services depends on both the scope of treatment needed and the home circumstances of the patient.

Important questions to be considered include: Is the needed technology available and safe for home use? What are the physical limitations of the home? Is the bathroom on the same floor as the bedroom? Is there adequate privacy to insure rest? How close is the home to emergency medical facilities? Are there family members or friends willing and able to assist the patient at home?

Another issue to consider when judging the appropriateness of home health care is the cost. Because of the rapid changes in reimbursement for home health care services, both by private insurers and by government programs such as Medicare and Medicaid, it is advisable to verify the extent of coverage before committing to home health services. This may be more difficult than it sounds. Often, an insurer will say that such a determination cannot be made until its reviewers look at the bill. Sometimes you can get information by prefacing your request with "... Assuming your reviewers find the services medically necessary...," then describe the type, frequency, and purpose of the desired services.

Although home health care is often a less expensive way

to receive services than in a hospital or other institutional setting, the intensity of services which need to be provided or the lack of insurance coverage may mean that some services will be more expensive for the patient if provided at home.

◻ WHAT KINDS OF HOME HEALTH CARE SERVICES ARE AVAILABLE?

Although the term "home health care services" is used almost universally to describe services delivered in the home to people with medical or psychiatric problems, a great deal of specialization has developed in the types of services provided by different agencies and professionals. Home health services can generally be divided into four major types.

Intermittent skilled services

"Intermittent skilled services" is a phrase taken directly from the federal government's Medicare/Medicaid regulations. It refers to a health care provider that comes to a patient's home to provide skilled services (or services that support skilled services) on a visit basis. Visits can range from 15 minutes to 2 hours; they are usually about 1 hour in length. These visits most often occur two or three times a week. In order for intermittent skilled services to be reimbursed by Medicare or Medicaid, the patient is usually required to have an acute health problem that requires skilled intervention to meet treatment goals. Patients also need to show improvement in their condition over time.

Hourly or shift services

Hourly or shift services are what their name indicates: home health services delivered on a regular hourly or shift basis. Often they substitute for or augment the skills of a family member caring for the patient. The services may vary from companionship once a week while the spouse does the shopping, to the services of a registered nurse 24 hours a day, 7 days a week.

High-tech services

High-tech services usually involve a product or piece of complex equipment that requires specific on-going servicing to make it useful to the patient. Intravenous antibiotic therapy or use of a ventilator at home are examples of high-tech services. Those who service high-tech products are often limited to supervising the use of their product or equipment only. They are not allowed to care for other patient needs.

Durable medical equipment

Durable medical equipment (often just called "DME") is equipment needed in the care of a patient at home and used over an extended period of time. Examples include a hospital bed, a wheelchair, or walker. Durable medical equipment is available from firms that specialize in providing medical equipment for home use and from agencies and organizations that make such equipment available as an adjunct to other home health services.

❐ WHO PAYS FOR HOME HEALTH SERVICES?

Home health services are paid for in a variety of ways:

- *Private insurance* is sometimes available. Coverage is usually limited to services that are "medically necessary," "reasonable," and less expensive than similar services in another setting.

- *Medicare* is the largest source of payment for intermittent skilled services, but numerous administrative restrictions apply. See *Issue 23: Understanding Medicare.*

- *Medicaid* programs from state to state cover many home health services as an alternative to more expensive institutional care. Financial limitations on eligibility must be met.

- *Direct purchase* involves payment by the patient or the patient's family.

- *Charitable organizations,* such as United Way, also contribute significantly to the costs of home health care provided by non-profit agencies.

Policies governing payment for home health services change frequently. Home health agencies should be up to date on coverage issues in their state and community and should be able to assist in determining the availability of coverage.

❒ SELECTING HOME HEALTH CARE AGENCIES

Before selecting a provider, write down what services and equipment likely will be needed, the hours of services required, and other characteristics desired. This will help you evaluate the answers to certain questions you or your parent will need to ask in making a selection. For instance, if your parent needs nursing care and physical or speech therapy, you should ask about the availability of those services. A selection checklist is found under *Tab 9* as *Form 14.1: Checklist for Selecting and Evaluating a Home Health Care Provider.* Important considerations include:

- ✔ Is the provider licensed? About 75% of the states have a licensing process for home health care agencies and professionals, but some only certify specific kinds of agencies, and many of the licensing laws do not extend to high-tech or durable medical equipment providers.

✔ Have complaints been made against this agency? If so, how have they been resolved? Does the agency maintain its own complaint resolution program? If so, how does this work?

✔ What is the agency's range of services? If it does not provide all the services your parent will need, does it have arrangements with other providers to arrange and coordinate additional needed services?

✔ Are the individual service providers trained and licensed or certified to provide services in the home? Some states require special training to provide services in the home.

✔ Is there a way to contact the agency on a 24 hour a day basis? If not, what provisions will be made for emergencies?

✔ Does this provider have a good professional relationship with your parent's physician or other primary health care professional? Ask your parent's doctor for recommendations.

✔ What are the costs of various services? How are charges calculated, by visit or by the hour? What is included in the standard charges?

✔ What is the agency's approach to family involvement in the caregiving team? Does it seem willing to be responsive and creative in including family and friends if they wish to be involved as active caregivers?

◻ EVALUATING THE QUALITY OF HOME HEALTH SERVICES

Evaluating the quality of the home health services your parent is receiving should be an ongoing, informal process. Six elements to look for are:

1. Is the provider punctual, courteous and professional? Does he or she take time to explain and teach essential caregiving skills? The provider is a guest in your parent's home and should behave as such. He or she should arrive at the prearranged time, respect the family's, as well as the patient's privacy, and ask politely for any assistance needed. When explaining or teaching, it should be to all concerned. Instructions should be left in writing (legible, easy to read), as well as given orally.

2. Does the home health professional evaluate the patient's progress and report to the physician frequently?

3. Is the agency or its personnel available when needed and responsive to complaints or special needs? This is particularly important when your parent's family is at a distance. Patients who are isolated from their family and friends sometimes become dependent on their caregivers and are afraid to complain, especially if prior complaints were not addressed.

4. Does the agency or its personnel help facilitate and coordinate other needed services? A close working relationship with your parent's doctor is especially important.

5. Does the agency provide periodic on-site supervision? Is the supervisor willing to speak candidly with you and your parent about concerns that either of you may have?

6. Does your parent's home health professional maintain patient confidentiality? Just as doctors and hospitals have a duty to respect the privacy and confidentiality of their patients, home health agencies and the professionals they employ must also provide patient care in a professional, confidential way.

❑ BECOMING A PART OF THE CAREGIVING TEAM

Once you and your parent have successfully selected a home health care provider and services are being delivered, you may be surprised at the degree to which the patient and the entire family become an active part of the caregiving team. You and other family members may have an opportunity to learn new skills such as bathing and shampooing a bed-bound patient without soaking the mattress, giving injections, or lifting your parent in and out of a chair or bed without hurting your back. Everyone involved will be working together to help your parent achieve and/or maintain the highest level of functioning possible.

Feel free to ask for the assistance you need. The home health care worker may not always be able to provide it directly, but should help you in identifying a resource that can.

One of the most important things a family involved in home caregiving can do is keep a regular set of "progress notes" on a parent's condition. Some families find it useful to keep a "diary" as a means of tracking a parent's condition and spotting changes and problems. A responsive home health agency and its professional personnel should be able to assist you in this. Your progress notes can be kept under *Tab 9: Forms and Family Notes*.

Home health services, like other health care services, are becoming more sophisticated all the time. When appropriately used and monitored, they provide an important alternative to receiving care in a hospital or nursing home.

Issue 15

Selecting A Long-term Care Facility

Long-term care facilities are becoming an increasingly important component in the continuum of care for older adults. As people live longer, the need increases for both Skilled Nursing Facilities (SNFs) and Intermediate or Custodial Care Facilities to manage care for persons who need regular medical or personal care attention which cannot be given in the home. Long-term care facilities are now frequently referred to simply as "nursing facilities."

This issue focuses on several key elements which go into making a positive move to a nursing facility. They are:

- Assessing when your parent needs a nursing facility;

- Talking with your parent about long-term care: a positive approach;

- Comparing long-term care facilities before making a final selection;

- Paying for long-term care;

- Easing the transition to a nursing facility; and

- Making the most of your visits.

It is never easy to decide to move to an institutional setting for care. However, sometimes only an institution such as a skilled or intermediate care facility can provide the kind of ongoing care your parent needs. This chapter should help you and your parent decide whether long-term care in a nursing facility is a good solution for your parent. If it is, the chapter will also provide guidance both in selecting the best possible setting for your parent and making that move as smooth and comfortable as possible.

❑ ASSESSING WHEN YOUR PARENT NEEDS A LONG-TERM CARE FACILITY

As your parent's need for medical or personal care increases, there are several options which should be considered. Your parent can continue to live in his or her own home with home care services; move to a setting which provides some personal assistance, such as a congregate care home; move in with a family member; or move to a long-term care facility.

Many people are unfamiliar with both the variety of home care services available and the alternative forms of retirement housing now available for persons who need only minimal to moderate assistance in daily living. For information on services available in the home, see *Issue 5: Arranging Support Services for Independent Living* and *Issue 14: Arranging Home Health Care*; for the range of housing options for older adults, see *Issue 6: Other Retirement Living Alternatives*. The availability of home support services or assisted living alternatives may make it appropriate to defer for some time the question of nursing home placement.

At some point, however, nursing home care may become necessary. For example, your mother is living at home and becoming so forgetful that safety has become a major concern. Or perhaps both parents have been living with

Hospital Discharge Planning Services

It is common for the subject of nursing home placement to come up for the first time when a patient is discharged from the hospital. For example, your eighty-four year old father, who has been managing up to now to live independently in his home, falls and breaks a hip. There is no one at home to give him the nursing care he will require while his hip mends. Yet, his condition is stable, and continued hospitalization is unnecessary.

It is now important to find an appropriate setting in which he can continue his recovery.

A hospital discharge planner, usually a nurse or social worker, works with a patient and the patient's family to find a post-hospital placement appropriate to the patient's need for continuing medical care.

In addition, hospitals often have transfer agreements with skilled nursing and intermediate care facilities in the area. These agreements give priority to patients being discharged from the hospital.

Discharge planning services are required as a condition for hospital participation in the Medicare and Medicaid programs. These services, and related transfer arrangements with nursing homes, can be of value to your parent and you because they offer professional help in identifying your parent's needs and placement alternatives.

a relative who can no longer meet their personal care needs. Perhaps the retirement home where your father-in-law lives calls him or you and says that he needs more care and supervision than that placement can provide. There are a number of different ways in which the issue can emerge. Once it has emerged, there are several steps which should be taken to achieve the best available placement.

Once the subject has been broached with your parent, it is important to assess accurately his or her needs. Long-term care facilities vary greatly in the range of services offered, and the cost of care varies according to the level of service provided.

Help with this needs assessment should normally be available from your parent's doctor or hospital. The nursing facilities you are looking at also should be able to help you evaluate the match between the services they are able to offer and your parent's needs.

Intermediate care facilities

Intermediate Care Facilities are designed for those who are incapable of independent living, but who do not need continual nursing care. These facilities provide supervision, some nursing care, rehabilitation and recreation, as well as room and board.

Skilled nursing facilities

Skilled Nursing Facilities are often used on a short term basis for continuing care after a hospital discharge. They also provide care for those whose chronic medical problems require continual nursing supervision.

The distinction between these two levels of care is an important one. For both financial and personal reasons, it makes good sense to select a facility which will provide services at the level needed. Keep in mind that some facilities operate both intermediate care and skilled nursing care units; this gives patients the flexibility of stepping up to a higher level of care if necessary.

Some basic needs assessment questions to ask before selecting a facility include:

- ✔ What personal care functions does your parent need help with? Can he or she bathe, dress, eat, use the toilet, and take care of personal grooming independently?

- ✔ Does your parent eat regularly, and eat healthy food? Are there special diet restrictions or nutritional needs?

- ✔ Can your parent walk independently or with an aid?

- ✔ What are your parent's medical needs? Can he or she manage medications? What are your parent's physical limitations?

- ✔ Does your parent experience significant confusion? Can your parent handle money? Is he or she experiencing depression or irrational anger?

If you and your parent experience difficulty in assessing what level of care is needed, your parent's primary care physician or other health care provider may be of assistance. If your parent has not had a thorough physical examination recently, it will be helpful to have one while considering a move to a nursing home. Such an examination will not only help you assess the level of care needed, it is also a standard requirement of both intermediate care and skilled nursing facilities.

❐ TALKING WITH YOUR PARENT ABOUT LONG-TERM CARE: A POSITIVE APPROACH

It is not easy to talk with a parent about moving to a long-term care facility. However, your parent should be the primary participant in the move unless mental impairment makes this impossible. Someone, either you or another family member, should begin the process with an initial conversation. When this conversation is held, the reasons for concern should be explained, and the positive aspects of the move—such as greater security, 24-hour care, increased medical assistance—should be emphasized. If you or another primary caregiver have reached the limits of your caregiving capacity, that should be stated in a loving but direct way.

This initial conversation may evoke intense feelings in both your parent and other family members. Guilt, anger, shame, fatigue, relief, and loneliness are common feelings for persons considering a move to a nursing home and for other family members. It is important to address those feelings honestly, and to work through them as well as possible. Other family members, a physician, social worker, or clergy can provide support for both you and your parent in this process. Often, feelings have their basis in a deep sadness about coming to this point of decision making. Sharing these feelings with others can help you and your parent gain perspective and insight at a difficult time.

As you talk with your parent about long-term care, try to listen carefully for the concerns he or she is expressing. Is your parent afraid of being abandoned? Does he or she have financial concerns? Does he or she have a realistic view both of his or her own needs and of what nursing facilities are like? Often it is helpful in these initial stages to visit several facilities "just to see" what they are like and to ask questions. Such low pressure visits may dispel some of your parent's concerns and misconceptions and some of your own. And they give you a basis for continuing the conversation.

Prepare yourself for a possible angry display of feelings by your parent. Anger is a normal reaction to grief, and grief is a common response in considering nursing home alternatives. Comments like, "It's difficult for me to say this…" or "It must be tough to hear me say these things…" are more honest and more helpful than a flat, "This will be the best thing for you." Both you and your parent know that a nursing home placement is often only the best of less than perfect options.

Even if your parent is confused, talk with him or her about the decision to move to a nursing home. Something of your attitude and commitment to continuing support will be understood, even if the words are not. When your parent arrives in a new environment, he or she will sense that something is different. Talk to a confused parent in preparation for the move as if he or she understands.

❏ SELECTING A LONG-TERM CARE FACILITY

It requires time and energy to find a good nursing home for your parent. Give yourself as much time as possible. The less time you have to consider options, the more likely it is that your "best solution" will not be available.

The fit between an individual and a particular facility is based on the unique features of both. Some facilities just feel right. Such intuitive feelings are important. However, there are some important points to observe and ask about as you compare different facilities. *Form 15.1: Nursing Home Selection Checklist* found under *Tab 9* provides a helpful way to organize the information you gather on this subject. Important considerations include:

- *Health and safety standards.* All long-term care facilities are licensed by the state, and professional survey teams evaluate them regularly. The results of the most recent of these "surveys" must be posted in the facility. When you visit a facility, ask to see the most recent survey. Talk with the administrator, admissions coordinator, or other contact person about the survey results. They should be able to give you important interpretive information about why out-of-compliance items existed and how they have been dealt with. Survey reports are not a perfect indicator of a nursing home's standards. Since the last survey, compliance with government standards may have improved or declined. However, survey reports do give a general sense of facility strengths and weaknesses.

- *Size of facility.* Nursing homes come in all sizes, and different sizes have their own mix of advantages and disadvantages. For example, a small facility may be more personal and homelike, but it may not have the range of services found in a larger institution. If your parent needs extensive rehabilitation, a larger facility might be a better match. If your parent is shy or fearful, he or she may be more comfortable in a smaller facility. As you evaluate alternatives, be sure to check how size affects the basic level of staffing and services provided.

- *Medical care.* Medical care under physician guidance is a large and important part of long-term care services, especially in a skilled nursing facility. Ask questions about your parent's physician's involvement in the facilities you visit. Does your parent's physician have other patients in this facility? Does the facility have a "medical staff" relationship with your parent's physician. Some physicians do not make nursing home visits, or only visit a limited number of nursing homes.

- *Ownership and management.* Who owns a nursing home (local owner/operator versus regional/national chain; not for profit versus investor owned) is less important than how the facility is managed. Nursing home administrators and directors of nursing services play very significant roles in a nursing home because they set the standard for the facility's values and commitment to patient service. You should ask how long the current management team has been in place and whether vacancies exist in key positions. You should also observe the attitudes of the personnel with whom you come in contact, and feel free to ask about their philosophy of patient service and family involvement.

- *Convenience.* Convenience is almost always a major factor in choosing a nursing home. A location close to family and friends will make it easier to visit your parent, and these visits will, in turn, contribute significantly to the quality of your parent's nursing home experience.

Along with these general issues, your parent's particular needs and preferences will help narrow the choices as you research long-term care facilities. Look for the special features that each facility offers. Some have "special care" units for residents with particular problems, such as hospice units for those with a terminal illness, rehabilitation units for stroke patients, sheltered care for those suffering from dementia. With some looking around, it is possible to find a good fit between your parent's circumstances and the alternatives available.

❑ PAYING FOR LONG-TERM CARE

Long-term care is funded primarily through private finances and Medicaid. More and more people carry long-term care insurance to cover all or part of the cost of nursing home care. As you and your parent consider the financial realities of long-term care, the following information about payment sources will be helpful.

Medicare

Medicare provides only limited assistance in paying for nursing home care. In order to receive Medicare funding for nursing home care, persons must meet specific, stringent skilled nursing care requirements under federal government guidelines and must receive care in a skilled nursing facility which has a Medicare contract. Because Medicare only covers specific types of skilled care, it will not pay anything for most long-term care needs. However, a person in a nursing home is eligible for Medicare coverage of physician visits and hospitalization just as he or she would be if living independently. For more information about general Medicare coverage, see *Issue 23: Understanding Medicare*.

Medicaid

Medicaid is a joint federal/state program administered by the state to provide medical assistance to low income persons. Many older adults pay privately for long-term care until their assets are depleted ("spent down"), and then become eligible for Medicaid coverage. Each state has different eligibility requirements, but all states have strict limits on the income, assets, and other financial resources a person may have and still qualify for Medicaid.

When a person becomes eligible for Medicaid funding of long-term care, that person's income—minus a small personal allowance—goes to the long-term care facility. Medicaid pays the difference in the person's daily care rate. Not all nursing homes agree to accept Medicaid residents. If finances are an issue for your parent, it is important to find out prior to admission if your parent's preferred facility is Medicaid eligible. This can prevent an otherwise potentially traumatic move to a new facility when the shift is made from private to public funding of care. For more information on Medicaid funding, see *Issue 24: Understanding Medicaid*.

Other sources of payment

A few older persons are entitled to financial benefits from the Veterans Administration. These may cover services in a Veterans Home or provide money for services in other facilities. If your parent is a veteran or veteran's widow, check for possible assistance from the Veterans Administration.

Private long-term care insurance

Individual and group policies for long-term care insurance are relatively new on the scene, but they are becoming increasingly popular. Policies vary in the coverage they provide. Some only cover skilled nursing services; others cover custodial care as well. Issues relating to selection and purchase of private long-term care insurance are discussed in *Issue 25: Private Insurance Alternatives*.

❑ EASING THE TRANSITION TO A NURSING HOME

Leaving home is rarely an easy task, and the transition to a long-term care facility can be especially difficult. It is a hard thing to give up independence, the material comforts and conveniences of home, the old neighborhood, and many less tangible things all at once. Such a transition can be made harder by illness or disability. However, family members can do much to ease the transition through organization and caring personal involvement. Helpful suggestions include:

- In helping a parent adjust to a move, it is important to be honest about the circumstances. If the family knows that it will not be possible for your parent to return home at a later date, that realization is probably best shared with your parent as well. False hopes and unrealistic expectations about returning home someday are not usually helpful in the adjustment process. Concerns about your parent's ability to understand and cope with the facts should be discussed with your parent's doctor, hospital discharge planner, social worker, or a case management professional, if one is available.

- Throughout the process of decision-making and moving, listen to your parent's concerns and try to address them. Find out what your parent can bring along to the chosen facility. Help to sort through things and decide on the possessions to be taken along. Such personal belongings are important. They represent a lifetime of experience and memory. Encourage your parent not to bring very valuable objects into the nursing home, as security is sometimes a problem. If there is a valuable item your parent is particularly attached to, you could bring it with you occasionally for a visit.

- If you have the time, carefully sort through your parent's possessions in advance of the move. Organize clothing that can be taken into the home. Label everything that your parent will take. With pictures and some other objects, it is helpful to label them not only with your parent's name, but with the subject of the picture or history of the object; this will enable staff to understand more about your parent through the picture or object, and they can then do a better job of relating to your parent.

- Leaving a beloved pet is often a significant concern of older persons. For many, the pet is as much "family" as are human family members. Who will take care of the pet? Can the pet visit in the nursing home? Will the animal have to be destroyed? All these issues need to be addressed with your parent.

- Before your parent arrives on moving day, it may be helpful to move some pictures and other special objects into the room to give a homelike, familiar atmosphere. Make advance arrangements for phone service if that is available and desired. If your parent desires a television set in the room, make appropriate arrangements. Share information with the staff about your parent's history, religious preference, dietary needs, and other important characteristics. Work with the facility to make moving day as positive and easy for your parent as possible. This will not only reduce the day's trauma for your parent, it will also let the nursing home staff know that you intend to remain closely connected to your parent and to monitor the care and personal attention he or she receives.

- Prior to or soon after moving day, notify your parent's friends and religious and social groups of the upcoming move. Help your parent take care of address changes for magazines and other mail.

- On the day of admission, plan to spend most of the day with your parent. It is important that he or she not feel that you are hurrying away. Such a move is exhausting, and there may be many new things to become familiar with: the staff, a new room, roommates, reduced privacy, a new dining room, and other changes. Listen to your parent's feelings and your own.

- When you leave, let your parent know specifically when you will be back. Having made that commitment, it is important to follow through, and to communicate with your parent as often as possible during his or her period of adjustment. It is important that your parent not feel abandoned in this new and still unfamiliar place.

- Each time you return to visit, it is a good practice to stop by the nurses' station to ask how your parent is doing. This reinforces the staff's understanding that your parent's care is important to you and the rest of your family, and that you wish to remain an active part of the team that is supporting and providing care to your parent. Checking regularly with staff also helps you stay on top of changes in your parent's medical condition.

❏ MAKING THE MOST OF YOUR NURSING-HOME VISITS

It is natural to care about how your parent is responding physically and emotionally to a nursing home placement. It is also a fact that most children of parents in nursing homes have busy lives, and so are unable to visit as often as they would like. Below your will find several tips on how to make the most of your nursing-home visits, both from the point of view of your parent and the nursing facility.

In dealing with your parent:

* Most of the time, tell your parent in advance when you will be coming to visit. Surprise visits are enjoyable and helpful for you in assessing how your parent is being treated, but if you tell your parent in advance of your visit, he or she can look forward to it, and, if necessary, rest up to be ready for it.

* Bring cookies or fresh fruit, or some other special food for your parent. Food in nursing homes tends to be bland because so many older persons are on some form of restricted diet. Think of a treat your parent might like and bring it along. This lets your parent know that you have been thinking about him or her. One important caution before bringing food into a nursing home: it is important to check with the nursing staff as to your parent's dietary restrictions. The staff will be candid with you about any potential problems and can help figure out an appropriate goodie.

* Bring a card, flowers, a plant, some small physical thing that will stay with your parent as a reminder of your visit after you have left. Especially if your parent is confused or forgetful, such tangible reminders of your visit may help him or her to remember it.

* If possible, check before you come for any things your parent needs or would like you to do, so that you come prepared.

In dealing with the staff:

* Every time you visit, make sure you talk with the staff responsible for your parent's care. This not only facilitates the transfer of important information, it also lets the staff know that you are watching the kind of care your parent is receiving.

* Vary the time of day you come and visit your parent. If the staff knows that you might pop in at any hour, it may make a difference in how early or how often your parent is bathed, helped to dress, encouraged to get out of bed, etc.

* If you have a concern or complaint, let the staff know directly and as graciously as possible. Check back to see if the problem has been taken care of.

* If you appreciate the care your parent is receiving, letters of appreciation, flowers, a box of candy for the staff, and other small gestures are helpful in conveying how you feel.

* If you live out of town or for some other reason can visit your parent only infrequently, you might want to make an appointment with a staff person to discuss your parent's care in a formal way whenever you are in town. This interaction will help the institution and you work more effectively as a team to give your parent the best possible care.

Adjustment to a nursing home may take a long time. You should continue to be a support to your parent throughout this time, both through visits and by contact with the facility's personnel. Check regularly with the staff about your parent's condition. Attend family orientation if possible. Some nursing homes offer support groups for family members which can be helpful for many. If invited to a team briefing about your parent, go and discuss your perspectives with the staff. Do not hesitate to bring up troublesome issues. If you have concerns about the care your parent is receiving, express those concerns promptly and candidly. Remember, however, to tell the staff and administrator about those services and characteristics your parent, you, and other members of the family especially appreciate. As in any service relationship, positive feedback is an excellent motivator.

If moving to a long-term care facility becomes the appropriate alternative for your parent, the experience can be a positive one both for your parent and for other family members. The amount of time you and your parent spend in advance selecting the right facility and preparing—both physically and psychologically—for the move will make a difference. So will your help and support on moving day and the days that follow.

Issue 16

Hospitalization

A hundred years ago, only the poor and those without families went to hospitals for medical care. Hospitals were seen as outside the mainstream, more useful for training physicians than for healing patients. These days, in contrast, the hospital is at the center of the health care industry. Especially for older adults, hospitalization for surgery, diagnostic testing, and medical care is a common occurrence.

As hospitals have grown in size, number, and sophistication, they have become self-contained mini-communities. You step inside the hospital door, and you enter a world which operates on its own rules, schedules, and rhythms, which may not be immediately obvious to those inexperienced in hospital protocol and procedure. Many people become intimidated in the hospital environment. They feel like outsiders, not knowing where to go for information or services. They are unsure of when to be more demanding, and when their expectations for personal care or communication are unrealistic. Illness and concern for one who is ill are, of course, stressful in themselves. Discomfort with the institution can add to a sense of vulnerability and uneasiness.

This chapter contains basic information about hospitals as institutions, their role in health care, and how that role is changing. The issue also covers strategies for working constructively with hospital personnel: what your legitimate expectations should be, what a patient can do for him/herself, what questions to ask, and how to work with physicians and hospital staff to get the best possible care for your parent. Because of the debilitating nature of many illnesses requiring hospitalization, and because of the pace and strangeness of the hospital environment, your parent may very well need your help as a support person and advocate during a hospital stay. This issue will help you be more confident and comfortable in that role.

❑ THE CHANGING HOSPITAL ENVIRONMENT

Why and how hospital care has changed

Until the mid-1960's, older Americans tended to avoid hospital care as much as possible. The majority of them had no health insurance; physicians and hospitals knew that older adults on fixed incomes could not afford hospital bills, and that care provided would often end up written off as charity care. In 1965, the United States Congress passed the Social Security Act of 1965 which instituted the Medicare and Medicaid programs. Under Medicare, virtually all persons age 65 and older became eligible for government funded hospital care. The population which had previously cost hospitals money became their most dependable source of revenue. Medicare reimbursed hospitals at the end of each hospital stay for all of the charges incurred by each Medicare patient. The system contained no incentives for either patients or physicians to consider the cost of care in treatment decisions.

The money which Medicare (and also Medicaid) fed into

the health care system fueled a significant revolution in medical technology. From Intensive Care Units (ICU's) to CT (Computerized Tomography) scanners to lasers in the operating room, medicine's technological advances have contributed to longer life and a higher quality of life for millions of people. Unfortunately, these same technological advances—and our increased use of them— have also driven health care costs steadily upward at more than twice the rate of inflation for other sectors of our economy.

In order to cope with rapidly increasing costs, Medicare in 1983 decided to change its system of payment to hospitals. Instead of reimbursing on a *cost basis* at the end of hospital stays, Medicare began paying *prospectively* for hospital care on a flat fee basis. The size of the fee for each patient is now based on what are called diagnostic related groups or "DRGs." The purpose of the DRGs is to give hospitals an incentive to provide more efficient and cost-effective care for patients. The hospital is paid the same amount for each patient with the same diagnosis— *regardless of length of hospital stay.* If a patient's care costs less than Medicare pays, the hospital keeps the difference. If a patient's care costs more than Medicare pays, the hospital bears the loss.

Many people have strong feelings about the new Medicare system of payment, both positive and negative. It is clear, however, the new system is proving effective in eliminating some unnecessary services and shortening hospital stays. Many procedures are now done on an out-patient rather than in-patient basis. Patients are also being discharged from hospitals sooner under the DRG system of payment, and physicians are encouraged to do only those tests and procedures which are medically necessary.

The hospital today

In this new, cost-conscious environment, hospitals have become busier, more intensive settings for medical care. Because average inpatient stays are shorter, patient days are fuller. There are more tests, more procedures, more therapies to squeeze into a shorter time. As the patients get busier, so do the nurses and other staff members. Nurses on a typical shift have many more complex tasks to perform than they did ten years ago. This leaves them less time for patient care extras, and may even cause delays in necessary care. Where nurses might previously have been available for a back rub and a lengthy chat, their time is now spent monitoring intravenous therapy ("IVs") and other complex medical equipment and dealing with a larger, sicker patient load.

Where hospital care ten years ago may have been inefficient, the problem now occurs that hospital personnel are very busy and sometimes overworked. This may make them seem inaccessible. People bustle in and out of rooms so quickly, it is sometimes difficult to ask questions or grasp what is going on. This does not mean that people who work in hospitals are uncaring. They are simply trying to do a large and complex job as efficiently as possible. As you support and act as advocate for your parent in a hospital setting, understanding the current pressures on hospitals and their staff will help you focus your requests and concerns on things that count—qualities and conditions of care that every patient has a right to expect.

❐ SELECTING WHICH HOSPITAL TO USE

Many communities are served by more than one hospital. If your parent must be hospitalized, several factors influence his or her hospital choice:

First, more and more insurance carriers are making special arrangements with a limited number of hospitals where patients will be given financial incentives to use those particular hospitals in return for a discounted rate. Such "preferred provider" arrangements are becoming increasingly popular as a method of controlling health care costs. Have your parent check his or her insurance coverage to see if it limits choice of hospitals.

Second, your parent will want to know which hospital the physician recommends. Although it is common for doctors to hold admitting privileges at more than one hospital, most will focus their inpatient practice at one facility.

Third, each hospital has its particular mix of strengths and areas of specialization. Your parent should discuss with his or her doctor which hospital has made a conscious commitment to treating older patients, and which has the specialized programs and equipment necessary to provide the kind of care needed for your parent. Many hospitals offer special benefits and conveniences to older adults and their families.

❑ WORKING WITH THE PHYSICIANS

In the hospital environment, the physicians are the quarterbacks; they call the plays. Nurses and other hospital staff members follow the physicians' orders. This is important to understand, because if you have questions about procedures or medications, and want them changed, the person who decides is usually a physician. So, for example, if your mother thinks she needs a higher level of pain medication, there is nothing a nurse can do with that request until the nurse can contact the doctor.

"Putting your foot down" with the nurse will get you nowhere.

Most physicians see their hospitalized patients on a daily basis. They schedule time in their days to do their hospital rounds. Patient visits are also frequently made by the "attending" physician's colleagues on a back-up basis (one doctor providing coverage for another), by specialists called in by the patient's primary physician, and by interns and residents ("house staff") employed by the hospital itself.

If you or your parent wishes to speak with a particular doctor, it is sometimes helpful to ask the nurse when that doctor usually comes in. Often the nurse can also write a note in your parent's chart that the patient or family wishes to speak to the doctor, so that he or she will know in advance to schedule a little extra time.

If your parent or you have questions or concerns about your parent's condition or care received, it is helpful to write the questions down before the doctor's visit. It is also helpful to write down the doctor's answers to questions, especially in a complex or stressful situation, so that accurate information will be passed on to the rest of the family and you will be able to avoid having to ask the same question more than once.

If your parent does not understand what a doctor is saying, or seems vague about what is going on, it may be helpful for you or another family member to be present during physician visits in order to ensure that important information is communicated and understood. You must have your parent's permission for this. If a person is capable of understanding medical information, communications with physicians are confidential unless that person asks members of the family to join in. Often, family involvement in treatment decisions begins as a natural and informal step with which everyone is comfortable.

It is common for a hospitalized patient to see a primary care physician and one or more specialists. Sometimes in such situations it is unclear who is in charge, and whether everyone is working from the same set of goals and assumptions. How to deal with this problem is covered in detail in *Issue 12: Making Appropriate Care Decisions.*

For more complete information about building a positive relationship with your parent's physicians, see *Issue 13: The Role of Physicians.*

❏ WORKING WITH THE NURSES

The quality of the nursing care is a key factor in your parent's hospital experience. While physicians decide what treatment is to be given, nurses provide the lion's share of patient care and have more constant patient contact than physicians. Nurses today are required to have a wide range of education and skills. They are responsible for basic patient care as well as complex procedures and monitoring high-tech equipment. In many states, nurses can qualify as advanced or certified specialists in such areas as anesthesiology and geriatric medicine. As other sectors of the economy have begun employing more women, the number of persons going into nursing as a profession has dropped radically. In many areas of the country, there is a shortage of qualified nurses, and hospitals are scrambling to find and retain good nurses. The first rule of creating a positive working relationship with your parent's nurses is to remember that R.N.s (Registered Nurses) are highly trained professional persons who deserve to be treated with respect.

Nurses generally work eight hour shifts, with three shifts scheduled per day. In some hospitals, nurses have the option of working either longer or shorter shifts. However, during each nursing shift there are certain tasks which must be done at certain times. When your parent is admitted to a hospital, it is a good idea to ask when shift changes and other busy times occur on your parent's ward or unit. Then you and your parent can schedule visits and any lengthy conversations with the nurses or special requests around these periods. For example, if your mother wants to speak with her nurse about a non-urgent request, it is probably best not to make that request while nurses are busy doing their rounds at the beginning of their shift. If you wish to see a nurse for a significant conversation, ask when during the shift would be the best time. Usually the nurse can give you a good sense of when he or she will be free.

If your parent has an urgent need, which can range from need for a bedpan or help getting to the toilet, to severe pain, or some other unexpected medical situation, do not be reluctant to call a nurse immediately. If no one answers the call button, walk to the nurses station and request help.

If the hospital staff is busy, there are some things you may be able to do to help them and your parent. Most nurses are happy to show you where to find extra pillows, blankets, clean gowns, ice, juice, and even extra food items. *Before getting food or water for your parent, make sure that he or she is allowed to have it and that the nurses are not monitoring food and fluid intake.*

Most nurses and other hospital personnel are persons who chose their professions because they enjoy patient contact and find satisfaction in serving others. The most important elements in developing a good working relationship with them are:

- Be sensitive to their schedules, and fit requests for time or non-essential needs into those periods when they are not already rushing to get tasks done.

- Sort out truly urgent requests from those which can wait a while. Then you can push harder to have the urgent requests handled immediately.

- Don't ask nurses to do things they can't do. If the nurse says you have to wait for a physician to change an order, then you need to find the physician, not put pressure on the nurse.

- Be responsive to the nurses and other care providers. If you think they are doing a good job, tell them so. If you have problems or concerns, tell them directly and try to get the issue resolved.

Nurses can be good friends and advocates for patients and families. Because they have so much patient contact, they are also a good source of information and practical advice. Working cooperatively with the nurses when your parent is hospitalized can greatly enhance the quality of the hospital stay.

❒ WORKING WITH OTHER HOSPITAL PERSONNEL

Because hospitals have become such complex organizations, it is likely your parent and you will have at least some contact with a variety of hospital personnel, both direct service providers and those who are involved in the "business" side of hospital care.

Charges and billing

These days, hospital bills are often settled between the hospital and an insurance carrier. For adults over the age of 65, Medicare is the largest single payer of hospital expenses. Some persons have private insurance to supplement what Medicare pays. In most cases, your parent will give all the necessary insurance information to the hospital before or at the time of admission, and the hospital will bill Medicare directly.

Often there is more than one bill generated during a hospital stay. Physicians such as surgeons and anesthesiologists send their own bills for the services they perform in the hospital. Laboratory tests performed on a preadmission basis may be billed separately as well. It is important to keep track of all the bills that come after a hospitalization. Keeping track of hospital and doctor bills is covered in *Issue 23: Understanding Medicare* and *Form 23.1: Medical Bills Payment Record.*

There are some hospital charges which Medicare does not pick up. Often these include optional services such as telephone or television. In some hospitals, patients pay for television on a daily basis.

If your parent or you have questions or disputes about a hospital bill, contact the hospital billing office immediately. Most hospitals have billing specialists to answer questions and review procedures to resolve potential disputes.

Complaints

Most hospitals have a standard protocol and trained staff to handle patient complaints about staff members, quality of care, or other problems. If your parent has a complaint, ask a staff member how complaints are processed. If that person cannot help you, contact the patient services or equivalent department. Make your complaint in the most matter-of-fact, rational way possible. It is usually necessary to put it in writing. The hospital will respond within a set period of time.

Discharge planning

Because patients are being released from hospitals as soon as possible, they often need a significant period of recuperation. Sometimes, though a patient no longer needs hospital care, he or she still is unable to return to independent living. Discharge planners are hospital employees who help patients organize the necessary care so that they can leave the hospital and either move to a less intensive institutional care setting—such as a nursing home—or move back home with home nursing care and other support. Though the main focus of the discharge planners' job is to get patients out of the hospital as quickly as possible, they are also a good source of information about available community resources which can be of help to your parent.

❏ THE IMPORTANCE OF SELF CARE

Though often if seems that the patient is passive in the hospital setting, with doctors, nurses, and others providing care, there is much which your parent can do for him or herself to help in the recovery process. Helpful kinds of self care include:

- Sharing information completely with physicians, nurses, and others. Often patients deliberately withhold important information about symptoms or activities from health care providers out of fear, embarrassment, or anger. Honest open communication is an important form of self care.

- Doing prescribed self-care activities. It is common for care providers to ask patients to perform activities on their own, from simple exercises in bed, to sitting in a chair, to walking or major physical

Consumer Checklist for Hospital Stays

✔ Use a hospital with an appropriate mix of facilities and services for treating older adults.

✔ At the time of admission, ask for the hospital's stay book or other patient/family guide to services and facilities.

✔ Work with your parent's doctor and with the hospital's discharge planner or other patient service coordinators to insure that your parent stays in the hospital as long as medically required and that post-discharge care at home or in another kind of facility is provided for.

✔ Keep small amounts of money at the hospital to pay for phone calls, newspapers, and any other small personal items the patient might need.

therapy. It takes a conscious effort for sick or uncomfortable patients to follow through on these prescribed activities, but the exercises and activities are important. Encourage your parent to do what has been asked. Offer to take a walk with your parent or talk with him or her when your parent is first trying to sit up after surgery. It will help your parent feel better and recover faster.

• Eating the hospital's food. One of the biggest compaints of hospital patients is that they don't like the food. Because patients are so inactive, they often find themselves without an appetite. It is important, especially for older adults, to try to eat despite the reasons for not eating. Your parent's body needs energy from food in order to recover and regain strength.

These basic kinds of self care may not seem very important compared to other aspects of hospital care. However, they are important for your parent's mental attitude and for physical recovery.

No one enjoys being hospitalized for a serious illness or other medical problem. However, understanding how the hospital works will make the institution seem like less of an alien environment. Hospitals today are institutions confronting rapid change. They are more concerned about costs than ever before. However, with rare exceptions, their primary focus is patient care and how to deliver the best care possible in today's health care environment.

Issue 17

Medications

Medications are an important part of modern health care, especially for older persons. They are beneficial in controlling many of the diseases and other health concerns that older adults experience. Even serious chronic diseases such as arthritis, high blood pressure, diabetes, and cancer can often be treated with drug therapy so that people live longer and with a higher quality of life than at anytime in the past. Sometimes, the right medication can prevent expensive hospitalization. And when hospitalization is required, drug therapy often can reduce the length of a hospital stay. While medicines play an important part in improving health and prolonging life, there are also risks in taking medicines. This issue addresses those risks, and how they can be best managed.

❏ RISKS OF TAKING MEDICINE

Drugs are powerful substances. Most people respond predictably to drugs. However, each person has the potential to react unpredictably to a given medication. Some factors that can affect a person's individual response to a particular drug include:

- age,
- presence of disease,

- use of other drugs,
- body weight.

Any single medical disorder may require the use of more than one drug to control that disorder. Or a patient may have more than one disease. For example, it is not uncommon for a person to have diabetes, emphysema, arthritis, high blood pressure, and angina all at the same time, and require 10 or 12 different medications for control. The more drugs and diseases, the more care required by all concerned to ensure that the benefits of drug therapy continue to outweigh the risks.

Although many medications may be necessary to control the medical problems of an individual, overmedication is a major concern of older patients, their families, and health care providers. Overmedication can occur when a person fails to stop using a drug as directed by the prescriber, uses other people's medications, takes a medication in excess of recommended amounts, or uses multiple medications with similar effects. For example, your father may see more than one prescriber. He may visit the family doctor for certain complaints, and specialists for other ailments. Because each of these prescribers works independently of the others, the result can be that none of them have an accurate knowledge of all the medical conditions for which your parent is being treated, or all of the medications he is using. Thus medications with similar effects can be inadvertently prescribed by two or more prescribers. *All older adults should have a complete, updated list of the medications they take—both prescription and non-prescription drugs—and they should take it with them each time they visit a health care provider.* A simple form for listing medications follows under *Tab 9* as *Form 17.1: List of Current Medications.*

Our society often has unrealistic expectations about drug

therapy. We often think that if we just could find that one right drug, our problems would be solved. People look for this magic in prescription drugs, in vitamin and mineral products, in herbal drugs, and in home remedies. Actually, no drug really cures. All any drug can do is promote the body's own ability to heal itself or mask symptoms of some underlying condition that may or may not be self-limiting.

For example, arthritis can be painful and limit the sufferer's activities. In cases where arthritis is very severe, *Prednisone* or a similar agent may be prescribed with instructions to decrease the number of tablets taken over a period of time. Because the relief provided by the drug can be so dramatic, the individual may decide not to reduce the dose of the drug under the mistaken impression that total pain relief is the goal of therapy. While the drug might give total pain relief at first and is safe for a short course, prolonged use at the high doses initially prescribed can lead to serious complications. Therefore, it is very important for people to understand the goal of therapy for each drug taken and have realistic expectations about therapy.

Although prescribers may carefully consider all the known factors that influence response to medications, it is still not possible to predict precisely an individual's response. Furthermore, not all responses to a medication are observable to anyone but the user. You don't know if your parent is experiencing blurred vision or feeling excessively tired, unless your parent tells you or the health care provider. Therefore, the patient and the patient's caregiver play an extremely important role in monitoring responses to medications and discussing medication effects with the health care provider.

❏ HELPING YOUR PARENT MANAGE MEDICATIONS

You may be worried that your parent is not taking his or her medications properly or is forgetting to take them at all. Unless your parent lives with you, you will not be present to monitor the medication regimen. However, there are specific ways in which you can be helpful to your parent and decrease the risks associated with taking medications, while assisting your parent in being as independent as possible in managing his or her own medication regimen. Four things you and your parent can do to ensure safe medication management are:

- get information about your parent's medications from the health provider,

- find out about your parent's medications from your pharmacist,

- set up a system for taking medications,

- know what to do when a medication causes side effects.

❏ GATHERING INFORMATION ABOUT MEDICATIONS

There may be a number of reasons why it is difficult for your parent to get all the information he or she needs about medications from a physician or other health care provider. Many older people simply do not feel comfortable asking questions of their doctors. It is also very likely your parent may be anxious about his or her health condition and may forget to ask, or may feel that the doctor is too busy and rushed.

However, you and your parent need to have basic information in order to manage medications safely. You also have the right to be given this information in a way that is readily understandable. The following questions cover the basics your parent or you needs to know and understand:

- *What is the name of the drug?* Is it a generic or trade name? This can help sort out duplications.

- *Why is the patient taking it?* What condition is to be treated? The prescriber can have this information put on the label by writing it on the prescription.

- *What is the intended purpose of the drug?* Sometimes a diagnostic term is meaningless. Stating the intended therapeutic effect (e.g. slowing the heart) is most useful.

- *How often should this drug be taken?* Does once a day mean in the morning with breakfast or at bedtime? Does three times a day mean with meals or every eight hours?

- *What is the correct dosage?* Capsules should not be cut in half. Tablets which do not have a grove or are hard and shiny also should not be cut in half. Liquids should be measured in measuring spoons or oral syringes, not tableware spoons.

- *How long should the drug be taken?* Antibiotics generally should be taken at least 5-10 days for simple infections. For prostatitis and some other infections, weeks of therapy may be needed for a successful outcome. Other medications are intended to be used for life (e.g. insulin in certain diabetics). Stopping too soon can cause treatment failure. Continuing beyond the intended length of therapy can lead to unwanted side effects.

- *What are the side effects?* Find out which ones are

to be expected and which tend to disappear with continued use.

- *What can be done to prevent side effects should they occur?* Some drugs cause dizziness with standing, so patients should be warned to stand slowly and with support.

- *What side effects should the patient report?* Some side effects are useful indicators of the success of therapy. Others indicate that the dose may be too high or too low or that the drug needs to be stopped.

- *Are there special instructions?* Some medications should not be taken with food; others should. Certain medications can cause drowsiness or decreased alertness, so that driving or other tasks may be hazardous. There are medications that require preparation, like mixing of insulin doses; others require certain skills for proper administration (inhalers, eye drops). Some medications have special storage requirements. All special instructions should be given both orally and in writing to prevent confusion.

- *What should be done if the patent misses a dose?* Everyone forgets to take a medication occasionally. Sometimes it is safe to take the dose as soon as it is remembered. Other times it is not safe, and one should skip the forgotten dose and continue with the next dose as scheduled. Be sure to ask!

- *Does this medicine replace anything currently taken?* Sometimes people have adverse reactions because they did not stop taking an old medicine when a new one was prescribed.

- *Does this medicine interact with anything the patient already takes?* Here is where your parent's list comes in handy. Ask your parent's doctor about interactions.

- *Is this medication necessary?* This question is important enough to be the first one asked. Sometimes providers feel pressured into prescribing medication to try to help the patient. Perhaps nondrug therapy can be tried first. If the complaint being treated is really a side effect of another medication, if that medication were discontinued or its dose adjusted, a new medicine might be unnecessary.

If your parent has difficulty remembering questions to ask, you might suggest that he or she prepare a list of questions to ask the provider about each medication. The above questions may serve as a guide.

☐ THE ROLE OF A PHARMACIST

Pharmacists are specially trained to understand and discuss medications. Pharmacists can give you and your parent a lot of information about the drugs your parent takes. However, you need to know what to ask for.

For example, one source of information about medicines is the patient information sheets found in some drug packages. These inserts typically list side effects, when to notify the physician, how often to take the drug, what to do if a dose is missed, and any other information the manufacturer thinks important. Your parent or you can request these inserts from your pharmacist. Additional information is available in books listed under *Tab 7: Resources.*

Your pharmacist should be able to speak with you knowledgeably about prescribed medicines, over-the-counter drugs, how to reduce the cost of medicines, side effects and interactions of drugs, and other special problems. Again, knowing what to ask the pharmacist will be important.

Over-the-counter medicines

It is likely that your parent will be taking at least one or two over-the-counter drugs as well as prescription medications. The substances in over-the-counter drugs may interact in a negative way with prescribed medicines. Be sure to ask the pharmacist if it is all right to take specific over-the-counter drugs as well as the other drugs being taken, or if there may be undesirable effects.

In many states, pharmacists maintain records of medications used by each patron. These records are called patient profiles. Potential drug interactions can be identified by reviewing these profiles prior to dispensing prescribed medications. However, the profiles usually do not contain information about nonprescription drugs or prescriptions purchased elsewhere. Therefore, whenever buying nonprescription drugs, ask the pharmacist about potential interactions.

Saving money—generic drugs, mail-order drugs

Drugs are expensive, and you and your parent may be looking for ways to reduce their cost. Generic drugs may be cheaper than brand name drugs, but there are some precautions that need to be considered. Generic drugs are similar in composition to the brand-name drugs, but they are *not* identical. Therefore, it is important to ask your pharmacist if a generic drug can be safely substituted for a brand-name drug.

Another possible way to save money on drugs is to purchase from a drug mail-order house. This can be an attractive method of purchase, but there are risks to be aware of. When obtaining your drugs by mail, you do not have direct contact with a pharmacist; so if you have questions, it may be difficult to obtain information. Also, when ordering from a mail-order pharmacy, you generally are required to purchase drugs in large amounts. Ordering large amounts of a drug should be avoided except when your parent has been taking a drug for a period of time and will likely continue to take that drug over a long period of time.

Other questions to ask

If your parent has arthritis or weakness in his or her hands, it may be difficult to open some of the child-proof caps that are on medication bottles. A pharmacist will be able to substitute another type of cap for your parent if your parent requests it. Your parent also may have difficulty reading the labels on the bottle. If asked, the pharmacist will prepare a label so it is readable.

If you or your parent has been instructed to cut a dose in half, check with your pharmacist for recommendations. There are tablet cutters that can be handy. On the other hand, some tablets and capsules are not meant to be cut, crushed, or chewed. The pharmacist can recommend alternate dosage forms such as easily measured liquids or other brands that can provide the appropriate dose without cutting tablets.

❐ SIMPLE ROUTINES FOR TAKING MEDICATIONS

It is not unusual for older persons to be taking six or seven different prescribed medications as well as two or three over-the-counter drugs. Keeping track of all those medications can be confusing. The pharmacist can be helpful in simplifying medication schedules. For example, some medications come in formulations that do not require multiple daily doses. Or, your pharmacist may be able to recommend a different drug that requires fewer doses but will produce a similar effect. Here are three simple rules for safely taking medications:

Rule 1: Dispose of old medications

Many people are reluctant to throw away old medications. Some people have drawers filled with such drugs. Some of these drugs will have lost their effectiveness or may not be the drug of choice for the health problem a parent currently is experiencing. Encourage your parent to return all old medications to the pharmicist for proper disposal. If for some reason that is not possible, ask a physician how best to dispose of the particular drugs in question. Clearing out old and unused medicines can prevent accidental use of medicines that might not be appropriate.

Rule 2: Organize a schedule for taking medicines

When your parent is taking four to five medications a day at different times during the day, it may be difficult to keep track of which medication to take at what time. Another common problem your parent may have is remembering whether he or she took the medication. There are several systems that can be easily developed so your parent will know:

- what medicine to take;
- when to take it;
- how to take it; and
- if medicine was taken.

Medication Check-Off Chart

A check-off chart can help your parent know if he or she has taken a certain medication. The names of drugs are listed on the chart as well as the times of the day each drug is to be taken. In addition, the amount of the drug to be taken should be listed. The chart can be placed in a prominent place in your parent's home where he or she will see it each day, and check off each medication as it is taken. A medication check-off chart follows under *Tab 9* as *Form 17.2: Medication Check-Off List*.

Daily or Weekly Container Method

Using special containers to organize medications is another method for safely adhering to prescribed dosages. This method may be helpful if your parent has mild memory problems and forgets to use the medication check-off chart. Medication dispensing containers may be purchased at the pharmacy, or you can improvise with something as simple as an egg carton. Mark the cups of the container or egg carton with the hours of the day medicines are to be taken. Be sure to mark whether the hours are A.M. or P.M. All medicines for the day should be put in the container each morning. Your parent then takes the medicines at the appropriate time of day. If your parent wonders if he or she has taken the medicine, he or she can look to see if it is still there. There are containers manufactured which can organize an entire week's medications at once. These are helpful if you or another caregiver do not see your parent daily.

In choosing this method, be sure that your parent (or the caregiver) is able to place the medications in the container accurately and then remembers to take them. If your parent has a severe memory loss, this method will not be appropriate.

Rule 3: Store medications safely

If there are small children in the home, all medication containers should be stored in a place that is not accessible. Some medications should not be exposed to the air or left in the daily or weekly container. Others need to be stored in the refrigerator. Be sure to check labels for these special instructions.

❐ PREVENTING ADVERSE EFFECTS FROM MEDICATIONS

Many medications can cause side effects which may or may not be harmful. Prior to starting a drug, your parent should be forewarned of possible side effects by the physician and pharmacist and by reading the patient information sheet accompanying the medicine. Your parent needs to understand which side effects should be reported to a health care provider.

In addition, many medicines cause reactions when they are combined with other prescription drugs, with over-the-counter medications, with alcohol or smoke. Finally, a drug reaction may occur due to a person's age or other variables (for example, altitude).

Interactions with over-the-counter drugs

Drug interactions are not limited to prescription drugs. Over-the-counter drugs such as cough and cold remedies, laxatives, sleeping products, aspirin, even vitamins, can cause an adverse reaction when combined with certain drugs. Many people do not consider nonprescription products as drugs with the potential to interact. To avoid potential drug interactions, a complete list of all substances used, *not just prescription drugs*, should be kept and shared with your parent's primary doctor.

Suggestions for Reducing the Risk of Adverse Drug Effects

1. Prepare an accurate list of currently used prescriptions, nonprescription drugs, vitamins, minerals, herbs, and any other products taken regularly to promote wellness or treat a bodily function.

2. Realistically estimate tobacco, alcohol, and other social drug consumption.

3. Share the above information with each prescriber and pharmacy your parent patronizes.

4. Ask what interactions might be present.

5. Ask what potential adverse effects may occur and what to do if your parent experiences any.

6. Use one pharmacy as a source for all prescriptions and nonprescription products.

When using nonprescription drugs, *read the small print.* Many nonprescription drugs are combination products. They contain several ingredients. For example, a variety of products contain aspirin plus other ingredients to treat pain or cold symptoms. Read beyond the trade name and find out exactly what is in the product your parent is taking. Ask the pharmacist for information about potential interactions.

Interactions with food, alcohol, and tobacco

Drugs can also interact with certain foods, tobacco smoke, and alcoholic beverages. A person who uses *Dyazide* and switches to a salt substitute without informing the physician could retain too much potassium and become ill. Certain antidepressants (categorically called monoamine oxidase inhibitors) can adversely interact with aged foods such as cheeses, herring, and red wines to cause increased blood pressure leading to severe headaches and an increased risk of stroke.

One need not be an alcoholic to experience significant adverse drug interactions between alcohol and medicines. The same holds true for cigarette smoke. Although heavy smokers are usually the ones considered to be at risk, passive smokers and the partners of smokers occasionally have adverse or poor reactions to drugs as a result of inhaling another's tobacco fumes.

Interactions between alcohol and other drugs affecting the brain (i.e. antidepressants, antihistamines, narcotic pain relievers) may be detected shortly after the combination has been taken. In other cases, the patient may take two interacting agents regularly for days or weeks before the results of the interaction are apparent.

Adverse drug reactions and age

Although drug interactions alone can cause adverse effects, changes in the way the body responds to medications are often a factor. Both the physical processes of aging and the progression of some diseases can be significant factors in adverse drug reactions. Therefore, it is important that people who take medications for long periods of time continue to see their prescriber on a regular basis. In some states, it is illegal to refill a prescription after one year has elapsed. Anyone on medication for a chronic illness or condition, even if responding well to therapy, should see the prescriber at least once a year to make sure that body functions have not changed. For example, many older people use the drug *Digoxin (Lanoxin)* for heart problems. As a person ages, the body's ability to eliminate the drug may decline. If the dose is not adjusted downward, the drug can accumulate, leading to potentially serious effects.

Conditions that may make adverse drug interactions more likely

Certain drug categories have a higher likelihood of interacting with other drugs and foods. Similarly, persons with certain health conditions are at greater risk for adverse reactions to drugs. The following table lists some of the conditions that may make a person more susceptible to drug interactions or to adverse effects from medicines.

Conditions that May increase Susceptibility to Adverse Drug Effects or Interactions

Alcoholism	Kidney problems
Anxiety	Liver disorders
Arthritis (or other conditions associated with chronic pain)	Lung problems, (e.g. emphysema, asthma, bronchitis)
Dementia	Parkinson's disease
Depression	Seizure disorder (epilepsy)
Diabetes	
Heart Problem (e.g. irregular heart rate, heart valve replacement, high blood pressure)	Sleep disorders
	Thought disorders
	Thyroid disorders
	Tuberculosis

Important: If your parent has one or more of the conditions listed, do not stop drug therapy without first discussing the consequences with your parent's physician.

Proper use of medications can and should be an important tool in your parent's management of acute and chronic medical conditions. If inadvertently misused, however, multiple medications and medication interactions can cause medical problems of their own. The key to effective management of medications is clear communication between your parent (and you, if you are involved in your parent's medical care) and your parent's physician(s) or health care providers. In today's age of advanced drug therapy, managing the use of medications requires gathering and organizing basic information concerning the identity, intended purpose, potential side effects, and potential interactions of the drugs your parent is taking.

Issue 18

Selecting and Working with a Family Lawyer

A lawyer who understands the legal issues associated with aging and the elderly can be an important resource for an older person and that person's family. A knowledgeable lawyer can serve as an adviser, a facilitator, and—if need be—an advocate. He or she can help your parents:

- develop a plan for handling future financial and personal affairs, including possible use of trusts, and preparation of a will, a durable power of attorney, and other related documents;

- sort out the maze of procedures, rules, and regulations that accompany most insurance and government health care payment programs; and

- make appropriate declarations concerning future health care decisions.

Although there are many ways a lawyer can be helpful, older people often are reluctant to consult one. They may never have consulted a lawyer in the past. They may fear high fees, or they may not know how to go about finding a lawyer skilled in handling the particular kinds of issues they face. Often, an older person will have a last will and testament that was drafted years ago, but changes in the law or within the family have left it out of date. Over the years your parents may have moved to a new community where they do not know an attorney; their lawyer may have retired; or they may simply want to find a new source for legal services.

This chapter discusses how to help your parents work positively with a lawyer, including:

- how to find a lawyer suited to their needs;

- how to control the cost of legal services and get as much value as possible for the money spent;

- where to turn if the fees customarily charged by lawyers are beyond your parents' means.

❐ RETAINING A LAWYER

Hiring a lawyer ought to be a straightforward, manageable task. It can be if your parents follow these basic rules.

Rule 1: Look for a lawyer who regularly provides the kinds of services your parents need.

Today the practice of law reflects the complexity of our society. As many aspects of modern life have grown more specialized, so has the orientation of many lawyers. We now have everything from entertainment law experts to high technology law experts. Your parents will need a lawyer with expertise in the legal issues which affect older adults.

If your parents' need is for a simple will with a durable power of attorney, they should look for a lawyer with a general practice, yet one whose general practice regularly includes preparation of estate planning documents. If your parents' estate is large enough to involve more sophisticated tax or financial planning concerns, or if they have special needs such as establishing a trust for a disabled child or minor grandchildren, they should seek legal counsel who specializes in estate planning. If the family needs help securing the appointment of a guardian for a parent with dementia, it may be best to consult a lawyer whose practice regularly combines estate planning with representation of the elderly and disabled and their families.

Rule 2: Be aggressive about asking for referrals, and be as specific as possible in describing the kind of lawyer you are looking for.

There are many excellent sources for lawyer referrals:

- friends and associates whose judgment you trust and who have hired a lawyer for the kinds of services needed;

- state and local bar associations and the lawyer referral services they frequently sponsor;

- advocacy and support groups such as the Alzheimers Disease and Related Disorders Association;

- other professionals, including accountants, insurance agents, bankers, clergy, and lawyers you may know but who do not practice in the field of law you or your parents require.

In being specific about what you or your parents are looking for, you will want to say something like this:

"I am looking for a qualified, accessible attorney who devotes at least a significant portion of his or her practice to handling issues confronted by older clients and their families. Can you recommend someone who can help me with . . . (preparation of a simple will and durable power of attorney; preparation of a 'living will'—directive to physicians concerning future health care preferences; appointment of a guardian; etc.)."

Rule 3: Before making a final selection, ask a few key questions, and be sure to make a note of the answers you receive.

Some of the questions to ask include:

- What percentage of your time do you spend handling the kind of matter I am interested in?

- How do you charge for your services? Some lawyers establish a flat rate for various standard documents, such as a simple will, a simple trust, or a durable power of attorney; others charge for their services on an hourly basis.

- If you charge on an hourly rate basis, can you give me a firm estimate of the time required—in effect an upper limit on the charge?

- Who will I be dealing with? Many lawyers employ and rely on younger lawyers and paraprofessionals; these persons can be excellent resources in helping your parents understand their legal options; they are also usually less expensive than the lawyer for whom they work.

Rule 4: Don't be reluctant to ask these questions of two or more lawyers before making a final selection.

Generally, lawyers will provide an initial consultation for no fee or a modest fee. Your parents should interview several lawyers and look for someone with whom they are comfortable and work well. Gathering comparative information can be helpful. Not only will it make for a more informed selection, it will also produce useful bits of information along the way.

Rule 5: State clearly the specific services you are seeking and what you can spend.

Don't be afraid to state exactly what your needs are and how much you are willing to pay. Recognize, however, that you may have to adjust your expectations based on input from lawyers you interview. You may discover that additional services are required, or that your circumstances are more complicated than you realized.

Your lawyer should initiate a discussion of fees at your first appointment, but if he or she forgets, you should make sure that the discussion takes place. Most lawyers also will follow up the initial appointment with a short "engagement letter" setting forth the services to be provided, who will be providing them, how fees will be determined, and what the total expenditure is expected to be. Once again, if the lawyer forgets, send a letter yourself summarizing points discussed at the first meeting.

Consulting Lawyer Directories

Many public libraries purchase one or more national directories of lawyers. One of the oldest and most widely used is called Martindale-Hubbell. In it you will find most lawyers in active practice, together with a brief biographical sketch. Martindale even includes an informal peer ranking. Look for a lawyer with an "av" rating ("a" for very high legal ability); "v" (for very high general recommendation) or a "bv" rating ("b" for high legal ability; "v" for very high general recommendation)."

❐ WORKING WITH A LAWYER

When an attorney-client relationship turns sour, it is more often because of poor communication than because of deficiencies in the services provided. A lawyer may fail to be specific with his/her client concerning the fees the lawyer intends to charge. A client may not be forthright in laying out his or her goals and the amount of money budgeted to meet them. When older persons are involved as clients, the risk of miscommunication and resulting frustration and disappointment increases because many older adults have trouble being direct.

A key to a good relationship with a lawyer is good communications. Your parents can help by clearly stating their needs and desires. They should insist that the lawyer also speak in specific, understandable terms. Here are some steps to encourage accurate communication between your parents, you, and your parent's lawyer—steps which will help ensure the effective delivery of legal services:

- *Understand who is the client.* The relationship between a lawyer and a client is like the relationship between a doctor and a patient. These are confidential relationships. The communications between a lawyer and a client are "privileged" communications which the lawyer must keep confidential. Your parents' lawyer represents your parents, not you. The lawyer may not ethically disclose to you privileged communications with your parent. The only way you may become part of the lawyer-client relationship—and part of the chain of communication—is to have your parent waive the attorney-client privilege by granting permission for you to participate. Such permission should normally be stated in a letter or other written document given to the lawyer, or at least confirmed by the lawyer in a letter to your parent.

- *Do your homework ahead of time.* Your parents will save time and money if they prepare for meetings with the lawyer. It might be helpful for them to review the legal issues discussed in *Tab 4* and identify the areas where assistance is needed. They should also identify specific questions that need to be addressed and locate copies of papers and records which may have a bearing on their legal problem.

- *Help the lawyer get the job done.* Depending on the nature of your involvement in your parents' attorney-client relationship, there may be things you can do to help make sure that work is successfully completed. For example, if important documents are prepared, such as a will, or durable power of attorney, make sure they are executed and placed in safekeeping. Having sought legal advice, your parents should complete whatever follow up is needed.

  Many times clients are frustrated by the complexity of even a simple will or durable power of attorney. "Legalese" can be difficult to read and understand; but in the real world, clients must expect to confront and work through complex legal jargon. You and your parents should be prepared for language and concepts that you do not fully understand. Don't be afraid to ask for clarification when you need to, and do so promptly.

- *Follow up.* It is good practice to provide prompt feedback to a lawyer. If you have received prompt, efficient, and understandable legal services, let your lawyer know you recognize that fact and appreciate it. You may even wish to send a short note expressing thanks. On the other hand, if you become dissatisfied with your lawyer, speak up at once. Let the lawyer know exactly what is wrong from your vantage point; chances are good that the cause of the problem is something that can be corrected.

- *Fee disputes.* If fees are disputed, many state and local bar associations offer attorneys fee arbitration procedures at no charge. If your parents take advantage of this service, they can expect to have an independent third party look at the fees they were charged and express an opinion on whether or not they are reasonable. The lawyer may also propose a compromise on the fees as an alternative to arbitration.

❐ ACCESS TO LEGAL SERVICES ON A LIMITED BUDGET

For many older people, the assistance of a lawyer may seem like a luxury they cannot afford. Fortunately, access to legal services is not entirely dependent on ability to pay. If your parents have limited means, consider these options:

- *Bar Association-sponsored programs such as Neighborhood Legal Service Clinics.* Many state and local bar associations operate programs to provide legal advice and assistance for those on a limited budget. These programs may be found in the Yellow Pages under lawyer referral services.

- *Government or privately funded legal services offices.* Many communities have government-funded or private, non-profit legal services offices that provide low-cost or no-cost representation to low income clients. These sources typically have a financial means test for eligibility.

- *Individual law firm "pro bono" programs.* Many law firms provide low-cost or reduced-cost legal services to persons who otherwise would be unable to obtain needed legal services. Occasionally, bar associations will keep rosters of such private "pro bono" (for the good of the community) programs. Another good place to learn about informal pro bono activities and sliding fee scales based on ability to pay is at the firm itself. Larger firms often organize pro bono committees, and a member or the chairperson of such a committee can provide information on what options the firm can make available to persons in your parents' position. In seeking to take advantage of private pro bono programs, your parents should be as specific as possible in describing their needs: for example, "my wife and I each need a durable power of attorney, but we are seeking this legal service on a restricted budget. Can you help?" Or, "Does your firm participate in a pro bono guardianship program that my father and our family could take advantage of?"

As in any professional service relationship, selection of a lawyer requires planning and follow through. A lawyer can be an excellent family resource, especially when making arrangements for the future, sorting out loose ends of a business or personal nature, or securing the appointment of a guardian. Following the steps outlined in this chapter should help your parents obtain effective legal assistance and reduce the risk of frustration, disappointment, and financial loss.

Issue 19

Estate Planning Considerations

Estate planning is a phrase used to describe the process of making a will and executing other related documents, such as a trust, a "living will," or a durable power of attorney. These are documents that will shape legal relationships, rights, and responsibilities in the event of future incapacity or death. Estate planning provides answers to questions like these:

- how will my property be distributed after my death, and who do I want to put in charge of that process?

- who will handle my financial affairs if I become incapacitated and am no longer able to handle them myself?

- what instructions do I wish to leave concerning medical treatments that I would refuse or accept, if I were incapacitated and unable to decide at the time the treatment was proposed?

- who will make important health care decisions for me if I become incapacitated and lose the ability to decide for myself?

Some people think estate planning is only useful or necessary for the wealthy. This is not true. It is in your parents' best interests, regardless of income, to set out in advance who can make business and health care decisions for them in case of their incapacity, and to designate who will inherit their estate, however modest.

This chapter describes what is involved in the process of estate planning. It will help you and your parents understand what steps and considerations usually go into such planning, and know some of the questions to be thinking about. However, helping your parents plan their estate usually means encouraging them to consult a qualified estate planning attorney.

❏ ALTERNATIVES FOR TRANSFERRING ASSETS ON DEATH

When death occurs, a person's property passes to others as the person has directed during his or her lifetime. There are four primary methods for giving this direction:

- a will;
- a community property agreement (in states which recognize community property);
- joint tenancies with right of survivorship (and other similar forms of property ownership);
- trusts established during a person's lifetime and that continue in effect upon death.

If no advance directions are given by a person who owns property, his or her property passes at death according to priorities established under state law.

Wills

A person's will may be simple or complex, depending on the size of the person's estate and the plan for distribution of property. A will serves many purposes. It states how property will be divided after a person dies. It also controls when property will pass. For example, your father's will might provide that his estate will pass to your mother for her lifetime, and then be equally divided among you and your siblings.

A will also names an executor whose responsibility it becomes to carry out the terms of the will, and it specifies what powers and responsibilities the executor will have.

For larger estates, a will and the planning that goes along with making a will may incorporate transfers of property, creation of trusts, and other steps designed to reduce or eliminate estate and inheritance taxes.

After a person dies, the will he or she leaves must usually go through "probate." Probate is the procedure through which a court recognizes the validity of a person's will and confirms the personal appointments (for example: executor, guardian, trustee), property transfers, and other provisions it contains. Probate also gives creditors of the deceased person a chance to make their claims. Probate is almost always accomplished with the active involvement of a lawyer whose fee is paid out of the estate. The executor and any trustees appointed under the will are also usually paid for their services. Many states have enacted probate reform laws which streamline the process and authorize implementation of the terms of a person's will with minimum court supervision.

Advising your parents on a new will or the updating of an existing will is their lawyer's job. As your parents consider drafting or updating their wills, these are some of the questions they will want to answer:

- how do I want my property distributed after my death?

- should I leave certain property in trust, rather than outright? If so, who do I want to act as trustee?

- do I wish to make any religious or charitable bequests? If so, to which organizations or causes?

- who should I name as executor (and trustee and/or guardian) under my will, and who will I designate as alternate if my first choice is unable to serve?

- are there ways of reducing the taxes my estate will have to pay?

- will probate proceedings be necessary?

The preceding section, *Issue 18: Selecting and Working with a Family Lawyer*, discussed the advantages of doing some basic homework before seeing a lawyer. Preparation on your parents' part can make their lawyer's work more efficient and affordable. Most lawyers work with a basic estate planning form, or at least can list the kinds of financial information and documentation they will need to see in order to help your parents in their estate planning. If your parents can find out what they will need, and then bring it with them when they see their lawyer, it will save time and money.

Community property agreements

Some states recognize community ownership of property. Under community property laws, property acquired through the efforts of either a husband or wife during marriage is presumed to be "community property." Community property laws may also permit spouses to enter into a "community property agreement" in which both agree that all their property will automatically become the sole property of the surviving spouse at the moment one of them dies. A community property agreement may be useful in certain circumstances to arrange for transfer of property on death without the need for probate. Your parents' lawyer should advise them whether a community property agreement is permitted under the laws of the state in which they live and, if so, whether it makes good sense in their situation.

Joint tenancies with right of survivorship

Most states permit two or more persons to hold property as "joint tenants with right of survivorship." When property is owned in this fashion, it normally passes automatically on the death of one of the parties to the surviving joint tenant or tenants. Creating joint tenancies with right of survivorship may have tax implications, so this strategy, too, calls for the advice of a lawyer or other tax advisor.

State law specifies what steps are required to create a joint tenancy with right of survivorship. In most states, for example, a joint tenancy with right of survivorship can only be created through a written document, expressly declaring the intent of the owner/transferor to create a joint tenancy in which his or her interests will pass automatically on death. Many people misunderstand the difference between joint tenancy bank or investment accounts and simply giving someone the authority as an agent to sign checks, make deposits and withdrawals, and take other administrative actions on their behalf. Under a joint tenancy, the entire account balance automatically passes to the joint tenant, regardless of what the person's will says; authority to sign checks and take other similar actions as an agent, on the other hand, conveys no ownership rights, either currently or at time of death. This difference makes it important to recognize when a joint tenancy with right of survivorship is intended and to follow the steps required by law to create it. It also highlights the importance of using correct procedures—usually a power of attorney—to authorize another to act as an agent in financial matters.

Some states recognize ownership of property in "tenancy by the entirety." A tenancy by the entirety is a special kind of joint tenancy in which a husband and wife own property together, with the property passing at death to whichever of them survives the other. As with other sorts of ownership by joint tenancy, it is important to establish clearly the intent of joint ownership in the appropriate legal manner.

Trusts

Trusts are another approach that can be used to transfer property without probate proceedings. A trust is a flexible estate planning tool which can be adapted to the needs of each individual's circumstances. It is easiest to think of a trust as a three-way arrangement involving: (1) a "trustor"; (2) a"trustee"; and (3) one or more "beneficiaries." The person who creates the trust is the trustor. The trustor transfers legal title to the trustee, who is charged with the responsibility of holding title to the property and managing it in a prudent way for the benefit of the beneficiary or beneficiaries. Thus, trusts are different from other property transfers in that title to the property and the right to the income or other beneficial use of the property are in separate parties. Normally, the trustee has all of the responsibilities and burdens of property ownership (and earns a fee for carrying these), while the beneficiary enjoys the benefits as provided under the terms of the trust.

Trusts are used for many purposes:

- to assure professional management of property—and to relieve the beneficiary of the burdens of property management;

- to take advantage of legitimate strategies for avoiding or reducing taxes;

- to arrange for a number of beneficiaries to share in the income or use of the trust property;

- to give a lifetime interest in property to one person, with ownership then passing to another beneficiary or group of beneficiaries, e.g. from children to grandchildren; and

- to provide financial security for minor children or a member of the family who is disabled.

Trusts may be either "testamentary trusts" or "living trusts." Testamentary trusts are those established under the terms of a will and are put into effect on the death of the trustor. Living trusts are created during the lifetime of the trustor and can be either revocable (subject to change) or irrevocable (no longer subject to change).

Living trusts can be structured so that the property included in the trust—potentially the entire estate of the trustor—passes at death according to the terms of the trust. If properly structured, a living trust can thus have the effect of bypassing probate proceedings concerning the trust property, because, under the terms of the trust and at the time of the trustor's death, the property is legally owned by the trustee (in trust for the named beneficiary or beneficiaries), rather than the trustor.

Intestacy (having no will)

If your parents make no will or other arrangement for the distribution of their property on death, it will pass under state laws governing "intestate succession." For example, state law might say that if a man dies without a will and is survived by his wife and two children, his estate, after payment of debts, taxes, and expenses of administration, will be divided by giving half to the wife and one quarter to each of the two children.

There are usually good reasons for not relying on intestacy laws for the distribution of one's estate. Most importantly, what the statue calls for and what the individual might choose for himself or herself could be quite different. Also, the costs of administration may be higher because no planning was undertaken to minimize expenses.

◻ TAX AND ADMINISTRATIVE CONSIDERATIONS

Estate taxes

Most estates are not subject to state or federal estate or death tax liability. Under federal law, an individual is allowed to pass up to $600,000 in property at death without tax liability. Most states exempt a similar amount from estate or inheritance taxes. Together, a husband and wife, with only basic estate tax planning, can leave $1.2 million to their heirs tax free. For large estates, or estates which approach taxable levels, tax planning is an important consideration, and an experienced lawyer should be consulted.

Costs of administration

Many people go to great lengths to avoid probate, hoping to avoid the high administrative costs that are often associated with probating a will. Probate can be expensive. If substantial administrative efforts are required, if there are disputes among interested parties, or if state laws and procedures are cumbersome and difficult, it may be desirable to develop an estate plan that does not involve a will. Avoiding probate may also have the advantage of avoiding having family and personal finances open to public scrutiny in the form of court records.

However, avoiding probate is not a goal to be pursued at all costs. Where streamlined probate procedures have been enacted, a probate proceeding can usually be completed at a reasonable cost. Further, trusts or other arrangements designed to avoid probate may themselves become expensive and difficult to manage. Finally, avoiding probate will not affect applicable federal and state tax requirements. Your parents' estate plan should use the tools which best serve their needs.

Ancillary probates

Where an individual owns real property in another state, a separate "ancillary" probate proceeding in that state may be required unless plans have been made to transfer the property outside of a probate proceeding. Ancillary proceedings can cause additional uncertainty and expense. The estate plan should make specific provision for ancillary probates or for some other mechanism to transfer out-of-state property.

❐ MANAGING FINANCIAL AND PERSONAL AFFAIRS IN THE EVENT OF MENTAL INCAPACITY

In addition to planning for the transfer of property on death, effective estate planning should address the possibility of future legal incapacity due to mental or physical disability. A person who is incompetent under applicable legal standards cannot be held legally responsible for his or her actions. For example, a person who is incompetent will not be bound to contracts or property transfers that he or she makes while incapacitated.

Business and financial decisions can be made on behalf of a person who is no longer competent in one of three ways:

- by an agent or "attorney-in-fact" under a durable power of attorney;

- by a trustee acting under the terms of a trust that was established while the person was still competent (but only for property held in the trust); or

- by a court-appointed guardian.

Durable powers of attorney

Of these three, the most flexible and least expensive approach usually is a durable power of attorney. A power of attorney is simply an authorization made by a person while legally competent for another person to act on his or her behalf. The scope of the authorization may be narrow (limited to particular acts or transactions) or broad. A broadly worded durable power of attorney will appoint another to act for a person in all but specifically excluded business and personal matters.

Durable powers of attorney are so named because under

the state laws authorizing them they continue in effect even after the maker becomes legally incompetent.

Durable powers of attorney can be structured so that they are effective either immediately or only upon disability. Those that take effect immediately have the advantage that the "attorney-in-fact," usually a spouse or child, can act immediately in case of an emergency or a disabling illness. When a durable power is effective only on disability, the attorney-in-fact may not act until it has been determined, in accordance with the procedure set forth in the power of attorney, that the maker is no longer competent. This determination usually calls for a judgment by a trusted person or a committee of persons named in the durable power.

While durable powers of attorney that take effect immediately require a high level of trust and confidence in the appointee (since the designated attorney-in-fact has rights over the personal and business affairs of the maker), there are strategies available for making sure the agent's power is used only at the proper time:

- the attorney in fact need not be a single person; two trusted family members or friends can be designated with the requirement that they act together.

- a durable power of attorney is revocable at anytime up to the point of incapacity;

- durable powers are sometimes placed for safekeeping in the hands of a trusted third party, other than the attorney-in-fact, as a sort of check and balance.

One important point to remember about a durable power of attorney is that it does not prevent the person who has given the power of attorney from continuing to act on his or her own behalf, even if that person becomes incapacitated. A power of attorney gives co-management authority to another person; it does not withdraw the giver's own powers. Taking away a person's power to act alone requires court appointment of a guardian. However, a durable power of attorney can be drafted to anticipate the possibility of a future guardianship, and the person giving the durable power of attorney can use it to state his or her preferences for who should serve as guardian, if one is later appointed by the court.

Management by a trustee

A trustee may be granted broad powers to act with respect to any property placed in trust. However, the procedures for establishing and maintaining a trust often are more burdensome and expensive than a durable power of attorney. Thus, unless there are other reasons to set up a trust, it usually is a less desirable tool for dealing with incapacity than a durable power of attorney.

Guardianships

A court-appointed guardian may also exercise a variety of powers on behalf of any person who has become mentally incapacitated. For a detailed discussion of this legal procedure, see *Issue 20: Guardianships.*

❐ LEAVING BINDING INSTRUCTIONS CONCERNING HEALTH CARE MATTERS

The law recognizes the right of all adults to make their own medical treatment decisions. This includes the right to choose among alternative treatment strategies and the right to refuse treatment all together. It also includes the right to execute "advance directives," including living wills and durable powers of attorney for health care.

Living wills

A majority of states permit individuals (while competent) to execute a directive to physicians, commonly referred to as a "living will." This document states the person's wishes concerning acceptance or refusal of life-sustaining treatment in the event of a terminal illness.

The form of the directive to physicians, and the legal requirements for a living will to be effective, vary from state to state, so it is important to use the correct form and follow the necessary procedural requirements for your state. A typical example is found under *Form 19.1: Living Will.* The correct form for your parents' state should be available from Senior Information and Referral or a health care provider.

Under most state laws, a living will must be witnessed by two persons who meet certain qualifications; for example:

- they may not be related to the person making the living will;
- they may not be designated as heirs under the last will and testament of the person;
- they may not have a claim against the estate;
- they are may be attending physicians; and
- they may not be employees of the physician or a health care facility in which the patient is being treated.

A living will may be revoked at any time by its maker, even after the maker ceases to be mentally competent. Revocation can be made by physically destroying the written document, executing a signed and dated statement of revocation, or verbally stating that revocation is desired.

Living wills serve a limited purpose because they cannot vest in another person the ability to respond immediately and flexibly to a wide variety of contingent circumstances. Such flexibility is best provided by a durable power of attorney for health care, as discussed below. However, living wills are recognized as important in assuring medical treatment decisions that conform to a patient's wishes (see *Issue 12: Making Appropriate Care Decisions*).

Durable powers of attorney for health care

Many states permit durable powers of attorney to be used to delegate health care decision making to another. The types of health care decisions covered by a durable power of attorney may include:

- authority to consent to medical and surgical care;

- authority to refuse treatment or withhold or withdraw life sustaining treatment under certain circumstances;

- authority to admit the person to a medical, nursing, residential, or other institution.

A single durable power of attorney can cover both health care and financial matters.

Good estate planning requires considerable forethought and organization. It also involves facing up to the uncertainties of the future. If your parents are reluctant to take on the chore of preparing or updating their estate planning, emphasize with them the positive aspects of the task. Estate planning enables them to express their preferences and thus retain greater control over their affairs, even in case they later lose the ablity to act alone. It also helps others by giving guidance for decisions that may have to be made in the future.

Issue 20

Guardianship

If the time comes when a parent can no longer make decisions because of mental or physical incapacity, and no durable power of attorney has been set up ahead of time (see discussion of durable powers of attorney in *Issue 19: Estate Planning Considerations*), a guardianship might be necessary.

You may realize that your parent is unable to manage a checkbook, keep track of assets, or pay bills on time. Overnight, the occurrence of a stroke or even a fall can trigger the sudden need for important decisions when the older person is unable to make them. Whether the necessity of considering a guardianship comes suddenly with an unexpected medical problem, or evolves slowly over time, it is always a difficult decision to make. However, a guardianship should be considered when it appears that physical, emotional, or financial damage could occur to your parent due to his or her inability to make decisions, and there is not an authorized surrogate decision maker to step in.

Guardianship is a legal proceeding under which a court supervised guardian is appointed to administer the affairs of a "ward," someone who is incapable of acting on his or her own. This issue explains the basic elements of a guardianship:

- what a guardianship is,
- how it is established,
- how a guardianship operates,
- who should serve as a guardian.

❏ WHAT IS A GUARDIANSHIP?

A legal guardian occupies a position of trust and responsibility. He or she is empowered to make essential deci-

How Do I Know
If my Parent Needs a Guardian?

There are no cut-and-dried standards of when a person should be legally declared incompetent and a guardian appointed. However, as you consider whether a guardianship might be necessary for your parent, you might ask the following questions:

- can your parent keep track of important documents, remember to pay bills on time, and manage a checkbook?

- is your parent's mind sufficiently clear that he or she can follow complex conversations about important financial or medical affairs, and make considered decisions?

- is your parent able to communicate his or her wishes clearly or consistently?

- does your parent exhibit signs of confusion and inability to focus?

sions for the one who is incapacitated. The laws of guardianship have been modified over the years, and most states now divide guardianship into two different types, full and limited. The states are concerned about protecting as much of a person's freedom and decision making power as possible. If your parent is fully incapable of making any personal, medical, or financial decisions, then a full guardianship may be required. However, if he or she needs help in some areas but not in others, then a limited guardianship can be tailored to meet specific needs by defining the areas where help is needed and giving a limited guardian the right to make decisions in those areas only.

For example, your mother may be able to live in her own home, make medical decisions, manage some daily living needs and simple financial transactions such as grocery shopping. She needs assistance, however, in investing her money, maintaining her home, paying bills, cooking, and bathing. In such an instance, a guardian's powers could be limited to managing assets, paying monthly bills, hiring help in the home, and providing an allowance for daily purchases. As time passes, if more help is required, the guardian can petition the court for increased powers.

❐ HOW IS A GUARDIANSHIP ESTABLISHED?

A guardianship is initiated by filing a request or petition with the court asking that the named person be declared incompetent and a guardian appointed to act on his or her behalf. The "petitioner" (the person who instigates the request for guardianship) must provide the court with clear evidence that a guardianship is necessary. To initiate this process, you should consult your parent's primary physician and your own lawyer.

Any guardianship, whether full or limited, requires a detailed letter from a physician outlining the patient's diagnosis and general medical condition, an opinion on how long the present incapacity will last, and the doctor's assessment of the person's ability to make decisions. As you consider the need for a guardianship, it is a good idea to discuss the matter with your parent's doctor so that he or she understands your goals in establishing a guardianship, and you understand the doctor's opinion of whether a guardianship is necessary and what areas it should cover.

You might also want to talk with your parent's lawyer, if the medical condition requiring guardianship is clear and there is no question of your parent contesting the action. If there is any doubt, your parent's lawyer owes his or her loyalty to your parent and will be unable to assist you.

Your lawyer may help you determine whether a guardianship is appropriate for your parent, and may be able to do the legal work necessary to set it up. In talking with your lawyer about a petition for guardianship, ask about his or her experience in guardianship law, as well as about fees. The laws governing guardianship are complex and change frequently. If your lawyer is not experienced in this area of the law, ask for a referral to a lawyer who is. Most lawyers are happy to provide this kind of referral. Keep interviewing lawyers until you find one that you trust, who has experience in setting up guardianships, and who is candid about the fees and costs involved.

The attorney you select will prepare the necessary papers and file the guardianship petition. After the petition is filed, the court will usually appoint an independent,

Guardianship vs. Durable Power of Attorney

A durable power of attorney is a more flexible and less expensive procedure for setting up substitute decision making authority than a guardianship. Planning ahead with a well drafted durable power of attorney will usually avoid the need for a guardianship.

However, this is not always possible. For example, your parent may not want to execute a durable power of attorney or may become incapacitated before doing so.

Also, if it becomes necessary to prevent a parent from taking actions on his or her own, a guardianship will be necessary. A guardianship takes the power to act away from the ward and gives it to the guardian. A durable power of attorney, in comparison, grants power to act to the designated "attorney-in-fact," but it does not prevent the person appointing an agent from acting as well.

temporary guardian, called a "guardian *ad litem,*" to investigate and represent the interest of your parent in the guardianship proceeding. The role of the guardian *ad litem* is to protect the rights of your parent and provide an independent report to the court on whether the proposed guardianship is appropriate. While the guardianship proceeding is going on, your parent is still presumed legally competent. Power to act on his or her behalf is not transferred until the court decides the matter and appoints a guardian.

The court will then hold a hearing to consider the guardianship petition and the report of the guardian *ad litem*. If there are no disputes and the court is satisfied that a guardian is necessary, the court will establish the guardianship, appoint the guardian, and specify the powers and duties of the guardian.

While most guardianships are established without controversy, disagreements can arise concerning the need for or scope of the proposed guardianship. For example, the guardian *ad litem* may object to the guardianship or suggest alternative ways to handle the proposed ward's business affairs. Other family members or interested parties may object to the proceeding or the proposed guardian. If these disagreements cannot be resolved among the parties, the court will conduct a trial to resolve the disputes.

❐ HOW DOES A GUARDIANSHIP OPERATE?

Each state has its own laws governing the scope and operation of guardianships. However, in all states the appointed guardian becomes the legal decision maker for the ward in all matters covered by the guardianship. All states require guardians to make periodic reports to the court; usually these reports are required annually. They include a detailed accounting of all actions taken, especially financial transactions. In most states, specific court approval of financial transactions is required. If you are appointed guardian of one or both of your parents, be sure to keep careful records of all financial transactions and arrangements entered into on their behalf.

Guardians, including guardians *ad litem*, are entitled to payment for their services out of the assets of the guardianship, unless the guardian is a friend or relative who agrees to serve without compensation. In some cases, guardianship costs may be paid by the state if the ward qualifies for public assistance. Guardians are also required to post a bond determined in relation to the amount of the estate's assets to assure that they faithfully perform their duties.

❑ WHO SHOULD SERVE AS GUARDIAN?

Generally, any competent adult of good moral character can be appointed as a guardian. Most often, the guardian will be a family member. This helps both to keep down the costs of the guardianship and to assure that the guardian is personally concerned about the well-being of the ward.

Most states also allow public agencies to serve as guardians if the ward qualifies for public assistance. In some states, private guardianship agencies may act as guardians. Your lawyer or Senior Information and Assistance can help direct you to non-family guardians if necessary.

If there is conflict among family members over who should serve as guardian, there are creative ways to try to resolve those disagreements:

- Have a family meeting to allow everyone time to present opinions and feelings. Sometimes an outside mediator or resource person such as a trusted family friend, clergy, lawyer, or social worker may help the family come to a consensus decision.

- Appoint co-guardians, using either two family members or one family member and one outside person to serve as guardians.

- Set up the terms of the guardianship so that the guardian needs to obtain written consent from certain family members before taking certain sorts of actions.

Remember that disputes that cannot be resolved amicably or that arise after the guardianship is already established often deteriorate into stressful, expensive court battles that serve the interests of no one.

Acting as a guardian demands considerable time and commitment. To take over any aspect of another person's life in order to protect them is a serious responsibility. As this issue makes clear, it can be a complicated process, but there are substantial rewards in knowing that you have provided for your parent either by acting as a guardian or by helping make sure that an appropriate guardian is found.

Issue 21

Older Adults as Consumers

Many older Americans are victims of illegal or unethical commercial practices. Questionable sales and solicitations aimed at older people can cause serious financial loss. Abusive activities involving smaller amounts of money can cause distress, embarrassment, confusion, and resentment.

Abusive practices range all the way from petty overcharges or a "hard sell" for unneeded items to outright frauds and swindles directed at the elderly over the phone, through the mail, or from door to door. This issue discussion looks at these unscrupulous business practices and criminal activities, the steps your parents can take to prevent being taken advantage of, and what to do if your parents are victimized.

☐ COMMON PRACTICES THAT VICTIMIZE SENIORS IN THE MARKETPLACE

Unethical or illegal practices that take advantage of older people are as diverse and plentiful as the promoters, pitchmen, and con artists that conceive and carry them out.

Telephone solicitations

There are a wide variety of schemes that use telephone

solicitations to contact victims. Since the elderly are often dependent on telephones for outside contact, they are particularly vulnerable to these appeals. Questionable operations involve such things as:

- *charitable solicitations* that are either outright frauds or operations at the edge of legitimacy, skimming off excessive "administrative fees" from contributions;

- *credit card schemes* that are designed to obtain a person's Visa or Mastercard number so that it can be used to make unauthorized charges;

- *home appointment schemes* where the caller may use various ruses to get an appointment for a home visit so a sales representative can put on a "hard sell;"

- *vitamins* and other health products sold over the phone by unscrupulous operators who make false or exaggerated claims exploiting the health concerns of older persons;

- *investment schemes* of all descriptions that are offered over the phone by promoters promising "once in a lifetime" opportunities;

- *low cost vacations, club memberships, and magazine subscriptions* in which older adults are misled or defrauded by telephone solicitors.

Telephone solicitations should always be viewed with suspicion. While many of the scams mentioned above can be peddled by other means, e.g. door-to-door or through the mails, the telephone provides quick and easy personal contact with potential victims. Lonely adults seeking friendly contacts are easy targets for sympathetic-sounding solicitors. Danger signs to watch for include:

- does the caller try to pressure your parent into an immediate decision or immediate payment?

- does the caller refuse to mail free information?

- does the caller apply pressure to get a credit card number?

These and any other situations that arouse discomfort or suspicions should *always* be avoided.

Door-to-door fraud

Door-to-door peddlers pose the same risks of fraud as telephone solicitors. These persons are trained to close a sale on the spot before the buyer can think things over or investigate. Anyone buying from a door-to-door agent should be very careful.

Home improvement schemes

Millions of dollars are lost every year on home improvement scams involving services that are bogus, unnecessary, or over-priced. These unethical practices range from simple overcharging to schemes where con artists offer homeowners a special deal on a repair job because they have "materials left over from a job they just finished down the street."

Auto repairs

The elderly (along with most of the rest of the population) are vulnerable to auto repair fraud because of lack of knowledge about the mechanical operation of cars. Abusive practices include overcharging, unnecessary repairs, and improperly done work. The best protection against this type of fraud is for your parents to find and deal with a mechanic they trust.

Other frauds

Other schemes designed to cheat consumers are constantly being invented and revived. Land promotions, mail order fraud, bait advertising, phoney prizes, fraudulent credit practices, and pyramid schemes, among countless others, constantly threaten to take advantage of unwitting consumers. It is impossible to anticipate every scheme that may be devised, but a healthy skepticism and cautious buying habits will help avoid most of these frauds.

❒ STEPS TO REDUCE THE RISK OF LOSS

There are several practical steps you and your parents can take to reduce the risk of loss in connection with consumer fraud.

1. Consumer protection measures can be discussed openly with your parents. Forewarned is forearmed. Perhaps a subscription to *Consumer Reports, Changing Times,* or another similar consumer advocacy/money management publication can serve to help your parents protect themselves from danger.

2. Support your parents' sound financial management; There is no stronger defense against fraud than a reasonable household budget and an investment strategy that makes good sense, relying on reputable advisers and brokers, and avoiding questionable promoters. Any investment opportunities should be checked out by a qualified advisor before money is committed.

3. Your parents should have a plan for their charitable giving and should stick to it in the face of all solicitations save those about which they have

firsthand knowledge.

4. Encourage your parents in sensible buying habits and attitudes. In addition to those already mentioned, these include the following:

- Comparison shop for both price and quality, particularly on major purchases. Get several bids for any home repair or improvement work.

- Deal with reputable merchants who have a long-term interest in maintaining satisfied customers.

- Read and understand any written contracts before signing. Be sure all of the terms of an agreement are in the written contract. Don't rely on oral assurances. Also, be sure to keep a copy of any signed contracts.

- Beware of "bait" advertising where consumers are lured by a bargain price and then manipulated into purchasing a higher priced article. *Remember, any deal that sounds too good to be true probably is!* Be especially wary of prizes, free gifts, or claims of deep discounts.

- Avoid any buying situation where the seller resorts to high pressure sales tactics. The standard rule here is: "if you feel uncomfortable, don't buy."

- Allow a self-imposed cooling-off period before completing any major purchase.

- Beware of medical quackery. Quacks thrive by selling bogus devices, treatments, and cures for incurable diseases and conditions. Hearing aids, dentures, eyeglasses, drugs, and vitamins are common problem areas.

❐ WHAT TO DO IF YOU BELIEVE YOUR PARENTS HAVE BEEN VICTIMIZED

If you suspect or know that your parents have been victimized, your first step should be to find out immediately what their legal rights are. There are a number of state and federal laws that are designed to help protect consumers from unethical business practices. Generally, these laws help assure that consumers receive adequate information to make an informed purchase decision and that they are provided adequate time to consider the decision. Some statutes grant consumers the right to cancel contracts within a certain time (usually three to seven days). Others require businesses to adhere to certain statutory procedures in dealing with customers. For example, with auto repairs, a customer may have a right to a written estimate that may not be exceeded by more than 10% without prior authorization. Laws can provide help, but time may be a critical element, so act promptly.

Consumer protection laws have their limitations. While outright fraud is illegal, it is usually difficult to prove or remedy. Prudent buying and investment practices will always be the consumer's best defense.

❐ WHERE TO GO FOR HELP

A good general source of information concerning your parents' legal rights as consumers is the Consumer Protection division of the state Attorney General's office. This office should be able to advise you on specific situations, or direct you to another agency for help.

There are a number of other government agencies that may be able to help.

1. *The Federal Trade Commission* (FTC) has responsibility for federal laws regulating door-to-door sales, fair credit reporting, and unfair credit practices.

2. *The Postal Inspector* of the United States Postal Service is primarily responsible for policing frauds committed through the mail.

3. *Cities and counties* may have local consumer offices to give advice and make referrals to other sources of assistance, if necessary.

4. *Small claims courts* provide an inexpensive forum in which to bring a legal action if you or your parents are victimized by an illegal business practice. Information concerning court procedures may be obtained from the clerk of the court or the local bar association.

If your consumer complaint involves a reputable firm, you may well be able to resolve the problem by contacting the firm directly. A prompt complaint that clearly describes the problem and offers a reasonable solution often will resolve the dispute.

Other non-governmental sources of assistance on consumer matters include:

- *the Better Business Bureau.* This is a voluntary organization of participating businesses whose goal is to promote fair business practices. The Bureau maintains information on whether complaints have been filed against a business in the past and will present your complaint to the business in an attempt to reach a settlement. The Bureau also provides an arbitration service to resolve disputes without going to court.

- *the local press and media.* Many local newspapers

and radio stations have consumer affairs departments that will look into complaints on behalf of consumers. These departments may also be able to guide you to other sources of assistance.

- *other advocates.* Depending on your location and the nature of the problem, there may be other nongovernmental sources of help. Legislators, local consumer groups, and organizations such as the American Association of Retired Persons (AARP), as well as trade associations, such as the Direct Marketing Association, may provide assistance on particular complaints.

Consumer protection for older adults is a serious issue. Adults who are least vulnerable to the types of fraud mentioned above are those who are not lonely or isolated, but who can depend on a personal network of family and friends to encourage and assist them in managing major purchases and investments. Good communication within the family will contribute to this support and to an improved awareness of consumer fraud risks.

5 Financial Issues

Issue 22

Financial Planning and Management

This issue covers two related topics: financial planning and financial management. The financial planning section discusses how to evaluate your parents' financial situation and how to help them plan for meeting their financial needs. The financial management section deals with issues that may arise if it becomes necessary to intervene in the day-to-day management of your parents' finances.

Typically, while parents remain healthy and independent, they will retain full control over the planning and management of their financial affairs. Ideally, they will have established a financial plan for retirement while they were still working. Adult children may have little or no involvement in this process.

However, as parents lose their ability to live independently, adult children may need to intervene in both the planning and management of their parents' financial affairs. This section will provide background information to help guide such intervention if it becomes necessary.

When to get involved

Families often have trouble discussing money in an open, constructive manner. Such discussions can evoke strong emotions. Jealousy, independence, self-esteem, and pri constructive manner. Such discussions can evoke strong emotions. Jealousy, independence, self-esteem, and privacy are all factors which sometimes inhibit open communication among family members about finances. If these barriers can be overcome, it is best for adult children to become acquainted early with their parents' finances. As a side benefit, this involvement may stimulate the adult children to begin thinking about their own retirement planning.

Often, however, adult children do not become involved in their parents' financial affairs until something goes wrong or until parents are forced into a major change. Circumstances may require the children to make important financial decisions for or with their parents with very little information from which to work. If financial issues arise at the same time the family is confronted with other problems, the task of sorting them out can seem overwhelming. Learning something about financial planning in advance will help you step into such situations and be more comfortable in making or helping to make decisions.

❐ FINANCIAL PLANNING

Financial planning is a process that many of us find intimidating. We have enough difficulty totaling up last year's financial results for Uncle Sam on April 15, and we are reluctant to take on the task of making realistic estimates and plans for the future. Yet, ignoring this task will not make it go away. Planning for the future use of financial resources will be important for your parents, even after they are no longer able to do the planning on their own.

The basic goal of financial planning in later life is to make sure there will be adequate financial resources available to meet projected lifetime expenditure needs. This planning process involves three steps:

1. gathering the necessary financial records and information;

2. evaluating needs and resources; and

3. preparing a budget.

Completing this process need not be an overwhelming task if it is approached in an organized fashion. Careful planning will be particularly important when considering any major change in living arrangements, such as a move into retirement housing. A thoughtful budget will help focus the planning on options which are within reach financially. It is far easier to plan for financial needs in advance than to be caught later in a financial crisis with few resources and alternatives with which to work.

Step 1: Gathering information

To begin the planning process, your parents should first assemble the financial information upon which plans and projections will be based. A good first step in this process is to locate the important records and documents that bear on your parents' finances. *Form 1.1: Helpful Personal Information* provides a checklist for locating and identifying these records and documents. Maintaining an up to date inventory of these documents and their location will make both financial planning and financial management much easier. A thorough inventory of financial records will also help assure that rights and benefits to which your parents are entitled are not overlooked.

Locating documents can be difficult, particularly if a parent suffers from memory loss or confusion. Sometimes records are misplaced or hidden, and an extensive search is necessary to recover them or obtain replacements.

From the records identified in *Form 1.1*, you can help your parents calculate their net worth. Net worth is the value of all assets they own minus the liabilities that they owe. It indicates the net value of all assets they have available to meet future financial needs. *Form 22.1: Net Worth Statement* provides a format for estimating net worth. The valuation estimates included should be realistic and based on current prices for which property could be resold. Generally, items of personal property such as furniture, tools, and personal belongings will be worth far less than they cost new.

Financial planning will also involve estimating your parents' future income and expenditures. If your parents expect to continue their present lifestyle, projections can be based on their current income and expenses. If their lifestyle is changing, or if they want to project the effect of changes into the future, they should gather information on what their income and expenses will be under the changed conditions. Try not to overlook any major expenditures that are likely to become necessary. You might suggest budgeting a contingency amount for unexpected expenses since it is easier to underestimate expenses than income.

Form 22.2: Household Budget lists the income and expense categories for which your parents or you will want to gather information. Make sure the relevant information is gathered for each category that applies to your parents.

You and your parents may need further information to estimate their future benefits from private pensions, profit sharing plans, or Social Security. In the case of private retirement plans, the Employee Retirement

Income Security Act (ERISA) requires the plan administrator to tell retirees or their authorized representatives about the retiree's rights and benefits under the plan. On request, the plan administrator will provide information such as:

- the type of pension benefit and whether it is fully vested;

- the benefit formula;

- projections of future benefit amounts or the amount a retiree has in the retirement fund;

- the benefit rights of a surviving spouse after the death of the retiree.

Questions about future Social Security benefits usually can be answered by your local Social Security office. Local senior advocacy groups also can help answer questions about Social Security benefits or advise your parents if they have a dispute with the Social Security Administration. See *Tab 7: Resources.*

The local Social Security office will provide a booklet entitled "How to Calculate Your Benefits" upon request. A statement of credited earnings and an estimate of benefit amounts may also be obtained free of charge by submitting Form SSA-7004 PC (Request for Earnings and Benefit Estimate Statement). Your local Social Security office can supply the request form, which must be signed by the beneficiary or an authorized representative. The government also publishes a comprehensive book on Social Security benefits entitled the *Social Security Handbook,* which is available in libraries or through the government printing office.

Many states now offer older adults property tax credits, exemptions, or deferrals. These can offer significant tax savings to your parents. Information on these programs can be obtained from your local property tax assessor or other official or agency charged with administering the tax on property.

Step 2: Evaluating needs and resources

The second step in financial planning is to organize the information gathered on income and expenses and to assess the adequacy of financial resources to meet financial needs. The information should be organized into a budget format such as *Form 22.2: Household Budget.*

Extending these financial projections over your parents' expected lifetimes provides an estimate of the adequacy of their financial resources to meet lifetime expenditure requirements. Included with *Form 22.2* is a list of yearly inflation adjustment factors based on 4% and 8% inflation rates, and a life expectancy table. If you first calculate the expected expenses for future years in current dollars and then multiply the total by the appropriate inflation factor for each year into the future, it will give you the dollar amount of expenses you can expect for future years at a given rate of inflation. While no one knows what the actual rates of inflation will be in future years, it is likely to be within the range of 4% to 8% per year. The life expectancy table will provide a guide for estimating how long resources must last, but remember the tables are based on averages. Your parents may live longer than or not as long as the average.

If initial budget calculations show insufficient income to cover projected expenses, you and your parents may want to consider other sources of funds. For example, if your parents own life insurance that has a cash value, a loan against the policy may provide additional funds. A good insurance agent will be able to describe the options available under your parents' policies and help your parents decide among various loan and payout options.

Home equity conversions are also a potential source of money. Many older people own their homes free and clear (or nearly so), but have little cash to meet living expenses. Recently, a number of approaches have evolved to allow this "home equity" value to be used to pay expenses, while still allowing the owners to continue to live in their home. These options include:

- *reverse mortgages*—where monthly loan payments are made to the homeowner based on the amount of equity in the home (The loan amount is repaid at a future date when the homeowner dies or sells the home).

- *deferred payment loans*—a long-term, secured loan under which repayment is deferred until the sale of the property.

- *sale/leaseback conversions*—where the owner sells the home to an investor while retaining the right to live in the property for life.

- *other home equity loans and credit lines*—in which banks and brokerage houses make loans or extend credit on the basis of a second mortgage against the property.

These and other similar arrangements provide mechanisms for making use of the equity in the home to pay living costs. In considering any such arrangements, however, be sure your parents understand clearly all the terms, conditions, and long-term costs of the entire transaction.

Finally, your parents may want to review projected expenditures for possible savings. Are there ways to cut back without undue hardship? Are your parents taking full advantage of available senior assistance programs? A careful review of these and similar items may help bring the budget into balance.

Reducing financial risks

In addition to evaluating the adequacy of financial resources, you and your parents may want to consider ways of reducing their exposure to undue financial risks. The greatest risks faced by most older adults are for health care, whether it be acute short-term emergencies or long-term care needs. If your parents have average resources (neither Medicaid-eligible, nor independently wealthy), they may want to review their insurance coverage and consider additional insurance to supplement Medicare coverage or to cover the cost of long-term care. See *Issue 25: Private Insurance Alternatives.*

Step 3: Prepare a household budget

After choosing how to allocate the available financial resources, your parents should prepare a final household budget that reflects these decisions. The budget will serve as a guide for future financial decisions. It can also sound an alarm if income and expenditures diverge significantly from the budget estimates.

If, despite all efforts, your parents cannot establish a balanced budget, the budget projections will help them and you identify how much more will likely be required and when these funds will be needed. For example, if other family members are going to contribute to make up the deficit, the budget will indicate when and how large a contribution may be necessary. Or, if you and your parents are considering public sources of financial assistance, for example, Supplemental Security Income (SSI) or Medicaid, the budget will help you plan to meet the eligibility requirements for those programs. When timing considerations are important, you may want to break down the budget projections on a monthly rather than annual basis.

Whatever your parents' situation, a thoughtful budget will help them obtain the best advantages from their financial resources.

☐ FINANCIAL MANAGEMENT

Financial management is largely a matter of:

- ✔ organization and judgment;
- ✔ reasonable and current record-keeping;
- ✔ timely attention to recurring obligations; and
- ✔ common sense in knowing when an expense is needed and affordable.

Older adults are often able to manage their financial affairs without family assistance. However, certain disabilities of age, particularly severe memory loss, may give rise to the need for intervention.

Does your parent need help?

It may not be obvious when a parent begins having trouble managing finances. The parent may be reluctant to acknowledge difficulties, and the effects of mismanagement may not appear immediately. Below are listed some specific signs that may indicate a need for help.

- Do you see evidence of reckless or impulsive decisions: major furniture purchases, lavish gifts for family members and others, expenditures which seem out of character?

- Has your parent become unreasonably frugal, unwilling to spend available funds for even basic necessities?

- Is your parent becoming vague or forgetful in other areas of life? For example, if your mother

Joint Bank Accounts or Power of Attorney

Normally, adding a name as an additional signer on a bank account does more than just authorize another person to pay bills. It creates a specific form of ownership for the funds in the account: joint tenancy with right of survivorship. Legal title to the funds in such accounts passes to the joint tenant at death, subject to claims by creditors of the deceased. This change in ownership should be taken into account if it seems appropriate to have a joint account.

Most banks also have standard form powers of attorney that can be used to authorize another person to manage an account without transferring an interest in the account to that person. The powers granted by a power of attorney will terminate at the death of the account owner. The authority will also terminate if the owner becomes mentally incapacitated, unless it is a durable power of attorney. See the discussion of joint tenancy and powers of attorney in *Issue 19: Estate Planning Considerations.*

is always misplacing her glasses, she might also be misplacing bills or other financial documents which require action within a certain period of time.

- Does your intuition tell you that something is amiss? For example, do you sense either excessive anxiety or lack of concern by your parent about financial matters?

All of these are possible signs that some level of help may be needed in managing your parents' finances.

As with financial planning, it is best for adult children to begin involvement in financial management before an acute need arises. Early involvement should focus on establishing procedures for managing financial affairs in case of an emergency. This subject might be raised, for example, when your parents discuss plans for wills, durable powers of attorney, or other estate planning issues. Topics that might be covered in early discussions include:

- Do your parents or you have a handy, inclusive listing of important financial documents and records and where they are kept? Trying to locate this information after an emergency or death occurs is often a difficult task.

- What arrangements have been made for handling ongoing finances in case of a disabling emergency? There should be a plan for managing major assets and paying obligations. For example, have your parents considered a power of attorney or joint tenancy for bank accounts? This would be helpful in case it becomes necessary for an adult child to take responsibility for paying bills.

How to get involved

If there already are indications your parent is experiencing difficulty in managing finances, more direct and immediate assistance may be required. Intervention can be difficult, and it should always be approached in a sensitive manner. The following ideas might help in this situation.

- Discuss your concerns with others whom you trust and who may be aware of the financial problems of your parent. These discussions may confirm your concerns or set them to rest.

- Find an appropriate opening to discuss financial problems, for example, when your parent talks about being tired or slowing down. Consult with others close to your parent about the best way to offer help. The time and manner in which the subject is broached will affect your chances for successful intervention.

- Give your parent the option of having someone other than you provide assistance. Another family member or an outside professional (accountant or bank trust officer) is a good alternative. This gives your parent a choice and may make him or her more comfortable with the idea of relying on someone else for help.

- Try not to link your offer of help with discovered financial mistakes of your parent. No one likes to be caught making mistakes; parents especially don't like to be caught by their children. Your intervention should not look like punishment. If you discover unpaid bills or other examples of financial mismanagement, talk with your parent about the problem. Let your parent maintain control in choosing an appropriate option.

- When discussing financial management issues with your parents, emphasize greater convenience, financial security, and peace of mind as their goals. Your own peace of mind may be important to you, but that should be kept in the background.

- Investigate some options and resources that are appropriate for your parent ahead of time so that your discussion can have more focus. Suggest specific ways you can help. Avoid vagueness which may be interpreted as evidence of an ulterior motive.

Areas for providing assistance

There are a number of separate areas in which financial management problems commonly arise. Try to focus your involvement in areas where problems are serious. Your parents may remain capable of handling most areas and need only limited assistance. Consider the following areas:

- *Medicare and other health care bills*—Keeping track of Medicare and Medicare supplement insurance paperwork is a daunting task for anyone. You may be able to set up standard procedures that your parents can follow with limited help from you. See *Form 23.1: Medical Bill Payment Record.*

- *insurance coverage*—There is a wide variety of insurance products marketed to older adults, and it is difficult for nonprofessionals to assess and compare policies. As a result, older adults sometimes end up with duplicate coverages or unnecessary and overpriced policies. Sometimes insurance coverage is overlooked or forgotten, or there is confusion about coverage and benefits. A trustworthy insurance agent can help assure that your parents' insurance is reasonable and appropriate.

- *tax and other records*—A common problem with memory loss, confusion, or lack of energy is increased difficulty in maintaining and organizing financial records. If a parent is having increasing difficulty with income tax records, you might help directly, or suggest a professional service to handle or help with this task.

- *bill paying and bank records*—A range of alternatives are available to assist with these tasks. In some cases, a hired bill-paying service might be best. In others, you might set a prearranged time each month to sit down with your parent and organize and pay bills together. Maintaining bank records and balancing the bank account are functions that you might assist with, or which banks will perform for a fee.

- *consumer purchases and financial assistance programs*—As discussed in *Issue 21: Older Adults as Consumers*, buying practices are aspects of financial management that may require monitoring and possible intervention. Another subject area worth reviewing is whether your parent is taking advantage of available programs that offer financial assistance to older adults. For example, many states offer a senior citizen property tax exemption or deferral to older homeowners with limited incomes, yet a large percentage of those qualifying don't apply. Similarly, discounts and special arrangements are available for a wide range of public and private services. Simply pointing these out, or perhaps helping your parent to apply for these programs, may save them substantial sums.

- *investments*—Income from savings and investments, such as stocks, bonds, annuities, and rental property can be a significant income source during retirement. If you are faced with taking responsibility for managing investments for your parents, either you must be knowledgeable about investing or you should seek the advice of some-

Financial Planners

If your parents need help with financial or investment planning, a professional financial planner
may be worth considering. Financial planners
work under a variety of compensation arrangements, from hourly charges to straight commis-
sions for investment products sold to clients. Financial planning is not yet a regulated profession
in most states, so there is little in the way of gov-
ernmental supervision or uniform quality standards on which to rely.

In choosing a financial planner, interview several
before making a decision. Obtain recommendations from friends and professionals whom your
parents trust, such as their lawyer, accountant, or
banker.

one who is. Many stockbrokers offer advisory
services, but be careful to choose a broker who is
experienced and will watch out for your parent's
interests. Independent investor groups, such as
the American Association of Independent Inves-
tors (AAII), can be a good source of information
on investments. There are also many books available on investment management and financial
planning, some of which are listed under *Tab 7:
Resources*. Many are available at your public
library.

Helping your parents to plan and manage their financial
affairs can be a delicate task. It requires sensitive judg-

ment concerning the need for assistance and tact in raising the subject with them. Try to be positive and specific in making suggestions. Simply criticizing the way your parents are handling finances is likely to do more harm than good. Let your parents know that you are available to help them in those areas where they need and are willing to accept assistance.

Issue 23

Understanding Medicare

Medicare is the federally funded program through the Social Security Administration which provides health care coverage for most American adults age 65 and over and persons who are disabled. Initiated in 1965, Medicare is now the largest single payor for health care in the United States. As health care costs have soared in the past two decades, Medicare has tried both to continue to provide coverage to the Medicare population and to contain the cost of care provided. This has resulted in a complex web of regulations and incentives which continues to undergo modification almost on a yearly basis.

This issue will acquaint you with the general structure of Medicare, and help you and your parent understand the limits of coverage and how the Medicare system of payment works.

❒ MEDICARE: PART A

Medicare Part A covers most services provided by institutional health care providers. These services include:

- hospital inpatient services;
- a limited amount of care in a skilled nursing facility;
- hospice care for the terminally ill;

- a limited amount of home health care services.

For all those who are Medicare eligible, Medicare Part A is automatically included when you enroll. There are no premiums to pay.

Hospital services

In 1983, Medicare reorganized its system of payment to hospitals to provide more efficient health care. If your Medicare-eligible parent needs to be admitted to a hospital for medical services or surgery, Medicare will pay that hospital a set sum based on your parent's diagnosis. This sum is based on the average cost of care for persons with the same diagnosis in the same region. The Medicare payment to the hospital covers charges for inpatient hospital care, including room, treatments and testing procedures, drugs, equipment, and nursing care. Limitations on Medicare coverage of hospital expenses include: restrictions on the *number of days* of hospitalization covered; the beneficiary's *deductible payment*; and the beneficiary's *co-payment requirement*.

- *Number of days of coverage* — Medicare will pay up to 90 days in the hospital during any "benefit period." A "benefit period" begins when you start receiving hospital or nursing home care covered by Medicare and ends 60 days after you are finally discharged. In addition, each person covered by the program is entitled to a lifetime reserve of up to 60 days hospitalization, though this reserve coverage is subject to a higher than normal patient co-payment. Care in a psychiatric hospital is covered by Medicare, but subject to a 190-day lifetime limitation.

- *Deductible Expense* — Medicare benefits are subject to an annual deductible that must be paid by the beneficiary before he or she begins receiving Medicare benefits. The amount of the deductible is adjusted from year to year. In 1991, for example, the beneficiary is required to pay for the first $620.00 of hospital charges.

- *Beneficiary co-payment* — Persons covered under Medicare Part A are also subject to a co-payment or "co-insurance" charge of $157.00 (in 1991) per day for the 61st through the 90th days of hospitalization. Persons using their lifetime reserve of 60 days must pay $314.00 per day (in 1991) for each reserve day of hospitalization.

Skilled nursing home care

Under the current system of Medicare payment to hospitals, the hospital's incentive is to release patients as soon as they no longer need hospital services. This means that in many cases, patients will be well enough to leave the hospital but not well enough to return home. Medicare covers the costs of care in a Skilled Nursing Facility on a limited basis (up to 100 days) for those in this situation. Nursing home coverage is subject to a number of conditions:

1) admission for nursing home care must follow a period of at least three consecutive days of hospitalization;

2) admission must be for further treatment of the same condition for which the person was hospitalized and must, generally speaking, commence within 30 days after hospital discharge;

3) the patient is responsible for $78.50 per day (in 1991) for each day of nursing home care over 20 in a given benefit period.

It is important to understand the limitation on nursing

home care provided through Medicare. *Medicare does not cover nursing home care as a long-term or "custodial" care alternative.* If your parent needs such care, he or she will have to pay for it privately, or if your parent does not have the necessary resources, such care may be covered by Medicaid—see *Issue 24: Understanding Medicaid.*

Hospice care

Medicare pays for hospice care for those who wish it and are suffering from a terminal illness. Hospice care is often covered by what is called the Medicare Hospice Benefit. In order for your parent to receive the Medicare Hospice Benefit, your parent's physician must certify that your parent has a terminal illness and is expected to live less than six months. Medicare then will pay a set sum to a Medicare-licensed hospice provider to provide care.

Not all hospice providers are licensed to receive payment through the Medicare Hospice Benefit. As your parent looks into hospice care as an option, this is one aspect of care to check on. Even if a hospice program is not licensed to receive the Medicare Hospice Benefit, Medicare may pay for some aspects of hospice care under home health care benefits. For more information, read *Issue 27: Hospice Care* or check with your local hospice provider.

Home health care services

Medicare covers home health care services for persons who are essentially confined to their homes, who need occasional skilled medical and nursing care, but do not need to be in an institutional setting. This includes persons recently released from a hospital or nursing home, and those with chronic health problems which require on-going treatment. The services which Medicare covers include: part-time or intermittent nursing care; physical, occupational, and speech therapy; medical social services; services of a home health aide under some circumstances; medical supplies and durable medical equipment.

Limitations of Part A coverage

There are limitations to all the services covered under Medicare Part A. Depending on the type of services, the limitations include number of days of coverage and patient payment of deductibles and co-payments. For example, in each calendar year that one or more hospitalizations occur, the patient is required to pay a special hospital inpatient deductible charge which is applied to the first day of care. In 1991, that deductible amount was $620.

❑ MEDICARE PART B

Medicare Part B is an optional part of the Medicare program. When a person enters the Medicare program, he or she must elect whether or not to subscribe to Part B services. If a person does elect Part B coverage, there is a premium to pay which is deducted from the person's monthly Social Security check. That premium has been increasing. In 1991, it is $29.90 per month.

For most adults, it makes sense to pay the Part B premium for the coverage it offers. The services which Medicare Part B covers include:

- physicians' services;
- outpatient hospital services;
- physical and occupational therapy;
- speech pathology services;

- x-rays, laboratory charges, and other diagnostic tests;

- durable medical equipment such as wheel-chairs, crutches, special beds;

- ambulance service;

- prosthetic devices;

- outpatient surgical and rehabilitation services;

- certain drugs.

The limitations on coverage through Medicare Part B include an annual deductible of $100 and a co-insurance payment of 20% of the Medicare approved charge.

The phrase "Medicare approved charge" is a significant one. For all services provided under Medicare Part B, Medicare determines what it believes is a reasonable charge. The charge is computed by Medicare using a formula which measures the fee actually charged by the physician (the actual charge) against fee standards in that community (the prevailing charge) and what the physician has previously charged for that same service (the customary charge). The Medicare approved charge is the lowest of these three charges. If the physician's fee is higher than the Medicare approved charge, the physician can bill the patient for the additional monies, but Medicare will only pay 80% of the approved rate.

> Example: Mrs. Johnson goes to see her physician and the physician charges her $90 for the visit. When Medicare receives the bill, it decides through its formula that the approved charge for this type of visit is $70. Medicare will then pay the physician 80% of that $70, or $56 (if the patient has already paid the annual $100 deductible). The patient must pay the balance, or $34.

Some physicians "accept assignment," which means they are willing to have the Medicare approved charge be the full charge for the service provided. The benefit to physicians is that if they accept assignment, Medicare pays them directly. The benefit to your parents is a lower total charge. Your parents should check with their health care providers about whether they accept assignment. It can mean a significant savings.

❒ ORGANIZING AND PAYING MEDICAL BILLS

Medicare has been a significant boon to the older population, but the paperwork involved in tracking and obtaining payment of bills is significant. Older adults are frequently overwhelmed by the confusing mass of paperwork that one moderately serious illness can generate. One of the earliest ways you might intervene in a parent's life is in helping keep track of, organize, and pay medical bills. A convenient form to help simplify this procedure is included under: *Tab 9, Form 23.1: Medical Bill Payment Record.*

As you help organize and pay your parent's bills under Medicare, two things will be helpful. First, all Medicare "Explanations of Benefits" are referenced by the date the service was provided. So keep track of the service dates on bills. Second, remember the distinction between the Medicare approved charge and the actual charge for service.

If you have a question about your Medicare benefits

All Medicare "Explanation of Benefits" forms list both the phone number you can call if there are questions about what Medicare has and has not covered, and the procedure for having Medicare benefits officially reviewed. Sometimes physicians submit their paperwork in such a way that benefits are reduced. A call to the physician's office may be enough to have the claim resubmitted properly. Other problems may also arise in processing. If you or your parent have any questions about what Medicare has covered, do not hesitate to call the number listed on the Explanation of Benefits form and ask questions or request a formal review. You can also request a publication called "Your Medicare Handbook," prepared by the Social Security Administration.

Because dealing with medical bills under Medicare can be so cumbersome and intimidating, many older adults do not take full advantage of the benefits which they have paid for. Encourage your parents to be diligent in following up on Medicare benefits and explanations. If your help would be welcome, then help. When a person is either struggling with a chronic illness or recovering from a short term illness, the stress involved in dealing with medical bills may be significant. Your understanding of the difficulty of the process, as well as your actual help, can both increase your parents' peace of mind and decrease their out-of-pocket medical expense.

Issue 24

Understanding Medicaid

The Social Security Act of 1965 initiated two major federal spending programs which sought to provide medical care for those in American society who could least afford it: Medicare for persons over the age of 65 and the disabled, and Medicaid for the poor. Medicare was discussed in the previous issue (*Issue 23: Understanding Medicare*). This issue focuses on Medicaid, the program for persons whose income falls below certain designated levels. Today, there are over twenty-four million Americans covered by Medicaid, about sixteen percent of them over the age of 65. This issue will address Medicaid in a general sense, but its primary focus will be on how Medicaid affects those age 65 and over.

The following discusses typical Medicaid questions. However, Medicaid eligibility rules and regulations vary from state to state, so be sure you or your parent comfirms the specific limitations applicable where he or she lives before counting on coverage under this program.

❒ WHAT IS MEDICAID?

Medicaid is a joint federal and state funded program to help pay for the cost of medical expenses for the poor. Each state designs and administers its own Medicaid program, and there is great variety among the states as to how Medicaid is organized, who is eligible, and what specifically is covered; but all states provide some coverage for low-income older adults for:

- payment of Medicare Part B premiums;
- payment of Medicare co-payments and deductibles;
- extended nursing-home care.

Of these covered items—and other items such as prescription drugs, eyeglasses, and hearing aids which are covered in some states—by far the most crucial and most expensive is Medicaid's coverage of long-term care in nursing facilities. Each year Medicaid pays for about half of the nursing-home care delivered in this country. Older persons who need long term care and who have modest assets quickly find their personal assets depleted, and thus become Medicaid eligible some time after they have entered a nursing home.

◻ MEDICAID AND NURSING HOMES

Income limits

Unlike Medicare, Medicaid is not automatically available to people just because they are over 65 or disabled. To qualify for Medicaid, a person's monthly income and overall resources must be below a specific amount.

For purposes of the Medicaid program, the word *income* includes all monthly or periodic checks from sources such as Social Security, pensions, the military, or annuities. Medicaid does *not* consider money generated from property owned, such as stock dividends, rents, or real estate contract payments, to be income. Instead, property generating a monthly income is treated as a *resource*. Resources are discussed in the section below.

States vary in terms of how much income a Medicaid applicant is allowed to have and still qualify for benefits. Some states only provide benefits for people with income below a specified amount. Other states have no specific income limit but instead allow participation on a sliding scale basis. For example, a person in a state that follows this sliding scale approach is eligible in terms of income as long as his or her monthly income is less than the cost of nursing-home care and other medical expenses; if the Medicaid reimbursement rate is $1500 per month and your parent's income is $1400 per month, your parent would be eligible for approximately $100 of Medicaid benefits each month.

For a married couple where one spouse needs nursing-home care, Medicaid will consider only the income owned by the spouse in the nursing home in determining income eligibility. So, if your mother is in a nursing home and her only income is $400 from Social Security, only that amount will be considered in determining her Medicaid eligibility. Income owned by your father would be disregarded.

As a general rule you should never assume your parents' income is too high to qualify for Medicaid. Check with your parents' state Medicaid agency to see if their income is within the allowed limits.

Resource Limits

In Medicaid terminology, *resources* are all property which a person owns, except income. Examples of resources might include a home, bank accounts, individual retirement accounts (IRAs) , insurance policies (with a cash surrender value), and vehicles.

In 1989 the maximum amount of resources Medicaid allowed a person in a nursing home to keep was $2000.

Congress periodically increases this amount in small increments. Certain resources are exempt or disregarded in determining if resources are below the allowable limit.

A list of exempt resources follows:

- the family home if a spouse or dependent relative is living in it; the home will also be exempt indefinitely for a single person if the person states that he or she intends to return home;

- one car, regardless of its value;

- all household furnishings and personal effects;

- life insurance with a face value less than $1500 (for life insurance with a face value above $1500, any cash surrender value will be included as part of the $2000 resource limit);

- a burial fund up to $1500. This amount will be reduced by any life insurance policies with a face value below $1500. Rather than setting aside a $1500 burial fund, a person can set aside an unlimited amount in an irrevocable burial trust.

❑ RESOURCE EXEMPTION FOR THE COMMUNITY SPOUSE

In addition to the property exemptions mentioned above, Medicaid will also exempt certain resources if a person in a nursing home is married and has a spouse not living in the nursing home. Medicaid refers to this person as the "community spouse."

In addition to the family home and one car, the community spouse of someone entering a nursing home can now keep the *greater* of $12,000 or one-half of the couple's total resources, up to a maximum amount of

$60,000. For example, if a couple's resources equal $20,000, the community spouse can keep $12,000 and $8,000 must be spent before qualifying for Medicaid. If the couple's resources came to $100,000, the community spouse could keep $50,000—half of the total—and $50,000 would have to be spent before the spouse in the nursing home would be eligible for Medicaid.

States have the option of liberalizing this formula, although the maximum resources protected for the community spouse cannot exceed $60,000 (not including the home and car). You should check with the Medicaid agency in your parents' state to see if more liberal resource exemptions have been adopted in that state for the community spouse.

If your parents' resources exceed $60,000, but you believe that one of them will eventually need Medicaid for nursing-home care, the amount over $60,000 will have to be spent. It does not matter how the excess is spent as long as it is for the benefit of your parents. For example, they could repair, pay off, or replace their home, buy a new car, or take a trip. However, federal law prohibits them from giving the excess amount away in order to come within the $60,000 resource limits.

If one of your parents went into the hospital or a nursing home *before* September 30, 1989, the rules regarding what resources are exempt for the community spouse will be very different. You will need to check with your parent's state Medicaid agency to find out what those rules are.

How much income can a spouse at home keep?

When there is a spouse at home, Medicaid makes an exception to the general rule that a nursing home resident's income goes to pay for nursing home care with Medicaid paying the balance owing.

Medicaid allows the community spouse to keep the *greater* of:

- all checks paid in the name of the community spouse; or
- a spousal allowance.

The minimum spousal allowance was $815 per month in 1989. In addition to this base amount, the allowance can be increased up to $1500 if the community spouse's shelter costs are high enough. Shelter costs include:

- rent or mortgage payments,
- utilities,
- property taxes,
- homeowners insurance.

States have the option of increasing the base amount of the spousal allowance, as long as it does not exceed $1500.

Can my parent give away property before applying for medicaid?

As mentioned above, a parent without a spouse will have to deplete almost all of his or her resources before qualifying for Medicaid. Parents frequently want to know whether it is possible to deplete resources by making gifts to family members before applying for Medicaid. The general rule is that a person will be ineligible for Medicaid funding for nursing-home care if his or her giving meets *all* of the following criteria:

- property is transferred to someone other than a spouse,

- for less than fair market value,
- within 30 months of applying for Medicaid,
- and the purpose of the transfer was to qualify for Medicaid.

There would be no penalty if property was transferred *more* than 30 months before applying for Medicaid. There would be no penalty if property was sold at a reasonable price. The penalty usually arises when a person makes a gift; however, there would be no penalty if a gift was made within 30 months for some purpose other than qualifying for Medicaid. The burden is on the Medicaid applicant to convince the state that the gift was for some other purpose than qualifying for Medicaid. This can become difficult if a person is in poor health or is already in a hospital or nursing home.

If the penalty applies, your parent would be ineligible for Medicaid nursing home benefits for up to 30 months from the date the property was transferred. The exact number of months of ineligibility would depend on the value of the property transferred, but the penalty cannot exceed 30 months.

Does the gift penalty apply to my parent's home?

Remember, your parent can *keep* the family home if

- a spouse or dependent relative is living in the home; or
- your parent states that he or she intends to return home.

If your parent gives away the family home or sells it at less than fair market value, the gift penalty discussed above will apply. There is a very limited exception to

Examples of How Much Income the Community Spouse Can Keep

Example 1:   Husband's income $1500
                     Wife's income $ 300
                                     $1800
Total

If the wife goes into the nursing home, the husband can keep the checks paid in his name—$1500. The wife's check will be paid to the nursing home and Medicaid will pay the difference. If the husband goes into the nursing home, his wife can keep the spousal allowance. This will be at least $815 and could be increased up to $1500 depending on her shelter costs. She would keep enough of the couple's total income to equal her spousal allowance, and the balance of their income would go to the nursing home.

Example 2:   Husband's income $ 700
                     Wife's income $ 500
                                     $1200
Total

No matter which spouse went into the nursing home, the community spouse could keep at least $815 of their total income. This amount could be increased up to their total income of $1200, depending on their shelter costs. Any amount above the community spouse's allowance would be paid to the nursing home and Medicaid would pay the difference.

the gift penalty that applies only to the family home. The home may be transferred without any Medicaid penalty to:

- a spouse;

- a blind, disabled, or minor child;

- a child who has lived with and cared for the parent for at least two years before the parent went into a nursing home;

- a sibling who has lived in the home for at least one year and has an ownership interest in the home.

Remember, rules and limitations vary from state to state. Be sure to obtain professional advice about the law in your parents' state before attempting any property transfer.

Will there be a problem with medicaid if I sell my parent's property?

Many children are in the position of having to liquidate their parent's property to pay for the parent's nursing-home care. Since the proceeds may not cover the entire length of stay, Medicaid may be needed in the future. Therefore, it is important to document that the property was sold at a reasonable price. This does not mean that you have to get a "top dollar" sale price, but the sale price cannot be so low that the state will consider the sale to be a gift.

It is also important to keep records establishing that the proceeds from the sale were spent for your parent's benefit. It is appropriate to deduct from the proceeds those costs incurred in selling the property and any money loaned to your parent before the property was sold.

❏ APPLYING FOR MEDICAID

If you think your parent may qualify for Medicaid, you or your parent should contact the Medicaid agency in your parent's state to learn about its application procedure. If your parent is already in a hospital or nursing home, there may be a social worker or discharge planner on staff who can help with the application process. In any case, make sure to ask for that state's limitation on income and resources. If your parent does not yet meet the financial guidelines, call back in several months, see if the guidelines have changed, and reevaluate your parent's financial situation.

Your parent has the right to request a hearing if an application for Medicaid is denied. Be aware of the time deadlines for filing an appeal. The procedure and time requirements for appealing are customarily included in the denial notice. If your parents do not have their own attorney, they should consult with the local bar association in their county to see what legal assistance is available. They may be eligible for free legal services to work on the appeal through their local legal aid office.

Medicaid is a complex and sometimes frustrating government program. However, it provides necessary resources for health care for many older adults, especially those needing long-term care. If you think your parent may be nearing the point of Medicaid eligibility, it makes good sense to contact the state Medicaid office and get all the pertinent information.

Issue 25

Private Insurance Alternatives

Nearly one half of all persons who reach age 65 will experience a period of extended illness or disability before they die; one out of every four will enter a nursing home. These sobering statistics and others like them have been a major source of anxiety for older persons and their families. Even with Medicare coverage, annual deductible and co-payment amounts and charges for services not covered by Medicare combine to create a significant risk of financial hardship for older adults. With nursing home costs averaging more than $2000 per month, and with the cost of health care continuing to rise well in excess of the general rate of inflation, most older adults should give careful consideration to the new available forms of private insurance designed specifically to meet health care costs not covered by Medicare.

This issue discusses the two major types of private health care insurance coverage that are designed to meet the needs of older adults:

- *Medicare supplement ("Medigap") insurance* which covers Medicare deductibles and co-payments, and may extend some benefits for costs that are only partially covered by Medicare; and

- *long-term care insurance* which covers long-term care such as care in a nursing home, home care, and adult day care up to certain limits.

❐ WHO SHOULD PURCHASE PRIVATE INSURANCE?

Your parents should consider purchasing Medicare supplement and long term care insurance, *unless:*

- ✔ they are or will be eligible for Medicaid;

- ✔ they have sufficient resources to cover any medical or long-term care needs that might arise, without depleting their assets; or

- ✔ they are already covered by an adequate employee benefit plan which will continue in effect throughout their lives, providing supplemental health insurance and long-term care coverage.

Medigap insurance and long-term care insurance cover different risks. There are currently no combined Medicare supplement and long-term care insurance policies. Your parents may wish to investigate both.

❐ MEDICARE SUPPLEMENT ("MEDIGAP") INSURANCE

Medicare supplement insurance covers Medicare gaps; that is, some or all of the following costs of medical services that Medicare does not pay:

- the annual deductible for Part A hospital and therapeutic skilled nursing care services;

- the Part A co-payment amount;

- skilled nursing care services beyond the 100 days per year covered by Medicare;

- the annual Part B deductible, for physician, hospital outpatient, laboratory, and ambulance services;

- part B co-payments of 20% of approved charges.

Although Medigap insurance policies cover Medicare deductibles and co-payments and, to differing degrees, pick up where Medicare leaves off, most policies do not cover types of medical expenses excluded from Medicare coverage. For example, both Medicare and Medicare supplement policies generally exclude such items as private nurses, regular check-ups, eyewear, hearing aids, dental care, some kinds of elective surgery, custodial care in nursing homes, psychiatric care, and self-administered drugs.

You should also note that many Medicare supplement policies use the same reimbursement base as Medicare. Some more comprehensive (and expensive) ones will pay the difference between the approved charge and the actual charge. The less expensive plans do not cover anything over the Medicare approved charge. For example, if a physician's charge for services is $150, and the Medicare approved charge is $100, most Medicare supplement policies pay only the co-payment of 20% of the approved charge or, in this example, $20. The difference between the actual charge and the approved charge—$50 in this case—is not usually covered. For this reason, using the services of a physician who "accepts assignment," or buying a 100% policy, can make a significant difference financially. For more information on Medicare approved charges and physician acceptance of assignment, see *Issue 23: Understanding Medicare*.

In comparing Medicare supplement policies, use *Form 25.1: Check List for Purchasing Private Insurance*. The key issues are:

1. *coverage*—Exactly what costs will be paid?

2. *waiting period for pre-existing conditions*—How long before coverage begins for illnesses or physical disorders that existed prior to purchase of the policy?

3. *renewability*—Few policies are guaranteed renewable. Under what circumstances can the policy be canceled?

4. *limitations and exclusions*—What services are limited or excluded from coverage?

5. *premiums*—How much will the coverage cost? Is there a provision to pay premiums on a monthly rather than annual basis?

6. *claims processing* —Some insurance companies with Medicare processing contracts are able to offer consolidated claims processing through which Medicare supplement coverage is paid at the same time as the Medicare payment itself. If other features of insurance coverage are about equal, coordinated claims processing can save you or your parent time and effort.

❐ LONG-TERM CARE INSURANCE

Like Medicare, medigap insurance does not cover long-term care in a nursing home or at home. Nursing home and home care coverage are provided by long-term care insurance which pays for the cost of skilled, intermediate, or custodial care. Some long-term care policies also cover home care services. Many long-term care insurance policies pay a fixed amount per day, after a prescribed number of days of care have elapsed; others pay a percentage of the cost or provide a lump sum for long-term care.

Long-term care insurance is inexpensive if purchased

early, but premium costs rise steeply for older applicants. There is also a great deal of variety in the amount of coverage among policies, so it is important to compare policies carefully.

In comparing long-term care insurance policies, the key issues are:

1. *coverage*—What levels of care are covered?

2. *benefits*—How much will be paid? Will it be a daily amount, a percentage of the cost, or the actual cost?

3. *prior care/hospitalization requirements*—What time period and levels of prior care are required before benefits begin? Some policies give a choice between three days of prior hospitalization or no hospital stay. Since most nursing home patients are not hospitalized prior to entering a nursing home, this is an important point to check.

4. *length of coverage*—How long will the benefits last? Do benefits decrease after a certain amount of time has elapsed? Are they reinstated after a period of non-use?

5. *waiting periods*—How long after entering a nursing home does coverage begin? Policies vary on how long the person insured must wait after entering a care facility before receiving benefits. These waiting periods are similar to deductibles, since the insured person must pay the full cost of nursing home care received until the qualification period has passed. Policies with no wait or a relatively short waiting period are more expensive than those providing coverage only after a longer period of time.

6. *eligibility*—Generally, no medical examination is required for long term care insurance, but pur-

chasers must qualify based on health criteria. Some companies will not write policies after an applicant reaches a certain age.

7. *inflation*—Is there a provision in the policy to increase the benefit amount (and the premium) as nursing home costs rise due to inflation? What is the inflation benefit based on? Especially for younger purchasers, a policy with an inflation rider may be worth the extra premium cost.

8. *renewability*—Few policies are guaranteed renewable. Under what circumstances can the policy be cancelled? Be careful in purchasing policies through the mail because state laws regarding renewability vary widely from state to state.

9. *limitations and exclusions*—What services are limited or excluded from coverage?

10. *premiums*—How much will the coverage cost? Can the premium be paid monthly rather than annually or semi-annually?

Also see *Form 25.1*

Home care policies

Newest on the market are separate home care policies and those that incorporate home care in policies with nursing home coverage. Like older policies, it is important to determine the levels of care covered and any limitations for receiving the most used services: custodial care and chore services.

There are excellent policies available that do not require nursing home or hospital stays before receiving benefits. Some policies will also pay for adult day care, meals, equipment, transportation, respite care, and nutrition services, as well as nurses, therapists, and drugs. Because many people would prefer to receive care in their own home, these policies should be considered.

Reviewing and updating existing long-term care coverage

Premiums for long-term care insurance are established at the time of purchase. The cost is higher for older adults, lower for younger and middle-aged persons. A younger purchaser will pay a lower premium, but over a longer period of time. Because there is a waiting period in most policies and because premium costs rise sharply as persons grow older, it may be risky to replace existing policies, even if a more attractive insurance product becomes available. Before purchasing new policies, existing policies and needs should be carefully assessed. A person should change to upgrade current coverage only if:

✔ better or less expensive coverage is available, and

✔ there are no major limitations (such as exclusion of pre-existing conditions) associated with the replacement coverage.

❑ MANAGING THE DETAILS

Keeping track of private insurance premiums and claims can be complex. Because policies may be cancelled due to late or forgotten premium payments, you should make sure your parents are able to handle their financial affairs alone, or find some acceptable way to help. You might suggest that you or someone else help with sorting out medical bill payments. Submitting necessary paperwork first to Medicare and then to a Medicare supplement insurer can seem a monumental task, especially for someone recovering from an illness. *Form 23.1: Medical Bill Payment Record* can help you or your parent track the medical bill payment process.

❏ CONSUMER RIGHTS IN PURCHASING INSURANCE

Both state and federal governments have adopted laws to help consumers make informed choices when buying insurance. For example, the law typically gives purchasers of Medicare supplement and long-term care insurance the right to return the policy within 30 days of purchase and receive a full refund. This 30 day "free look" lets purchasers reconsider their purchase and make sure the coverage is what they want. In some states, a longer "free look" period is provided for policies sold by mail.

Regulatory agencies that supervise the insurance industry recommend that purchasers of Medicare supplement and long-term care insurance use their 30 day review period to:

- read the policy and any information or fact sheet accompanying the policy;

- ask questions and seek clarifications where appropriate; and

- return an unwanted policy within the "free look" period and by certified mail, return receipt requested.

❏ WHERE TO TURN FOR FURTHER HELP

Understanding Medicare supplement and long-term care insurance policies, and being able to compare competing insurance products are challenging tasks in the best of circumstances. You or your parents should expect to invest time and energy gathering information and making an informed choice about what products meet their needs and budget. Fortunately, there are several sources of help and information.

Insurance agents

Agents who represent one or more insurance companies in the Medicare supplement and long-term care insurance markets will be glad to provide you or your parents with information on the products they offer. A reputable agent in your community or in your parents' community can be an excellent—and affordable—place to start. Normally, your parents should be prepared to comparison shop. They should screen an insurance vendor in the same way they would a lawyer, accountant, or financial advisor. The goal is to find someone who is:

- experienced;
- regarded in the community as honest and capable;
- recommended by other professionals such as your parents' lawyer, physician, or accountant; and
- knowledgeable concerning the insurance products for which your parents are in the market.

Insurance brokers

Insurance brokers, by law, represent the buyer and have access to all insurance carriers. They can recommend the most appropriate coverage and find an insurer. If the broker is experienced in the type of insurance you want, he or she may be more reliable than an agent whose selection of policies is limited.

Independent insurance consultants

Today, there are independent professionals available in most larger communities who do not themselves offer insurance products, but who will assist purchasers on a fee basis. Often, the experience and objectivity of such a consultant will save time and money and also result in better coverage being purchased.

The state insurance commissioner

The state insurance commissioner's office or other state agency responsible for supervising insurance companies may provide a free telephone information line or volunteer counselors and free brochures or booklets dealing with Medicare supplement insurance, long-term care insurance, and other kinds of insurance specifically marketed to older adults.

It is important to bear in mind that Medicare supplement and long-term care insurance are relatively new on the market. Because insurance vendors are just beginning to have experience with the number and expense of claims, the benefits offered under these products change regularly. You or your parents will need to read and compare policies carefully. Good supplemental health care insurance products can provide your parents with significant protection against major health care costs. However, as with any other significant purchases, it is important to shop carefully and purchase the products that will best meet your parents' needs.

Issue 26

A Good Death

In this death-defying society, the phrase "a good death" may seem jarring at first. But all of us die at some point. Many of us have ideas about the way we would like to die. Some people wish a sudden death. Others would prefer time to plan, to say good-bye, to get ready. While each person's vision is different, most adults do have some feelings about how they wish to die, and as they grow older, their preferences grow stronger.

Of course, we do not have full control over the moment or means of our dying. However, as death draws nearer, there are often choices which can be made which support a person in dying in a manner close to their vision of a good death.

❑ TALKING ABOUT DYING

Children, even children who are middle-aged themselves, often experience difficulty talking with parents about death. Especially when a parent is gravely ill, family members are reluctant to speak directly of dying. Even if the sick person brings up the subject herself, the family tries to change it. All are to participate in a conspiracy to deny the present reality, as if through denial, they might make it go away.

Most older adults who are ill have questions, concerns, and ideas about dying and need a place to talk about them. Family members who are reluctant to discuss death may be doing the dying person a disservice. If a parent indicates a desire to talk, or if you feel it is time, such discussions can result in lower stress and a heightened sense of peace for everyone. Talking about death, especially when death seems near, may not be easy. The conversation can be very emotional and draining. It will require sensitivity on your part. However, such conversations can make possible a new level of closeness and confidence for both you and your parent.

Initiating the discussion

Often, before a parent is ill, there are opportunities to initiate a preliminary discussion about your parent's vision of a good death. A friend dies suddenly, and in conversation your mother says, "I'd hate to die like that." Her comment is an opening for you to ask some general questions about her feelings about death. How does she want to die? How would she feel if her only option for survival meant being placed on a respirator for an indefinite period of time? In case of a cardiac arrest, would she wish to be resuscitated? How about tube feeding? Organ donation? Would she like to die at home or in a hospital?

Obviously, you should not take a previously casual conversation and use it to rattle off a checklist of options, especially if it makes your parent uncomfortable, but it is an opening to learn about feelings and to say, "You know, I never want to be in this position, but someday I may have to make some decisions about life and death matters on your behalf. I'd really like to sit down with you one day and talk about this, so if I am in that position, I'll know I'll be doing what you want." Having once said that, it is important to follow up gently but persistently in the near future.

When a parent is ill

When a parent is ill, the discussion becomes more intense. He or she is looking at real options, not hypothetical situations. If a parent brings up the subject of dying, accept it matter-of-factly, and let your parent lead you in the discussion. With some encouragement, a parent will usually share concerns and preferences and give you a chance to ask questions. It will be important to check back with your parent from time to time. Sometimes a person's preferences change. You might help by saying, "What if X happens? What would you like done?" Help your parent think about final things he or she would like to do to get some closure on life. If your father says, "I'd just like to see my grandson one more time before I die," offer to help make that happen. If face to face contact can't happen, suggest a phone call, or even better, a letter or videotape.

If your parent does not want to talk

If a parent who is seriously ill does not talk about dying, there can be many reasons for it. One reason might be that he or she doesn't wish to distress you. You can initiate the conversation with some sensitivity as to timing. Be honest. It is perfectly all right to say, "You know, I really hope you get well, but seeing you sick like this makes me realize that we've never talked about what you want done in case of an emergency." If your parent indicates that he or she doesn't want to talk about it, drop the subject. If your parent does want to talk, you have your opening.

❒ CONCERNS OF THE DYING

Persons who know that their life expectancy is limited have a number of different types of concerns and preoccupations. The most common ones are discussed here.

Medical treatment concerns

People with limited time left to them are concerned about their quality of life through that time. In older persons, there are often trade-offs to be made between aggressive treatment of a medical problem and the desire for improved quality of life, or pain control vs. alertness. For example, if your parent has cancer, there may be chemotherapy treatments which give some chance of extended life, but which also cause persistent extreme nausea. As an advocate for your parent, your job is to follow up on any treatment concerns your parent has, see what the options are, and help your parent make the decision which is best for him or her.

Family concerns

Often, people who are dying want to tie up what they perceive to be loose ends in their lives. Family relationships or relationships with close friends may be some of those loose ends. There may be wrongs to be righted, apologies to be made, feelings to be expressed, or other sorts of reconciliations envisioned. When possible, encourage your parent to say the things which he or she believes need to be said—or make the gestures he or she believes need to be made. If face to face communication is impossible, letters can be a wonderful gift. Some people who are dying want to write letters to family and friends to be opened after their death. This is healthy. It is a way of expressing their idea of a good death.

Financial concerns

Sometimes a dying person, especially one with a dependent spouse or other, becomes almost obsessed with leaving financial affairs "in order." For example, you see your father with little energy and he wants to use it calling up his pension fund administrator or calculating what social security payment your mother is entitled to. Again, this is normal. It is a way of exerting control and being responsible in a situation where control is hard to come by. Be understanding. Offer to help your parent find the necessary information, and make the necessary financial arrangements. As well as helping your parent, it puts you in a better position to be of help to surviving dependents after death occurs.

Life tasks

At the end of a life, sometimes a person will embark on final projects which he or she wishes to complete as a symbol of bringing life to a sense of completion, rather than just letting it run out. Such projects may include visits to loved ones, trips to significant places, living through Christmas, making a special quilt, planting bulbs to bloom in the spring. Encourage your parent in such projects, and when possible, help bring them to completion. We all need the satisfaction of setting goals and reaching them.

Spiritual concerns

As death approaches, it is natural to wonder what occurs beyond the moment of death. Some persons have a sense of peace about approaching death; others feel apprehension. Many people wish to plan funerals or memorial services in advance, to choose music and readings, or write statements to be read. If a person has had a strong religious affiliation throughout his life, visits from clergy and other members of a religious community may provide an opportunity to discuss spiritual concerns. Frequently, someone who has not been overtly religious throughout life starts talking about God and what might happen to him or her after death. If you know a chaplain or clergy person who you think could have a helpful conversation with your parent, suggest to your parent that you call that person and set up an appointment. In the absence of such an outside person, be prepared to listen yourself. Draw your parent out. Listen to your parent's beliefs and feelings. Wherever possible, be or at least respectful of the beliefs expressed. This is not a time to debate your parent's religious beliefs of lack thereof. Be supportive. What your parent needs is the inner resources to face death with dignity.

❑ WHOSE DEATH IS THIS?

Remember, everyone has a different idea of a good death. Your task with a parent facing death is to be an advocate for him or her, to help put together the elements which will make his or her life complete, which will bring joy, fulfillment, and a sense of peace at the end of a long and full life.

❑ GETTING HELP

Sometimes your parent's understanding of a good death will be very different from yours. Sometimes the task of helping your parent die seems overwhelming. Whatever your particular circumstance, it probably will be helpful for you to have a person that you consider to be your primary source of support in this endeavor. That person may be another family member, a friend of yours, a friend of your parent. It doesn't matter who it is, as long as it is someone with whom you can talk freely, express your feelings, laugh, cry, get restored. It is exhausting work to help a parent die. It is normal to need help. Your responsibility is not only to help your parent, but also to come through the experience intact. The best caregivers and advocates are those who know when and how to take care of themselves.

Issue 27

Hospice Care

During the Middle Ages, the term "hospice" was used to signify a place where weary pilgrims could stop, rest, and refresh themselves before continuing on with their journey. In 1967, a British physician, Dr. Cicely Saunders, began using the term to symbolize a new kind of care for the dying. In a London suburb, she founded St. Christopher's Hospice which cared for its patients by offering supportive care and pain control. The patients at St. Christopher's came there because they had reached a point in their various illnesses where they were no longer looking for a cure. They wanted to make the most of the time left to them, to live out their lives at the highest level of quality possible, even if that compromised how long they would live.

Since its beginnings in 1967, the hospice movement has spread quickly throughout the world. In the United States alone, there are now over 1500 hospice programs affiliated with the National Hospice Organization. These programs serve over 100,000 patients a year, and are recognized by patients, physicians, and insurance carriers as providing a high quality, cost-effective medical alternative for persons with limited life expectancies.

❐ WHAT SERVICES ARE PROVIDED BY HOSPICE ORGANIZATIONS?

Hospice organizations vary greatly in size and range of services offered. However, all hospices generally agree that basic hospice care should include the following elements:

- Home based care whenever possible. Because home based care of the terminally ill is not always possible or consistent with the patient's desires, there are many excellent in-patient hospice programs.

- Care which focuses on the emotional, social, and spiritual needs of a dying person and that person's family, as well as on physical and medical needs.

- Care which is controlled as much as possible by the patient, working together with the family and the hospice staff.

- Support and services provided by an interdisciplinary team composed of physicians, nurses, social workers, chaplains, and trained volunteers.

- Nursing care and support available for patients and primary caregivers on an on-call basis, 24 hours a day, 7 days a week.

- Care directed at effective pain and symptom management, so that the patient can be alert and comfortable as much as possible, enhancing quality of life and promoting interaction with family and other loved ones.

- If a patient's symptoms cannot be managed at home, in-patient care provided in as pleasant and homelike an atmosphere as possible, where family and friends are encouraged to be present.

It is rare for hospice patients to undergo surgery or extensive intravenous therapy, except when necessary for effective pain control. Instead of focusing on curative medicine, hospice care concentrates its services towards making the dying patient as comfortable as possible, both physically and emotionally, in the last months and days of life.

A major part of the hospice program centers around the patient's family and friends. Professional hospice team members and trained volunteers work with each patient's primary support system—usually family or close friends—both to teach those persons how to manage care for the patient, and to give them the necessary physical, emotional, and spiritual support to do the job.

For example, if your father were dying of lung cancer and you and your sister decided to take care of him at home, hospice team members would provide the two of you with needed items—a hospital bed, commode chair, or other necessary equipment—and extensive training. Nurses might teach you to administer medications, watch for troublesome symptoms, and perform other nursing services. A home health aide would teach you how to perform essential personal care with a bed-bound patient. A volunteer might offer you support and encouragement as you learned these new tasks, or come and stay with your parent for a few hours while you got out of the house. These persons would continue to check in with you, reevaluate your father's needs, and provide the changing level of care necessary until your father died. After his death, they would offer continuing supportive care for you as you worked through your grief.

❒ WHO IS ELIGIBLE FOR HOSPICE CARE?

Generally, hospice programs care for persons in the last six months, or less, of life. Sometimes patients come to hospice because they have decided on their own that they want no more treatments which aggressively try to cure their disease. Sometimes a physician has told the patient that there are no further options for cure. In either of these situations, and the others which can develop, it is important for persons entering hospice to have three things:

1. An understanding of their disease prognosis—that they have been diagnosed with a terminal illness—and also an understanding of the kinds of services hospice provides and does not provide.

2. The cooperation of their personal physician who is willing to work with the hospice team to provide care.

3. A family member or close friend who is willing to be the primary caregiver, providing and managing care at home for the patient.

All three of these components must be in place in order for hospice care to be effective in the home. The patient must understand and consent to the kind of care he or she will be receiving; the physician must be willing to support this kind of care; and there must be a primary caregiver who will be with the patient through the dying process.

It needs to be stressed here that although hospice care offers a desirable alternative to conventional medical treatment for many people, it is not for everyone. A person who is still looking for a cure or one who does not want to work with a caregiving team is not a good match for hospice care.

If your parent has a terminal or potentially terminal illness and might want to make use of hospice services in the foreseeable future, it may be helpful to set up an initial meeting between your parent and a representative of a local hospice. Such a meeting would help you and your parent learn what hospice services are available in your community, see if there is a potential match, and decide whether and when to initiate hospice care.

❑ WHO PAYS FOR HOSPICE CARE?

Because of patient support of hospice services, and because hospice care is generally less expensive than conventional medical care, most private insurance carriers, as well as Medicare and Medicaid, now provide reimbursement at some level for hospice care. In the last few years, Medicare has adopted the Medicare Hospice Benefit which pays the hospice organization a prospective (before services are rendered) set fee for each patient. For more general information on Medicare and prospective payment, see *Issue 23: Understanding Medicare.* In order to qualify for the Medicare Hospice Benefit, the patient's physician must certify that the patient is expected to live six months or less. Hospice care must be provided through a hospice agency which has been approved by Medicare to provide services. The Medicare Hospice Benefit includes:

- nursing care,
- medical equipment and supplies,
- respite and in-patient care,
- counseling,
- therapies, and
- physician services.

If the patient lives longer than the expected six months, or if for some reason, hospice services cost more than the

Medicare hospice benefit covers, hospice organizations are still required to provide care to the patient.

If there is no Medicare approved hospice in your community, or if your parent elects not to apply for the hospice benefit, he or she can still be covered for some services under regular Medicare benefits. The billing and coverage will be different, however. The hospice staff or local Medicare representative can help you understand the difference in coverage.

❒ WHAT IMPLICATIONS DOES HOSPICE CARE HAVE FOR THE FAMILY?

Even fifty years ago, it was common for people to die at home, surrounded by loved and familiar faces and possessions. Now, most people die in hospitals or other institutions, surrounded by tubes and monitors and other technological equipment. Hospice care seeks to take death out of this institutional setting and relocate it as a natural, if difficult, part of life.

The families who have been supported by a hospice program in caring for their dying loved ones almost universally consider it a positive, empowering experience. Hospice team members are trained to be sensitive to the needs of patient *and* family. If your mother wants to die at home, and you wish to support her in this, but are worried whether you can provide the care she needs, hospice will give both training and emotional support. Hospice programs also offer the option of respite care—having someone else care for your parent for a few hours or a few days so that you can have a break—to provide much needed time for rest and renewal. Sometimes, caring for a dying parent seems an overwhelming task; hospice care works to make it manageable.

Some people worry about having a dying parent in the home if children are present. They are afraid it will be a negative or frightening experience for the children. You need to assess your own child's or children's needs and strengths, and their relationship with your parent. However, it is helpful to know that for many families with children, taking care of a grandparent at home while he or she is dying turns out to be a source of great family strength and positive energy. Your children, like you, will need education and support for this to be a good experience, but with the needed support, it can be a rare time of closeness and caring for them and can teach them much about life and family values.

Clearly, if your parent makes a choice for hospice care, and you are involved as a primary caregiver, the experience will have a significant impact on your life. It will be both physically and emotionally draining. However, it can also be deeply satisfying for you as well as your parent. If you might be involved in a caregiving role to your parent in a hospice setting, you should feel free to talk with hospice personnel yourself. Find out what the expectations are of you and exactly what kind of help is available. Talk with persons who have cared for a parent or other relative or friend with hospice support and see how they experienced that relationship. It is a major commitment. Take time to make a good decision for yourself.

Hospice care is not for everyone. However, for those who choose it, it can provide compassionate, sustaining care for the dying and their families. It is an option well worth considering.

Issue 28

Practical Issues Surrounding Death

For many people, the death of a parent is their first experience of dealing personally with the dying process. There may be issues of grief and loss to work through; necessary support for a surviving spouse or other dependent of the parent who has died; friends and relatives with whom to laugh and cry and remember. Or if your parent has lived into his or her high 80's or 90's, death might be a more isolated experience because close friends have already died, and there are few close relatives.

Whatever the emotional context of a person's death, there are always a number of practical and business issues to be dealt with at the time of death and in the weeks that follow. Sometimes these nitty-gritty matters come as a rude and painful distraction in the midst of great loss; other times, the necessary rhythms of wrapping up loose ends bring with them a sense of healing and completion. Whether it is helpful or hard, the business must get done. This issue will help you to understand what must be done and how to make the practical aspects of death as easy as possible.

❒ WHAT HAPPENS WHEN DEATH OCCURS?

If your parent dies in a hospital or other care facility

The great majority of persons in this country die in hospitals or other institutional settings. If a parent dies when you are not in the facility, the hospital or institution will call you or whoever they have listed as the primary contact person. If you live close by, whoever calls will probably ask if you wish to come by and see your parent one last time before the body is released to the funeral home. Different people have different feelings about the value of seeing a person's body after he or she has died. It can be a helpful thing to do if having that time either aids you in assimilating the reality that the person has died or gives you a private time to say your good-byes and bring your relationship to a sense of completion.

If you are with your parent in the institution when death occurs, and you see that your parent has died, you should go and tell a nurse. Either a doctor or a nurse will come into the room to officially pronounce that death has occurred. You will then have some time, if you wish it, to be with the body, call in other close family members who wish to be there, and say your good-byes. Later, the staff will help you gather up your parent's personal belongings. If your parent dies in a nursing home and has many belongings there to sort through and pack, the institution will usually give you a few days to do it, unless they need the bed immediately.

At the institution there will be papers to sign and decisions to make. Depending on the circumstances of your parent's death, a hospital may want permission to perform an autopsy or to use some of your parent's organs for transplant purposes. You should know that under some circumstances the hospital or local medical examiner or coroner is required by law to perform an autopsy. And under federal and state law, hospital personnel are now required in situations in which there is a potential for successful organ transplantation to ask the family about that subject. These are difficult subjects to confront immediately upon death, but the law requires they be dealt with. It will be easier if you have thought about them in advance and had some conversation with your parent and other family members about preferences. There is a place for you to make note of such preferences in *Form 1.1: Helpful Personal Information.*

If either autopsy (unless required by law) or organ donation raises serious issues based on religious beliefs or other personal concerns, and your parent never expressed a clear preference, you may certainly refuse the requests. However, they are worth considering. Many people are comforted that out of the experience of death may come either new knowledge about disease (through autopsy) or the gift of restored health to another (through organ donation).

An institution will also need to release your parent's body to a licensed funeral home. You will be asked if you have a preference about which funeral home to use. Your parent may have made plans, and even prepaid for services, from a specific funeral home. That is something to check for if your parent has filled out *Form 28.1: Planning a Funeral/Memorial Service.* If you have no preference about funeral homes, you may ask the institution to select one for you. You will be given a form to sign authorizing release of the body. You do not need to wait at the hospital for the funeral director to come for the body. You may go home, and call the funeral home later in the day or on the next day to make an appointment to go and make appropriate arrangements.

If your parent dies at home

If your parent expects to die at home because of a progressive illness, you should ask your parent's physician or other health care provider in advance what to do when death occurs. The law differs from state to state, but usually in such cases there is no need to deal with the medical examiner or other law enforcement personnel.

If your parent dies at home unexpectedly—for example, from a heart attack or stroke—you should call 911. A police officer and an aid car will come. They will help you make the necessary arrangements.

❒ NOTIFYING OTHERS THAT YOUR PARENT HAS DIED

When a parent dies, some names will come to you immediately as persons who should be contacted. Close family; good friends; your parent's minister, priest, or rabbi; your parent's lawyer and physician. Some calls you will want to make yourself. Other calls have to be made, but you do not need to make them. When a death occurs, both your friends and your parent's friends, as well as other family members, will want to be of assistance. It makes sense to let others help in passing the word. With friends, for example, or a church or community group, often you can make only one call and ask that person to organize informing others from that circle of acquaintances.

If there are many calls to be made, keep a list of who has been contacted. That way, there is less chance someone important will fall through the cracks.

❒ WORKING WITH THE FUNERAL HOME

Normally, within 24 hours of your parent's death, you should be in contact with the funeral home to set up an appointment with a funeral director. Funeral homes offer a wide range of services at the time of death. These usually include:

- transporting the body from the place of death to the funeral home;

- preparing the body for burial, arranging for a casket and other necessary items for burial, or arranging for cremation;

- working with the family and, if desired, a priest, rabbi, or minister for a funeral or memorial service;

- providing time and space for visitation and a funeral or memorial service;

- assisting in the preparation of an obituary and funeral notice for the local newspapers;

- completing the necessary paperwork for the death certificate, and obtaining certified copies of the death certificate for the family (Be sure to ask for an adequate number of certified death certificates. You will need one for each life insurance policy or pension your parent carried, and several more for processing your parent's Last Will and Testament and other financial business. A good rule of thumb is to request at least ten copies);

- transporting the body and family members (if desired) to the funeral or memorial service and/or to the cemetery.

Some funeral homes also offer to support groups and bereavement counseling for family members of the person who has died.

Contrary to what some people believe, most funeral directors are professionally trained persons who provide these services with compassion and integrity. The role they play in a community is a necessary one, and most do their work sensitively. However, it is important to realize that funeral directors deal with people who are in an especially vulnerable state. When someone you love has just died, you need to make quick decisions on painful issues, such as whether they prefer burial or cremation, what kind of casket to buy, where to buy a burial plot, what kind of service to have. Some of these decisions may involve the outlay of significant amounts of money and may also be emotionally charged, so they become more complicated.

Though most funeral directors will not deliberately use guilt and emotional manipulation to encourage families to purchase high priced goods and services, the following suggestions will minimize the risk of making decisions about which you feel angry or regretful later on.

- Never send one family member alone to see the funeral director. If possible, have two or three family representatives go, one of whom should be more detached from the pain of the loss than a spouse, or sometimes even a child.

- Most funeral homes offer a basic minimum service package. Additional services beyond that are charged individually. Make sure you understand what is included in the basic service, and what will be charged for additional services. Have the funeral director spell out the charges in writing. If you have questions about whether you want or need some of the services offered, go home and think about it, then call back with your answer.

- Money does not equal love. Many people think they must buy an expensive casket or provide a lavish funeral to show their love for the one who has died. This is not true. Buy only those goods and services that seem reasonable to you. In most cases, a total outlay of $1500 to $2500 for funeral expenses is considered reasonable.

The appointment with the funeral director is usually a part of the business of death that people dread. Arranging for caskets and funeral notices is no one's favorite chore. Try to schedule your visit far enough after your parent's death that you and significant others have had a night's sleep and have had some time to talk among yourselves about the kinds of arrangements that seem best to you.

If your parent has joined a memorial society or entered into some other form of prepaid funeral plan, you and other family members will have fewer decisions to make. However, you will also have less control. If your parent has made arrangements with which you are uncomfortable, you normally have little choice but to accept your parent's arrangements and understand that they represent your parent's wishes.

❒ PLANNING A FUNERAL OR MEMORIAL SERVICE

After one they love has died, most people find it helpful to participate in some structured ritual of celebration, remembrance, and letting go of the person who has died. Depending on the religious tradition and individual tastes of the deceased person and his or her family, this ritual might range from a Requiem Mass followed by an elaborate wake, to setting a time for family members and friends to get together informally to talk about the one who has died. Such services, both formal and informal,

Memorial Societies and Prepaid Funeral Plans

Nonprofit memorial societies have spread rapidly in the last fifteen years in response to the high cost of traditional funeral services. Persons wishing to join a memorial society usually pay a nominal initiation fee, and then are guaranteed a basic minimum of services at the time of their death at lower than market costs.

Services provided and costs vary from community to community. Many memorial societies require that a person join several days before the time of death in order for services to be provided.

Pre-paid funeral plans are offered by many funeral homes so that older adults can organize in advance the kinds of funeral services they would prefer at the time of death. Persons purchase services while they are alive and competent, and are usually guaranteed that there will be no further charges, even if costs increase from the time of the contract to the time the person dies.

It will be helpful to you and other family members to find out in advance of your parent's dying if he or she belongs to a memorial society or has purchased portions or all of a prepaid funeral plan.

can be a source of comfort and strength, gathering together the community of grief to laugh and cry and remember together.

Below is a list of questions which will help you in planning a funeral or memorial service for your parent.

- Did your parent leave any specific instructions about the kind of service that he or she would want? Did those instructions include specific requests for readings, music, a person to preside, or a place where the service was to be held?

- When will it be convenient for the service to take place? Do close family and friends have schedules which have to be worked around in planning the time and place of the service?

- Where will the service take place? If your parent belonged to a church, synagogue, or other religious community, when can it schedule a service?

- Who will officiate at the service? Will it be a minister, priest, rabbi, family member, or friend? Do you want an organist, soloist, or other provider of music, and how will those arrangements be made?

- Are there readings, music, pictures, or any other elements which you think would be especially meaningful to you or others as part of the ceremony?

- Do you want to choose someone to deliver a formal eulogy? Do you or other family members wish to offer some personal words of remembrance at the service?

- Do you wish to have visiting hours (a time when people can see the body, say a private good-bye, and speak with the family) before the service?

This custom varies from community to community.

- Will there be any kind of reception or other informal gathering of friends and family after the service? Where will it be held?

If you work through a church or other religious community, your contact in that community will undoubtedly have other questions to ask you about the service. However, it is best to think about the questions outlined above before you meet with whoever will be in charge so that you have some idea of what you want.

☐ OTHER PRACTICAL ISSUES

Along with the major issues of dealing with the death when it occurs—talking with the funeral director, and planning for a funeral or memorial service—there are other practical tasks large and small which should be attended to in the days and weeks following your parent's death.

- You will want to contact your parent's lawyer regarding the content of his or her will (if one exists) and any other legal business which needs to be attended to.

- You (or whoever has been appointed under your parent's will as personal representative of the estate) should contact your parent's bank, financial planner, pension administrator, life insurance company, and any others with whom your parent had significant financial dealing to inform them of the death. Many of these persons will want certified copies of the death certificate, especially if they are paying out benefits or transferring them to a surviving spouse or joint tenant.

- You should remember to cancel club memberships and magazine subscriptions, and have mail delivery stopped or transferred.

- If your parent was a regular contributor to a church or other community groups, you might wish to honor the rest of that year's financial commitment and let the agency or institution know that your parent has died.

- Outstanding bills need to be collected and paid, but this should always be coordinated with other aspects of handling the estate.

- One of the difficult things to do usually is to go through your parent's personal possessions—clothing, papers, mementos, furniture—in order to sort it, sell or give away what the family does not want to keep, and make arrangements for the rest. Like visiting the funeral home, this is a task that is easier if shared among two or more family members.

Funeral vs. Memorial Service

Some differences in usage may develop in individual communities, but, generally speaking, a funeral is a service of remembrance of a person where the body in the casket is present and the service culminates in or is followed by the burial of the body. A memorial service does not have the body present or the element of delivering the body to its final rest; usually it focuses almost exclusively on the celebration and remembrance of the life of the one who has died.

Taking care of all the business that needs to be sorted out after a death can take weeks or even months, depending on how your parent's affairs were organized. It is tiring and emotionally draining work. If you can, share the responsibilities with other family members, do hard tasks with another person, and don't take on too much at one time. It is normal to feel overwhelmed at times with the finishing up of things.

When a death occurs, there are often many pieces of information that are convenient to have readily at hand: key persons to contact; location of safe deposit box and key; location of other valuables; location of will and insurance policies. Much of this information can be gathered in one place using *Form 1.1: Helpful Personal Information*. Another form under *Tab 9* is *Form 28.1: Planning a Funeral/Memorial Service*. Completing this form with your parent will provide an opportunity to register any preferences which are meaningful to him or her about a funeral or memorial service. Filling out these forms before your parent dies will also make the job of the family easier, both practically and emotionally, as you work through the business of your parent's death.

Issue 29

Letting Go

One of the realities of death is that it means separation. If your parent is dying, then both you and your parent are dealing with issues of separation. Both of you, in different ways, must move through a process of letting go.

❏ LETTING GO: YOUR PARENT'S TASK

The end of life brings with it diminishing energy and strength. It also brings an awareness of solitude. No matter how many loved ones surround us, or how close we come to living our ideal of a good death, dying is still a journey that we ultimately experience alone.

Because of these two separate but related realities, many people prepare for death through a gradual process of letting go. The process begins much earlier than the perceived approach of death. One might look at all of adult life from adolescence to full adulthood to aging as a process of letting go. In adolescence, we start discarding some possibilities and pursuing others. Most of us learn that we will not be prima ballerinas, major league pitchers, or President of the United States. In our twenties, most of us choose careers; we choose life partners; and though our choices may be good ones, we turn our backs on other life possibilities. Childhood and college friends drop out of our acquaintance. We let go of them.

Growing older

As we grow older, a variety of choices and life events cause us to let go of many of our dreams, plans, relationships, and aspirations while we achieve others. We hope in mid-life that there is a balance achieved between hopes fulfilled and hopes slipped by the wayside. That balance is central to our adult equilibrium. It allows our self-definition as persons.

As a person reaches old age, there are often fewer achievements, fewer fulfillments, and more losses. Letting go becomes a constant activity. In old age, most friends and significant others are lost through death. Older adults lose energy, jobs, and the external reaffirmation of self-worth that work brings. They may experience loss of mobility, independence, health, and a sense of being in the center of things. Learning to live in a smaller and smaller world is often a primary task of aging. In Issues 9 and 10, the problem of depression in older persons was discussed. One of the major reasons for depression in persons in this age group is the weight of accumulated losses which follow too quickly, one upon another. In dealing with your parent, try to be aware of the number and kinds of losses your parent is facing. Often those losses are substantial and understanding them will help you be supportive.

Facing approaching death

When death approaches, the letting go process is accelerated and changed. The dying person has to prepare to leave behind all of life's possessions, relationships, pleasures, and concerns. In the leaving process, the person will have a decreasing amount of available energy. Therefore, he or she needs to set priorities.

Often, family members will perceive a lessening of interest in the world around as an unhealthy sign of deterioration in the dying person. In fact, it is appropriate behavior. The dying cannot take this world with them on their journey, so they let go of it in pieces. It is not unusual for those facing death to lose interest in world events, in pastimes which were once important to them, even in some once-central relationships. "My mother just doesn't seem to care about her grandchildren anymore," observes a concerned daughter. "I tried to cheer her up by showing her their pictures, and she just didn't respond." Grandmother was letting go, an appropriate task for a woman weeks from death.

This does not mean that we should assume that loved ones who are dying are always depressed and concerned only with themselves, or that we should not try to share our lives and joys with them. Rarely does one let go of all that is important before death. Your parents need your love, your concerns, your real relationship with them through the dying process. But if they seem distracted or disinterested, do not be hurt. It does not mean that they don't care or that you have failed. They are merely doing a final part of their life's work—letting go of life to accept death.

❏ LETTING GO: YOUR TASK

The death of a parent is never easy. Even if your parent has lived a long and full life, or if he or she was sick and death seems a kindness, still it is a major loss. Ours is not a society which does a good job of supporting the task of grieving, but grief is important. Your grief is important. Be kind to yourself; take time to grieve.

What is normal grief?

It is normal to experience a whole range of emotions as a parent dies. There is sometimes sorrow, although that may come later. If the dying has been long or painful, or if you have given much time to the care of your parent, an initial feeling of relief or freedom is common. So is fatigue. So is a sense of feeling unanchored or lost. Your relationship with your parents is usually the longest experience of relationship in your life. In this mobile society, often your parents are the only people you know who have known you since childhood. When one or both parents die, you lose not only your relationship with them, but a perspective on your own life. That loss takes time to assimilate and recover from.

Grief and conflict

Even in the happiest of families, parents and children go through periods of conflict and disinterest, as well as times of closeness. Death brings with it a need to sum up the relationship, to bring it to a close. It may take some time, but eventually your coming to terms with your parent's death will take in the parent who supported and disciplined you as a child, the parent you fought with in adolescence, the parent with whom you developed a new relationship in adult life.

After the death of a parent, it is not unusual for all the unresolved issues of the parent-child relationship to re-emerge in one form or another. You may feel anger, frustration, guilt. Though it is not rational, people often feel they should bury their parent-child conflicts when they bury their parents. It may not be that easy. Part of the grief process is letting go of the unresolved issues which are commonly part of the parent-child relationship.

Understanding the grieving process

Grief is the way in which one person lets go of another. Though everyone grieves differently, there are some common parameters. The stage of acute grief for a parent can last from a few days to a few months, depending on the particulars of the relationship. It is common for those suffering acute grief to exhibit signs of depression—loss of appetite, difficulty sleeping, sadness, emptiness, lack of interest. The sense of numbness or unreality which sets in at the time of death is replaced by a sense of loss and coming to terms with that loss.

Especially if you and your parent lived together or spent a great deal of time together, many outside "triggers" can bring on this sense of loss. A time of day that you and your parent were always together comes around; her favorite song plays on the radio; you cook her favorite meal. Father's Day arrives and this year you have no father. It is normal for these environmental cues to trigger your grief. It is normal to want to talk about both your feelings and your parent. You tell stories and you laugh. You tell stories and you cry. The talking, the laughing, and the crying are part of the healing process. Healing is accomplished by releasing feelings, working through them, and letting go of them.

Grieving from a distance

If you live a distance from your parent or for some other reason interacted with him or her infrequently, your grieving may be a longer, more unpredictable experience. It is common for those who live at a distance to think they have passed through their grief quickly, only to burst into tears a year and a half later because they smell their mother's perfume, or receive some other unexpected reminder of the person they have lost. The reason for this extended grief period is the infrequency of these reminders. If you did not regularly interact with your parent, it is easy to think everything is back to normal. You are not bombarded with triggers in the same way that you would be if your parent's life had been more closely bound up with yours. Then when you are reminded, you are surprised. There is not much you can do to change this process, but understanding it may make you feel more in control. Long distance talks with other family members can be helpful. Talking with a spouse or friend can be helpful. Again, grief is an essential part of healing. It is the feeling and expressing of your grief which will allow you to move beyond the pain of loss.

The gift of remembering

Although acute grief does end, there always will be moments when remembering a parent will be easy and other moments when it is hard, when it hurts. Your child graduates from college and you wish so much that Grandmother could be there. Christmas comes, and the place at the head of the table seems empty. If you have loved your parents, there will always be times when the reality of their deaths is sad for you.

Part of letting go is learning to find comfort and joy in your memories, in the stories you can remember of your parent. Memory is a great gift. It keeps your relationships with loved ones alive even when the persons themselves have died. Children—your own children, nieces, nephews, god-children—often love to hear stories of a previous generation. Share your stories with them. Those stories are family treasures. They keep alive the connection between generations.

❑ UNRESOLVED GRIEF

Occasionally, for a number of reasons, persons get stuck in the grieving process. The block may have to do with the particulars of the relationship between you and your parent. It may be caused by other stresses in your life. Whatever the cause, if you are having trouble dealing with the death of a parent, get help. There are a variety of kinds of help available in most communities. Check your community's resources and use them.

How do you know when your grief is not normal?

As stated earlier, each person grieves differently. Some people process their grief internally; some are more comfortable talking it out. Many people feel a gradually diminishing sadness; others describe their experience as intensely painful episodes separated by long periods of time when they are not actively dealing with the loss. There is no constant, no ideal standard by which to measure your experience. However, some guidelines are helpful.

- If you experience significant physical symptoms of depression after the first few weeks following the death, you should consider seeking help. Physical symptoms to watch for include: trouble sleeping, lack of appetite, constant fatigue, irritability, lack of concentration. A good place to start with any of these symptoms is your primary care physician. Have a check up. If there is not a medical explanation for your symptoms, seek help elsewhere.

- If your grief significantly disrupts the patterns of your life, your ability to work, your current relationships, your accustomed pastimes, then you will want to seek help.

- If your friends, family, or colleagues whom you trust suggest you need help, listen to them.

Where to find help

There are many sources of help available to those suffering from unresolved grief. You need to choose the kind of counseling or group experience you would be most comfortable with and would find most valuable.

- *individual counselors* —There are many psychiatrists, psychologists, masters of social work, pastoral counselors, and others who work with persons who are grieving. Get some referrals from your physician, clergyperson, or a local health provider (such as a hospital, home health agency, or hospice). You should also check your health insurance coverage to see whether such counseling is an included benefit.

- *support groups* —Many people find it helpful to join or form a group to share the grieving process and provide mutual understanding and support. For some, such a community experience is available informally within a circle of friends and acquaintances. However, most people who want such a group must seek it out. Many social service agencies and health care providers offer or sponsor bereavement support groups on an ongoing basis. If not, they should be able to make a referral to a program in your community.

In choosing a setting in which to address issues of unresolved grief, the most important consideration is finding an environment that is comfortable and trusting enough for you to enter into the experience, deal with the issues that are troubling you, and allow healing to take place. The goal of grief work is not to banish sadness, or even necessarily to work out unresolved issues between you and your parent. The goal is to come to an acceptable sense of closure and to go on with your life work, which is living toward the future.

7 Resources

Where to Start in Each State

DIRECTORY OF STATE AGING
INFORMATION SOURCES

> *Prepared by the National Association of State Units on Aging and reproduced here with its permission.*

Many State Agencies on Aging have established state-wide toll-free telephone numbers for aging-related information and referral. Illinois has a national toll-free number so caregivers living in other states can locate services for relatives living within Illinois. Many states also have special hotlines for problems related to nursing homes, elder abuse, and Alzheimer's disease.

The following directory lists the telephone numbers for the State Agency on Aging, state or national toll-free numbers, and special hotlines. If no toll-free number is available, contact the State Agency on Aging through the regular number listed.

A State Agency on Aging is an agency of state government designated by the governor and state legislature to be the focal point in the state for all matters concerning older citizens. The term State Agency on Aging is a generic term. The specific title and location in state government varies from state to state. In your state the State

Agency on Aging may be a commission, an office, a department, a bureau, a council, a board, or an aging and adult services program. Because of the Older Americans Act, State Agencies on Aging exist in every state and U.S. territory and in the District of Columbia.

ALABAMA
Commission on Aging
2nd Floor
136 Catoma Street
Montgomery, AL 36130
(205) 242-5743
Information and Referral
In State (800) 243-5463

ALASKA
Older Alaskans Commission
Post Office Box C
Juneau, AK 99811-0209
(907) 465-3250

ARIZONA
Aging and Adult
Administration
Post Office Box 6123 - 950A
Phoenix, AZ 85005
(602) 542-4446
Information and Referral
Maricopa County Northern
Arizona: (800) 352-3792
Pima County Southern
Arizona: (800) 362-3474

ARKANSAS
Division of Aging & Adult
Services
Post Office Box 1417,
Slot 1412
Little Rock, AR 72201
(501) 682-2441
Information and Referral
(501) 682-8150

CALIFORNIA
Department on Aging
1600 K Street
Sacramento, CA 95814
(916) 322-5290

COLORADO
Aging and Adult Services
1575 Sherman St., 4th Floor
Denver, CO 80203-1714
(303) 866-5931
Information and Referral
(303) 866-3851

CONNECTICUT
Department on Aging
175 Main Steet
Hartford, CT 06106
(203) 566-8645

Information and Referral
In State: (800) 443-9946
Out of State: (203) 566-7772

DELAWARE
Division of Aging
1901 North Dupont Hwy.
New Castle, DE 19720
(302) 421-6791
Information and Referral
In State: (800) 223-9074

DISTRICT OF COLUMBIA
Office on Aging
2nd Floor
1424 K Street, NW
Washington, D.C. 20005
(202) 724-5622
Information and Referral
(202) 724-5626

FLORIDA
Program Office of Aging &
Adult Service
Building 2, Room 237
1317 Winewood Boulevard
Tallahassee, FL 32301
(904) 488-8922
Hot Line – Elder Abuse
In State: (800) 96-ABUSE

GEORGIA
Office of Aging
Suite 633
878 Peachtree Street NE
Atlanta, GA 30309
(404) 894-5333

GUAM
Division of Senior Citizens
Post Office Box 2816
Agana, Guam 96910
(671) 632-4141/4153/4162

HAWAII
Executive Office on Aging
Suite 241
335 Merchant Street
Honolulu, HI 96813
(808) 548-2593
Information and Referral
In State: (800) 468-4644

IDAHO
Office on Aging
State House, Room 108
Boise, ID 83720
(208) 334-3833

ILLINOIS
Department on Aging
421 East Capitol Avenue
Springfield, IL 62701
(217) 785-2870
Information and Referral
In State: (800) 252-8966
Out of State: (800) 252-8600
Hot Line – Nursing Home
In State: (800) 252-8966

INDIANA
Division of Aging Services
Post Office Box 7083
Indianapolis, IN 46207-7083
(317) 232-7020
Information and Referral
In State: (800) 232-7000
Hot Line – Nursing Home
In State: (800) 545-7763
Adult Abuse
In State: (800) 545-7763

IOWA
Department of Elder Affairs
Suite 236
914 Grand Avenue
Des Moines, IA 50309
(515) 281-5187

KANSAS
Department on Aging
122-S Docking Office Bldg.
915 S.W. Harrison
Topeka, KS 66612-1500
(913) 296-4986
Information and Referral
In State: (800) 432-3535

KENTUCKY
Division of Aging Servies
CHR Building - 6th West
275 East Main Street
Frankfort, KY 40621
(502) 564-6930
Information and Referral
In State: (800) 372-2973
Hot Line - Long Term Care

Ombudsman
In State: (800) 372-2991

LOUISIANA
Office of Elder Affairs
Post Office Box 80374
Baton Rouge, LA 70806
(504) 925-1700

MAINE
Bureau of Elder and Adult
Services
State House Station #11
35 Anthony Avenue
Augusta, ME 04333
(207) 626-5335
Hot Line – Long Term Care
Ombudsman
In State: (800) 452-1912

MARYLAND
Office on Aging
Room 1004
301 West Preston Street
Baltimore, MD 21201-2374
(301) 225-1100
Senior Information and
Assistance
In State: (800) AGE-DIAL
(800) 243-3425

MASSACHUSETTS
Executive Office of Elder
Affairs
38 Chauncy Street
Boston, MA 02111
(617) 727-7750

Information and Referral
In State: (800) 882-2003
TDD: (800) 872-0166
Hot Line – Elder Abuse
In State: (800) 922-2275
Alzheimer's Information
In State: (800) 351-2229

MICHIGAN
Office of Services to the
Aging
Post Office Box 30026
Lansing, MI 48909
(517) 373-8230

MINNESOTA
Board on Aging
444 Lafayette Road
St. Paul, MN 55155-3843
(612) 296-2770
Information and Referral
In State: (800) 652-9747
Hot Line – Long Term Care
Ombudsman
In State: (800) 657-3591

MISSISSIPPI
Council on Aging
421 West Pascagoula Street
Jackson, MS 39203-3524
(601) 949-2070
Information and Referral
In State: (800) 222-7622
Hot Line – Personal Care,
Nursing Home, Hospital
Complaints
In State: (800) 227-7308

MISSOURI
Division on Aging
Post Office Box 1337
Jefferson City, MO 65102-1337
(314) 751-3082
Information and Referral
In State: (800) 235-5503
Hot Line – Elder Abuse/
Neglect
In State: (800) 392-0210

MONTANA
The Governor's Office on
Aging
State Capitol Building
Capitol Station, Room 219
Helena, MT 59620
(406) 444-3111
Information and Referral
In State: (800) 332-2272

NEBRASKA
Department on Aging
Post Office Box 95044
Lincoln, NE 68509-5044
(402) 471-2306

NEVADA
Division for Aging Services
Suite 114
340 North 11th Street
Las Vegas, NV 89101
(702) 486-3545
Information and Referral
In State: (800) 243-3638
(800) AGED-NEV

NEW HAMPSHIRE
Division of Elderly & Adult
Services
6 Hazen Drive
Concord, NH 03301-6501
(603) 271-4680
Information and Referral
In State: (800) 852-3345
Hot Line – Long Term Care
Ombudsman
In State: (800) 442-5640

NEW JERSEY
Division on Aging
101 South Broad Street
CN 807 South Broad &
Front Streets
Trenton, NJ 08625-0807
(609) 292-4833
Information and Referral
In State: (800) 792-8820

NEW MEXICO
State Agency on Aging
4th Floor
224 East Palace Avenue
Santa Fe, NM 87501
(505) 827-7640
Information and Referral
In State: (800) 432-2080

NEW YORK
Office on Aging
2 Empire State Plaza
Albany, NY 12223
(518) 474-3585

Information and Referral
In State: (800) 342-9871

NORTH CAROLINA
Division of Aging
693 Palmer Drive
Raleigh, NC 27603
(919) 733-3983
Information and Referral
(State Care Line)
In State: (800) 662-7030

NORTH DAKOTA
Aging Services
State Capitol Building
600 East Boulevard, 2nd Fl.
Bismarck, ND 58505
(701) 224-2577
Information and Referral
In State: (800) 472-2622

OHIO
Department of Aging
9th Floor
50 West Broad Street
Columbus, OH 43266-0501
(614) 466-5500
Hot Line – Nursing Home
Complaints
In State: (800) 282-1206

OKLAHOMA
Aging Services Division
Post Office Box 25352
Oklahoma City, OK 73125
(405) 521-2281

Hot Line – Elder Abuse
In State: (800) 522-3511

OREGON
Senior & Disabled Services
Division
313 Public Service Building
Salem, OR 97310
(503) 378-4728
Information and Referral
In State: (800) 232-3020

PENNSYLVANIA
Department of Aging
231 State Street
Harrisburg, PA 17101-1195
(717) 783-1550
Hot Line – Alzheimer's
In State: (800) 367-5115
Paid Prescriptions Problems
In State: (800) 225-7223
Hot Line – Fraud and Abuse
In State: (800) 992-2433

PUERTO RICO
Governor's Office for
Elderly Affairs
Call Box 50063
Old San Juan Station
San Juan, PR 00902
(809) 721-5710
Information and Referral
(809) 721-4560

RHODE ISLAND
Department of Elderly
Affairs
160 Pine Street
Providence, RI 02910-3708
(401) 277-2880
Information and Referral
In State: (800) 322-2880
Hot Line – Alzheimer's
In State: (800) 244-1428

SOUTH CAROLINA
Commission on Aging
Suite B-500
400 Arbor Lake Drive
Columbia, SC 29223
(803) 735-0210
Information and Referral
In State: (800) 868-9095
In Columbia:
(800) 735-0210

SOUTH DAKOTA
Office of Adult Services &
Aging
700 Governors Drive
Pierre, SD 57501
(605) 773-3656
Information and Referral
In State: (605) 773-3556

TENNESSEE
Commission on Aging
Suite 201
706 Church Street
Nashville, TN 37243-0860
(615) 741-2056

TEXAS
Department on Aging
Capitol Station
Post Office Box 12786
Austin, TX 78741-3702
(512) 444-2727
Information and Referral
In State: (800) 252-9240

UTAH
Division of Aging & Adult
Services
120 North 200 West
Post Office Box 45500
Salt Lake City, UT 84103
(801) 538-3822

VERMONT
Department of Aging &
Disabilities
103 South Main Street
Waterbury, VT 05676
(802) 241-2400
Information and Referral
In State: (800) 642-5119

VIRGINIA
Department for the Aging
10th Floor
700 East Franklin Street
Richmond, VA 23219-2327
(804) 225-2271
Information and Referral
In State: (800) 55-AGING
(800) 552-4464
Hot Line – Nursing Home

Complaints
In State: (800) 552-3402

VIRGIN ISLANDS
Senior Citizens Affairs
Department of Human
Services
19 Estate Diamond
Fredericksted
St. Croix, VI 00840
(809) 772-4950 Ext. 46

WASHINGTON
Aging & Adult Services
Administration
Mail Stop QG-16
Olympia, WA 98504
(206) 493-2500
Information and Referral
In State: (800) 422-3263
Hot Line – Nursing Home
Complaints
In State: (800) 562-6028

WEST VIRGINIA
Commission on Aging
Holly Grove - State Capitol
Charleston, WV 25305
(304) 348-3317
Information and Referral
In State: (800) 642-3671

WISCONSIN
Bureau on Aging
Post Office Box 7851
Madison, WI 53707

(608) 266-2536
Hot Line - Long Term Care
Ombudsman
In State: (800) 242-1060
Hot Line – MEDIGAP
Claims
In State: (800) 242-1060

WYOMING
Commission on Aging
139 Hathaway Building
Cheyenne, WY 82002
(307) 777-7986
Information and Referral
In State: (800) 442-2766

Other Major Resources on Aging Issues

GENERAL INFORMATION AND ASSISTANCE

American Association of Retired Persons (AARP)
National Office
1909 "K" St. N.W.
Washington, D.C. 20049
(202) 872-4700

National membership organization that provides a broad range of products and services to older Americans.

Children of Aging Parents
2761 Trenton Road
Levittown, PA 19056
(215) 945-6900

Information and referral services; programs for caregivers of older adults, including caregiver support group assistance, counseling, a newsletter, and educational programs and literature.

Gray Panthers
1424 16th St. N.W.
Suite 602
Washington, D.C. 20036
(202) 387-3111

Advocacy group that focuses on issues of concern to the elderly, such as Medicaid, mandatory retirement, age discrimination, and housing.

National Council on The Aging
600 Maryland Avenue S.W.
West Wing 100
Washington, D.C. 20024
(800) 424-9046

National membership organization primarily engaged in providing information and resources to professionals serving older Americans.

National Council of Senior Citizens
925 15th St. N.W.
Washington, D.C. 20005
(202) 624-9500

An advocacy organization for the elderly.

OWL—Older Women's League
730 11th St. N.W., Suite 300
Washington, D.C. 20001
(202) 783-6686

National advocacy organization, with focus on issues concerning older women, such as Social Security, pay equity, health care. Offers a variety of publications concerning these and similar issues.

FINANCIAL

Office of the Inspector General

U.S. Department of Health and Human Services
P.O. Box 17303
Baltimore, MD 21203-7303
Hotline (800) 368-5779

Handles complaints regarding fraud, waste, or abuse in Medicare, Medicaid, and Social Security.

Social Security, Medicare and Supplemental Security Income (SSI) Information Line
(800) 234-5772

Answers to questions regarding Social Security, Medicare, or SSI.

Department of Veterans Affairs (V.A.)
810 Vermont Ave. N.W.
Washington, D.C. 20420
(202) 233-4000

Information and referral for programs administered by the Department of Veterans Affairs.

HEALTH CARE

Alzheimer's Disease & Related Disorders Association
700 East Lake St., Suite 600
Chicago, IL 60601
(800) 621-0379

Information on Alzheimer's disease and research; referrals to local organizations and support groups.

American Cancer Society
1599 Clifton Road N.E.
Atlanta, GA 30329
(404) 320-3333
(800) 227-2345

Cancer information and referral to local societies for further information and programs.

AMC Cancer Research Center
1600 Pierce St.
Denver, CO 80214
(800) 525-3777

Current information on cancer, including causes, prevention, methods of detection, diagnosis, rehabilitation, and treatment. Also gives information on treatment facilities and counseling services.

American Council for the Blind
1155 15th St. N.W., Suite 720
Washington, D.C. 20005
(800) 424-8666

National membership organization of the blind and visually impaired. Provides information and referral services and various other programs for the sight impaired.

American Diabetes Association
1660 Duke St.
Alexandria, VA 22313
(800) 232-3472

Information, support, and referral services relating to diabetes.

American Heart Association
7320 Greenville Avenue
Dallas, TX 75231
(800) 242-1793

Information and referral services regarding heart disease.

American Lung Association
1740 Broadway
New York, NY 10019
(212) 315-8700

Information concerning lung disorders.

Arthritis Foundation
1314 Spring St. N.W.
Atlanta, GA 30309
(404) 872-7100
(800) 283-7800

Education, support, and social services through local chapters around the country for people with arthritis and their families.

Cancer Information Service
Department of Health and Human Services
(800) 422-6237

National Cancer Institute information service. Provides information about cancer to the public, but does not diagnose or recommend treatment programs.

Health Information Center, Office of Disease Prevention and Health Promotion, Public Health Service
P.O. Box 1133
Washington, D.C. 20013-1133
(800) 336-4797

A central source of information and referral for health questions.

Huntington's Disease Society of America
140 West 22nd St.
New York, NY 10011-2420
(212) 242-1968
(800) 345-4372

Information and referral services for victims of Huntington's disease; also answers questions on presymptomatic testing.

National Eye Care Project Hotline
P.O. Box 6988
San Francisco, CA 94101-6988
(800) 222-EYES

Information on free eye examinations for low income seniors who have not had an eye examination for three years.

National Hearing Aid Helpline
20361 Middlebelt Rd.
Livonia, MI 48152
(800) 521-5247

Directory for referrals to specialists in local areas; consumer information for purchase of hearing aids.

National Jewish Lung Line
1400 Jackson Street
Denver, CO 80206
(800) 222-5864

Information on a variety of lung diseases and disorders.

National Parkinson's Foundation
1501 N.W. 9th Avenue
Miami, FL 33136
(800) 327-4545

Information and literature concerning Parkinson's disease.

Simon Foundation
P.O. Box 835
Wilmette, IL 60091
(800) 237-4666

Help for those experiencing loss of bowel or bladder control. Various educational publications regarding incontinence.

HOSPICE

National Hospice Organization
1901 North Moore Street
Suite 901
Arlington, VA 22209
(703) 243-5900

Organization representing approximately 1,700 hospice programs nationwide. Provides referrals to local hospice programs.

HOUSING AND LONG-TERM CARE

American Association of Homes for the Aging
901 "E" Street N.W.
Washington, D.C. 20004
(202) 296-5960

Represents retirement living and long-term care facilities.

American Health Care Association
1201 "L" Street N.W.
Washington, D.C. 20005
(202) 842-4444

Represents many of the nation's skilled nursing and intermediate care facilities.

INSURANCE

American Council of Life Insurance,
Health Insurance Association of America
1001 Pennsylvania Avenue N.W.
Washington, D.C. 20004-2599
(800) 635-1271

Answers general questions and sends materials about life and health insurance. Does not handle complaints regarding insurance claims.

LEGAL

National Senior Citizens Law Center
1815 "H" Street N.W.
Suite 700
Washington, D.C. 20006
(202) 887-5280
(800) 783-6725

Advocacy program for senior citizens issues such as Social Security, Medicare/Medicaid, public and private pensions, and age discrimination.

RECREATION AND TRAVEL

Elderhostel
75 Federal Street
Boston, MA 02110
(617) 426-8056
(800) 346-7835

Non-credit educational programs for seniors, offered at colleges and universities around the world.

Society for the Advancement of Travel for the Handicapped (S.A.T.H.)
26 Court Street
Brooklyn, NY 11242
(718) 858-5483

Membership group that promotes travel opportunities and services for disabled persons.

SAFETY

National Safety Council
444 North Michigan Ave.
Chicago, IL 60611
(800) 621-7619

Information on all aspects of safety and accident prevention.

Publications on Subjects of Concern to Older Adults and Their Families

The Family CAREbook. Kenny, D. and Oettinger, E., Editors; Seattle: CAREsource Program Development, Inc. (1991)

The Family CAREbook – Large Print Forms. Looseleaf 8-1/2" x 11" forms supplement; Seattle: CAREsource Program Development, Inc. (1991)

Read Easy—Large Print Libraries for Older Adults. Ring, A.; Seattle: CAREsource Program Development, Inc. (1991)

If you are unable to locate any of the listed publications at your local bookstore, CAREsource publications and other titles flagged with a CARESOURCE are available by calling (800) 448-5213 or (206) 625-9128 or by writing:

CAREsource Program Development, Inc.
505 Seattle Tower ◆ 1218 Third Avenue
Seattle, WA 98101-3021

Aging – General

The Encyclopedia of Aging. Maddox, George L., et al; New York: Springer Publishing Co. (1987)

Successful Aging: A Sourcebook for Older People and Their Families. Avery, Ann C.; New York: Ballantine Books (1987)

When Your Parents Grow Old. Shelly, F.D.; New York: Harper & Row (1985)

Why Survive? Being Old in America. Butler, Robert N.; New York: Harper & Row (1985)

Caregiving and Family Relations

Aging is a Family Affair. Thompson, Wendy; Cincinnati: Seven Hills Books (1989)

Care of the Elderly: A Family Approach. Pinkston, E. & Linsk, N.; New York: Pergamon Press (1984)

Caregiving: When Someone You Love Grows Old. Gillies, John; Wheaton, IL: H. Shaw Publishing (1988)

Counseling Elders and Their Families: Potential Techniques for Applied Gerontology. Hert, J. & Weakland, J.; New York: MacMillan Publishing Company (1979)

Family Caregiving and Dependent Elderly. Springer, Diane, and Brubaker, Timothy; Beverly Hills, CA: Sage Publishing Co. (1984)

Growing Old: A Handbook for You and Your Aging Parent. Tomb, David A.; New York: Viking Penguin, Inc. (1986)

How to Care for Your Parents: A Handbook for Adult Children. Levin, N.J.; Washington D.C.: Storm King Press (Distributed by Random House) (1987)

Helping Elderly Parents: The Role of Adult Children. Cicirelli, V.; Boston: Auburn House (1982).

Miles Away and Still Caring: A Guide for Long-Distance Caregivers. AARP Pamphlet (1986)

Taking Care of Your Aging Family Members: A Practical Guide. Hooyman, Nancy and Lustbader, Wendy; New York: The Free Press (1988).

Understanding Aging Parents. Lester, Andrew and Judith; Philadelphia, PA: The Westminster Press (1980)

You and Your Aging Parent. The Modern Family's Guide to Emotional, Physical and Financial Problems. Silverstone, Barbara and Hyman, Helen K.; New York: Pantheon Press (1982)

Death and Dying

The Grief Recovery Handbook. James, John W. and Cherry, Frank; New York: Harper and Row (1989)

How to Survive the Loss of a Love. Colgrove, Melba, et al; New York: Bantam (1984)

It's Your Choice: The Practical Guide to Planning a Funeral. Nelson, Thomas C.; Washington D.C., AARP Books / Scott, Foresman and Co. (1987)

Questions and Answers on Death and Dying. Kubler-Ross, Elizabeth; New York: Macmillan (1974)

Financial Issues

The Complete and Easy Guide to Social Security and Medicare. Jehle, Faustin F.; Frasier Publishing Company, Annual Editions.

The Dow Jones-Irwin Guide to Retirement Planning. Vicker, Ray; Homewood, IL: Dow Jones-Irwin (1987)

Marshall Loeb's Money Guide. Loeb, Marshall; Boston: Little Brown and Company, Annual Editions.

Policy Wise: The Practical Guide to Insurance Decisions for Older Consumers. Chasen, Nancy; Washington D.C.: AARP Books/Scott, Foresman and Company (1987)

Securing Your Retirement Dollars. Weinstein, Grace; Washington, D.C.: American Council of Life Insurance — Health Insurance Association of America (1984)

The Social Security Handbook. Social Security Administration; Washington D.C.: United States government Printing Office, Annual Editions.

What to Do With What You've Got. Weaver, Peter and Buchanan, Annette; Washington D.C., AARP Books/Scott, Foresman and Company (1987)

Your Social Security. Social Security Administration (pamphlet free at Social Security Offices).

Health, Food, and Fitness

CARE SOURCE *Diet for A Small Planet*. Lappe, Frances M.; Ballantine Books (1987)

CARE SOURCE *Fit for Life I*. Diamond, Harvey and Diamond, Marilyn; Warner Books (1988)

CARE SOURCE *Fit for Life II: Living Health, the Complete Health Program*. Diamond, Harvey and Diamond, Marilyn; Warner Books (1988)

Fitness for Life: Exercises for People Over 50. Berland, Theodore; Washington D.C.: AARP Pamphlet (1987)

CARE SOURCE *Jane Brody's Good Food Book*. Brody, Jane; New York: Bantam (1987)

Handbook of Nutrition, Health and Aging. Watkin, Donald M.: Parkridge, NJ: Noyes Publications (1983)

Healthful Aging. Burdman, Geri M.; New Jersey: Prentice Hall (1986)

 How to Have Your Cake & Eat it Too! Diet Cooking for the Whole Family: Diabetic, Hypoglycemic, Low-Cholestrol, Low-Fat, Low-Sale, Low Calorie Diets. Mac Rae, Norma M.; Anchorage, Alaska: Alaska Northwest, Second Edition (1985)

 Love, Medicine and Miracles: Lessons Learned About Self-Healing from a Surgeon's Experience with Exceptional Patients. Siegl, Bernie S.; Harper & Row (1990)

Health Care (See also Health, Food & Fitness, Home Care, Mental Health and Counseling, and Nursing Homes.)

 Mayo Clinic Family Health & Medical Guide. Mayo; Greenwillow (1990)

 Old Enough to Feel Better: A Medical Guide for Seniors. Gordon, Michael; Johns Hopkins (1989) Revised Edition

Second Opinion: Your Comprehensive Guide to Alternative Treatments. Rosenfeld, Isadora; New York: Bantam Books Inc. (1988)

Alchoholism

Al-Anon Family Groups (B-5). AFG Inc., PO Box 862, Mid-Town Station, New York, New York 10018-0862

Alcoholics Anonymous. World Service Organization, PO Box 459, Grand Central Station, New York, New York 10163

Alzheimers

 The Thirty-Six Hour Day. Mace, Nancy L., and Rabins, Peter V.; New York: Warner Books (1989)

Arthritis

 The Arthritis Help Book: A Comprehensive Guide to Understanding Your Arthritis. Lorig, Kate; Addison, Wesley, Third Edition (1990)

 Guide to Independent Living for People with Arthritis. Arthritis Health Professions Association and the Patient and Community Services Department of the Arthritis Foundation; Atlanta, Georgia: Arthritis Foundation (1988)

Cancer

American Cancer Society: Complete Book of Cancer Prevention, Detection, Diagnosis, Treatment, Rehabilitation, Care. ACS Staff, Edited by Holleb, Arthur I., M.D.; Doubleday (1986)

Choices: Realistic Alternatives in Cancer Treatment. Morra, Marion, and Potts, Eve; New York: Avon Books (1990)

 Triumph: Getting Back to Normal When You Have Cancer. Morra, Marion & Potts, Eve; New York: Avon Books

Chronic Illness

Beyond Rage: The Emotional Impact of Chronic Physical Illness. Le Maistre, Jo-Ann; Alpine Guild (1985)

Living with Chronic Illness: Days of Patience and Passion. Register, Cheri; Free Press (1987)

 Mainstay: For the Well Spouse of the Chronically Ill. Strong, Maggie; Penguin (1989)

Depression

The Good News About Depression: New Medical Cares &Treatments That Can Work for You. Gold, Mark S., and Morris, Louis B.; Bantam (1988)

Diabetes

 The American Diabetes Association / The American Dietetic Association, Family Cookbook. Prentice Hall, Three Volumes, Revised Edition (1987)

The Diabetic Book: Help for Diabetics, Families and Friends. Bierman, June, and Toohay, Barbara; Jeremy Torcher; Distributed by Houghton Miflin, Revised Ed.

Diabetes In The Family. Runjan, J. and the American Diabetes Association Staff: Prentice Hall (1987)

 The Diabetic Woman: All Your Questions Answered. Jovaovic, Lois, Bierman, June, and Toohay, Barbara; Jeremy Torcher, Distributed by St. Martin's Press (1988)

Hearing

Hearing and Deafness. Davis, Hallowell and Silverman, Richard S.; Holt Reinhart & Winston, Inc. (1978)

Heart

 American Heart Association Low-Fat, Low-Cholestrol Cookbook. Edited by Grundy, Scott and Winston, Mary; Random House (1989)

 Heartmates: A Survival Guide for the Cardiac Spouse. Levin, Rhoda F.; Prentice Hall

Huntington's Disease

Toward A Fuller Life: A Guide to Everyday Living with Huntington's Disease. Werbel, Eileen; Huntington's Disease of America: New York (1990)

Multiple Sclerosis

 Multiple Sclerosis: New Hope and Practical Advice for People and Families. Rosner and Ross; Prentice Hall (1987)

Multiple Sclerosis: A Guide for Patients and Their Families. Scheinberg, Labe C. and Holland, Nancy J.; Raven (1987)

Parkinson's Disease

Parkinson's Disease: Guidelines for Patient and Families. Duvoisin, Roger C. M.D. Third Edition: Raven (1984)

Parkinson's Handbook. McGoon, Dwight C.; Norton (1990)

Sight

Growing Older with Good Vision. (Pamphlet) National Society to Prevent Blindness; Schaumburg, Illinois

---

Stroke

How to Prevent a Stroke: A Complete Risk Reduction Program. Rodale Press: Emmaus, Pennsylvania (1989)

Stroke: A Guide for Patients and Their Families. New York: McGraw Hill (1979)

Home Care

All About Home Care: A Consumer's Guide. National Home Caring Council: New York (1983).

 Home Care for the Elderly: A Complete Guide. Portnow, J. and Houtmann, M.; New York: McGraw-Hill (1987)

Home Health Care Solution: A Complete Consumer Guide. Nassif, Janet Zhun; New York: Harper and Row (1985)

Home Safety and Convenience

Housing Interiors for the Disabled and Elderly. Raschko, Bettyann; New York: Van Nostrand Reinhold (1982)

Planning Your Retirement Housing. Sumichrast, Michael, et al.; Washington D.C.: AARP Books/Scott, Foresman and Company (1987)

Legal and Consumer Issues

Essential Guide to Wills, Estates, Trusts, and Death Taxes. Soled, Alex J.; Washington D.C.: AARP Books/Scott, Foresman and Company (1988)

Estate Planning Guide. Kess, S., and Weslin, B.; Chicago: Commerce Clearing House. Annual Editions.

Medications

Advice for the Patient: Drug Information for the Patient (Consumer Edition). United States Pharmaceutical Convention, Inc.; Rockville, MD

About Your Medicines (Consumer Edition). United States Pharmaceutical Convention, Inc.; Rockville, MD (1991)

 Consumer Guide to Prescription Drugs. New American Library (1991)

 The Pill Book. Simon, G.I., et al.; New York: Bantam Books. 3rd rev. ed. (1986)

Mental Health and Counseling

The Dance of Anger. Lerner, H.; New York: Harper and Row (1989)

The Experience of Old Age: Stress, Coping, Survival. Lieberman, M.A., and Tobin, S.S.; New York: Basic Books (1983)

The Psychological Aspects of Chronic Illness. Greg, Charles H., Robertus, Judy and Stone, J. Blair; Springfield, IL: Charles C. Thomas, Publishers (1989)

To Be Old and Sad: Understanding Depression in the Elderly. Billig, N.; Lexington, MA.: Lexington Books (1987).

Nursing Homes

 Choosing a Nursing Home. Goldsmith, Seth B.; Prentice Hall (1990)

Choosing a Nursing Home. A Guidebook for Families. Richards, Mary et al; Seattle, WA: University of Washington Press (1985)

Long Term Care of Older People: A Practical Guide. Brody, E.; Human Sciences Press (1977)

Travel

 Get Up and Go: A Guide for the Mature Traveler. Malott, Gene and Adele; San Francisco: Gateway Books (1989)

Other

The Gadget Book: Ingenious Devices for Easier Living. LaBuda, Dennis ed.; AARP Books/Scott, Foresman and Co. (1987) Updated 5 April 1991

Glossary

AARP (American Association of Retired Persons)—This organization is dedicated to enhancing the quality of life of older Americans. It provides a wide range of services from mail-order drugs to political lobbying to consumer information.

Adult Day Care—These facilities provide regular daytime care to older adults for purposes of social activity, personal enrichment, and daytime coverage for a primary caregiver who is employed. Some adult day care programs offer physical and occupational therapy, counseling, medical treatment, or other health care services in addition to a social program.

Adult Family Homes—These are private residences licensed to provide room and board for a small number of (usually four) older adults. They are sometimes called adult foster homes or board and care.

Advocate—Senior advocates are persons or organizations who represent the interests of older persons. Generally, the term "advocate" is used for a more informal relationship than a fiduciary relationship such as an attorney or guardian. Advocates and advocacy groups operate in a number of specialized areas relating to senior citizen programs and issues.

Annuity, Annuitant—An annuity is the regular payment of money for life or for a specified period of time. The receiver or beneficiary of such payments is the annuitant.

Area Agency on Aging—The local or regional agency established under the Federal Older Americans Act to coordinate and provide a wide variety of services to the elderly. The Area Agency on Aging operates the Senior Information and Assistance telephone information and referral service.

Assignment—In the Medicare program, a physician who accepts assignment is paid directly by Medicare in return for agreeing to accept the Medicare approved charge as the full charge for services. The patient must still pay 20% of the approved charge as a "co-payment."

Attendant Care Service—This form of home health care involves a trained attendant assigned to provide personal care and some medical supervision for the client.

Attorney in Fact—This is a legal term for the person designated through a power of attorney to act for another person.

Caregiver—A caregiver is a person who directly provides some form of service, assistance, or support to another.

Care Management—As distinguished from caregiving, care management responsibilities involve arranging for and coordinating caregiving services which are provided by others.

Chore Services—This term encompasses a wide variety of home services to allow an older person to continue to live independently at home. Generally, chore services do not include skilled health care services.

Congregate Care Homes—This form of retirement housing provides separate apartments for the residents and a variety of support services such as meals, transportation, personal care, housekeeping, and social activities.

Congregate Nutrition Sites—In such programs, group meal service is provided for older adults at local senior or community centers, often including transportation services to and from the meal site.

Conservator—In some states, a conservator is the same as a full guardian of a person and that person's estate. In other states, a conservator is a guardian of an adult as distinguished from a guardian of a child. The conservator of an estate or of any property is appointed by the court to care for that estate or property.

Continuing Care (Lifecare) Communities—These are facilities which offer a variety of housing arrangements for older adults, including alternatives from independent living to nursing care facilities to meet the lifetime needs of residents.

Co-payment—Out of pocket payments for services covered by insurance are called co-payments or co-insurance. These payments can either be a flat per service fee or a percentage of the total fee. For example, Medicare Part B requires a 20% co-payment by the enrollee for covered services. Medicare pays only 80% of the approved charge.

Custodial Care Facilities (Intermediate)—This type of nursing home care provides a high level of assistance for daily living activities, such as meals and personal care, but does not provide regular skilled medical services. Custodial care is not covered by Medicare or most private health insurance.

Decedent—A decedent is a person who has died. The term is used frequently in the course of estate settlement.

Deductible—The deductible is the amount of expense that an insured person must incur before an insurance carrier becomes liable for payment.

DRG (Diagnostic Related Group)—DRGs are illness categories defined by the Medicare program for purposes of paying hospitals for services provided to enrollees. Each hospital admission is categorized by DRG and the hospital is paid a flat fee based on that DRG, regardless of actual length of hospitalization.

Discharge Planning—Discharge planning a service provided through hospitals to help place a convalescing patient in an appropriate care setting and to arrange necessary support services so that the patient can leave the hospital as soon as possible . Discharge planners are often very knowledgeable about community resources available for assisting older patients to maintain an independent lifestyle.

Durable Power of Attorney—This legal document is usually executed as part of a person's estate planning. In it, the person names an "attorney in fact" to act on his or her behalf in business and/or health care matters.

Estate Planning—Estate planning is the process of creating and preserving one's property during one's lifetime and arranging for its transfer at one's death through making a will or following other legal procedures.

Guardian—A guardian is a person appointed by the court to control and manage another person's affairs and/or property. Most typically, a guardian is appointed to manage the affairs of an adult who is incapable of looking after his or her own affairs.

Guardian Ad Litem—A guardian ad litem is an individual appointed by the court for the purpose of investigating and representing the interest of the person for whom a guardianship is requested.

Home Health Care—This term describes health care services provided in the home, usually under the direction of a licensed home health care agency or an independent registered nurse.

Home Sharing—Home sharing is an arrangement among several older individuals to share a residence. Many communities have formal or informal coordinating services to help seniors locate house mates who wish to share a home.

Hospice Care—Hospice care for the terminally ill and their families emphasizing pain management and controlling symptoms, rather than on seeking a cure; it is offered by many hospitals on an in-patient basis and at home by home health and hospice agencies.

Integrated Care Communities—These housing facilities offer a wide range of alternatives from total independent living to skilled nursing facilities. These facilities are designed to allow residents to remain within the community as their needs for assistance grow.

Intermediate Care Facility—*(See Custodial Care Facility)*

Intestacy— Intestacy is the state of being without a will. If a person dies intestate, the person's property passes to the heirs as required by the applicable state statute.

Life Care Communities—*(See Continuing Care Communities.)*

Living Will (Directive to Physician)—This legal document gives a physician instructions concerning desired medical treatment in the event a person becomes terminally ill and also loses the ability to communicate his or her wishes at the time.

Long-Term Care Insurance—This type of private insurance is designed to cover costs of nursing home care or sometimes services in the home which make nursing home care unnecessary.

Meals on Wheels—This community-based meal service delivers frozen meals to the homes of older adults at a modest charge.

Medicaid—Medicaid is the federal/state program which pays for health care needs of low income individuals who meet the program qualifying standards.

Medicare—This federal program provides health insurance for Americans age 65 or older and disabled persons.

Medicare Approved Charge—This is the official payment base for Medicare Part B reimbursement. The Medicare Approved Charge is determined through a standard Medicare formula. This charge may be less than the provider's actual charge.

Medicare Supplement Insurance (Medigap)—These are private insurance programs designed primarily to cover Medicare deductibles and co-payments.

Mobile Market—A mobile market provides grocery delivery service to older persons who cannot do their own shopping.

Net Worth—Net worth equals the total value of a person's estate. Net worth is determined by subtracting the sum of all liabilities from the sum of all assets.

Power of Attorney—This legal document gives another person (the "attorney in fact") legal authority to act on one's behalf. A *durable* power of attorney is one which continues to be effective even though the person granting the power of attorney has become mentally incapacitated.

Preferred Providers—Some health care providers contract with insurance companies to provide care at a discounted rate, in return for the insurance carrier giving consumers financial incentives to use these preferred providers.

Representative Payee—This is the legal term for a person or organization authorized to receive and administer benefit payments (Social Security, Supplemental Security Income) for a person deemed incapable of acting financially for him or herself. Banks often act as representative payees.

Respite Care—Respite care is temporary care for a person provided by a home health agency or other provider in order to give rest and personal time to the person's regular caregiver.

Senior Information & Referral—This telephone assistance and referral service is operated by the Area Agency on Aging in each community. It is the primary access point for identifying services and resources for older adults.

Skilled Nursing Facility—A nursing home which provides skilled nursing care and other medical services to chronically ill patients and those recently discharged from the hospital is a skilled nursing facility. A skilled nursing facility provides a higher level of care than an intermediate or custodial care facility.

Support Groups—Support groups provide emotional support, information, and companionship for persons experiencing a common problem.

Term Insurance—Term insurance is a form of life insurance having no cash surrender value and furnishing insurance protection for only a specified or limited period of time.

Trust—Trusts are a form of ownership under which property is held and managed by a person or institution (the trustee) for the benefit of other persons or institutions for whom the trust was created (the beneficiaries). The creator of a trust is commonly referred to as the settlor, grantor, or trustor.

Van Services—This transportation service by van is provided for older adults who need assistance. Pick-up and delivery is generally by advance appointment. Cost for such programs varies from community to community.

Ward—The legal term for a person whose affairs are being managed by a court appointed guardian.

9 Forms and Family Notes

Form 1.1
Helpful Personal Information

PERSONAL INFORMATION

	Husband	Wife
Name		
Home address and phone		
Social Security No.		
Medicare No.		
Medicaid No.		
Armed Forces ID No.		
Drivers License No.		
Consent given for organ transplant(s) in case of death	Yes ☐ No ☐	Yes ☐ No ☐

EMERGENCY CONTACTS

Family members		
Physician		
Clergy		
Neighbors		
Close friends		
Other		

CHILDREN

Record name, address, and phone number

_____   _____
_____   _____
_____   _____
_____   _____
_____   _____
_____   _____
_____   _____
_____   _____
_____   _____
_____   _____
_____   _____
_____   _____
_____   _____
_____   _____

OTHER CLOSE RELATIVES

Record name, address, and phone number

_____   _____
_____   _____
_____   _____
_____   _____
_____   _____
_____   _____
_____   _____
_____   _____
_____   _____
_____   _____
_____   _____
_____   _____
_____   _____
_____   _____

HOUSEHOLD SUPPORT

Record name and phone number

Chore service
agency
_____   _____
_____   _____

Personal care
attendant
_____   _____
_____   _____

Other
_____   _____
_____   _____

HEALTH CARE PROVIDERS

Record name, address, and phone number

Primary care
physician
_____   _____
_____   _____
_____   _____

Physician
specialists
_____   _____
_____   _____
_____   _____

Hospital
_____   _____
_____   _____
_____   _____

Home health
provider
_____   _____
_____   _____
_____   _____

Other health
provider(s)
_____   _____
_____   _____
_____   _____

Pharmacist
_____   _____
_____   _____
_____   _____

INSURANCE
Record company/policy name, policy number, and agent's name

Primary health
coverage
(usually Medicare)
_____ _____
_____ _____
_____ _____

Medicare
supplement
_____ _____
_____ _____
_____ _____

Long-term care
insurance
_____ _____
_____ _____
_____ _____

Auto insurance
_____ _____
_____ _____
_____ _____

Homeowners
insurance
_____ _____
_____ _____
_____ _____

Life insurance
_____ _____
_____ _____
_____ _____

LEGAL AND FINANCIAL SERVICES
Record name, address, and phone number

Attorney
_____ _____
_____ _____
_____ _____

Accountant
_____ _____
_____ _____
_____ _____

Financial advisor
_____ _____
_____ _____
_____ _____

Record bank name(s), branch(es), account number(s), and signer(s)

Checking account _____ _____

_____ _____

_____ _____

Savings and
investment
accounts _____ _____

_____ _____

_____ _____

LOCATION OF IMPORTANT RECORDS

Safe deposit box
and keys _____ _____

_____ _____

_____ _____

Estate Planning Documents

Will _____ _____

_____ _____

_____ _____

Living will _____ _____

_____ _____

_____ _____

Durable power of
attorney for
health care _____ _____

_____ _____

_____ _____

Other Legal Documents

Contracts and
promissory notes _____ _____

_____ _____

_____ _____

Divorce records _____ _____

_____ _____

_____ _____

Partnership
agreements _____ _____

_____ _____

Financial Records

Tax returns for
prior years

_____ _____
_____ _____
_____ _____

This year's tax
information

_____ _____
_____ _____
_____ _____

Check register
and savings
passbooks

_____ _____
_____ _____

Pension, IRA,
Keogh, and other
deferred comp-
ensation records

_____ _____
_____ _____

Real estate
documents

_____ _____
_____ _____
_____ _____

Insurance policies
and premium
payment records

_____ _____
_____ _____
_____ _____

Health care
expense and reim-
bursement records

_____ _____
_____ _____
_____ _____

Records
concerning prepaid
funeral plan, burial
plot, etc.

_____ _____
_____ _____
_____ _____

LOCATION OF PERSONAL PROPERTY

_____ _____ _____
_____ _____ _____
_____ _____ _____
_____ _____ _____
_____ _____ _____

Form 3.1
Checklist for Selecting a Private
Case Management Professional

NEEDS ASSESSMENTS—WHAT SKILLS AND SERVICES ARE WE LOOKING FOR IN A CASE MANAGER

	Strong Need	Some Need	Not Sure
1. Nursing Home	☐	☐	☐
2. Arranging Support Service:			
a. Meals	☐	☐	☐
b. Transportation	☐	☐	☐
c. Daytime Programs	☐	☐	☐
d. Social Programs	☐	☐	☐
3. Other Residential Alternatives	☐	☐	☐
4. Monitoring Home Health Care	☐	☐	☐
5. Arranging Psychological Services	☐	☐	☐
6. Coping with Depression	☐	☐	☐
7. Drug or Alcohol Abuse Problems	☐	☐	☐
8. Other:			
_____	☐	☐	☐
_____	☐	☐	☐
_____	☐	☐	☐

QUESTIONS TO ASK CONCERNING QUALIFICATIONS AND REFERENCES

Providers:

1. How long has the person or agency been providing private case management services in this community? _____ _____

2. What academic and professional credentials does the provider have? _____ _____

3. How many years of practical case management experience does the professional you will be working with have? _____ _____

4. What is the provider's range of services? _____ _____

5. How does the provider charge for services?

    a. Flat Fee _____ _____
    b. Hourly Rates _____ _____
    c. Monthly Retainer _____ _____
    d. Commission or Markup on Services Coordinated _____ _____

6. How will the provider keep in contact with the family? _____ _____

7. What references can be given (physicians, hospital discharge planners, public agencies, others)? _____ _____

Form 4.1
Household Safety and
Convenience Checklist

ACCIDENT PREVENTION

Date checked:

Bathroom

_____ _____

✔ Grab bars installed in bath /
shower

_____ _____

✔ Non-skid surface in bath /
shower

_____ _____

✔ Water temperature reduced to 120°   _____ _____

✔ Floor surfaces dry and clean

_____ _____

Interior Stairs and Landings

✔ Handrails on both sides of stairs   _____ _____

✔ Lighting adequate   _____ _____

✔ Floor coverings in good repair   _____ _____

✔ Traffic areas free of obstacles   _____ _____

Bedroom

✔ Furniture placed safely   _____ _____

Kitchen

✔ Floors dry and in good repair

✔ No sharp metal edges

✔ Safe stool for reaching

Other living space

✔ Throw rugs removed or secured to the floor

✔ Other floor coverings in good repair

✔ Traffic areas adequately lighted

Exterior Walkways, Stairs and Landings

✔ Adequate lighting

✔ Traffic surfaces free of obstacles (e.g. snow)

FIRE SAFETY

Prevention

✔ Hazardous materials removed or properly stored

✔ Electrical appliances checked and in good order

✔ No overloaded outlets or extension cords

- ✔ Chimneys and flues cleaned if heavily used ﹘﹘﹘ ﹘﹘﹘
- ✔ Light bulbs appropriate size and wattage ﹘﹘﹘ ﹘﹘﹘
- ✔ Heaters located away from flammable materials ﹘﹘﹘ ﹘﹘﹘

Safety Devices

- ✔ Smoke detector/alarms properly placed; batteries checked recently ﹘﹘﹘ ﹘﹘﹘

Ability to Respond

- ✔ Escape routes and reporting procedures understood ﹘﹘﹘ ﹘﹘﹘

SECURITY

- ✔ Doors and Windows ﹘﹘﹘ ﹘﹘﹘
- ✔ Locks in good working order ﹘﹘﹘ ﹘﹘﹘

Lighting

- ✔ Exterior areas well lighted and free of unnecessary vegetation ﹘﹘﹘ ﹘﹘﹘

Communications

- ✔ Phone next to bed ﹘﹘﹘ ﹘﹘﹘
- ✔ Emergency numbers clearly visible ﹘﹘﹘ ﹘﹘﹘

CONVENIENCE AND LIVABILITY

✔ Telephone placement   _____ _____

✔ Lighting adequate   _____ _____

✔ Drafts reduced   _____ _____

✔ Beds and chairs easy to get
into and out of   _____ _____

Remember: safety assessments should be updated at regular intervals.

Form 5.1
Questions to Ask a Chore Service Provider

This form contains the questions you or your parents should ask in selecting an individual or agency to provide chore service in their home. Space has been left after each question to write down and compare answers.

PART I—SERVICES OFFERED

1. What services are needed? Can the individual or agency provide needed services?

   - Light housekeeping
   - Heavy housekeeping
   - Meal preparation
   - Laundry
   - Personal care (help with bathing, grooming, getting dressed, etc.)
   - Shopping
   - Transportation to and from appointments
   - Companionship
   - Home improvements or maintenance
   - Yard upkeep

2. Will the individual providing the services have his or her own car to use for errands?

   - If yes, will his or her insurance cover trips in connection with employment?

   - If no, is your car insured while driven by an employee?

   _____

3. What is the rate of turnover in personnel? Can you request and expect to have the same service providers over time?

   _____

PART II—RATES

1. How will the individual or agency charge for services provided? What are their current rates?

   _____

2. If you are dealing directly with a chore worker, will he/she be your employee or a self-employed independent contractor? This is relevant for tax purposes.

   _____

PART III—QUALIFICATIONS AND SUPERVISION: HELP THROUGH AN AGENCY

1. Are agency personnel treated as employees of the agency and supervised accordingly, or do they act as independent contractors?

   _____

2. Does the agency provide training and orientation for its new chore service workers? How detailed is it?

3. What are the experience and qualifications of the worker who will be serving in your parents' home?

4. What are the experience and qualifications of the agency's supervisors?

5. What is the agency's procedure for employee supervision and evaluation? Will a supervisor visit your parent's home from time to time to see how things are going?

6. Does the agency have a procedure for addressing client or family concerns and complaints?

PART IV—QUALIFICATIONS AND SUPERVISION: HELP YOU HIRE YOURSELF

1. What is the individual's experience with this kind of work? Be specific in discussing the services you are expecting the applicant to provide.

2. How long was the individual at his/her last placement? Why did that relationship end?

3. What are the minimum/maximum hours the individual can work?

_____

4. What will be the best way for you and your parent to provide feedback on the individual's performance?

_____

5. Will it be possible to renegotiate hours and services as your parents' needs change?

_____

PART V—REFERENCES AND AFFILIATIONS

1. Is the individual or agency recommended by knowledgeable persons in the community or by past satisfied families? Taking time to check out the references you are given is always a good idea.

_____

_____

_____

Form 6.1
Checklist for Choosing a Retirement Living Facility

This form lists many of the factors older adults should consider in evaluating retirement housing alternatives. The importance of each factor will vary depending on a person's or couple's current needs and preferences as well as the services and facilities they anticipate needing in the future. Factors to consider are organized into three groups: Part I lists factors to consider before visiting a facility; Part II lists questions to ask about the facility and the services it offers; and Part III lists conditions to observe.

PART I—FACTORS TO CONSIDER IN ADVANCE

Facility Name:

_____ _____

Location

1. Located in a geographic area of choice?

   _____ _____

2. Convenient for visits by (and to) family, friends, and health care providers?

   _____ _____

3. Adequate transportation connections?

   _____ _____

4. Adequate support services?

   _____ _____

Reputation

5. Does the facility have a good reputation in the community?

   _____ _____

PART II—QUESTIONS TO ASK ABOUT A RETIREMENT LIVING FACILITY

Service

1. Are these services provided or available?

    - Housecleaning   _____ _____

    - Laundry   _____ _____

    - Personal care   _____ _____

    - Social and recreational programs   _____ _____

    - Transportation services   _____ _____

    - Food services or meal preparation, including ability to meet special dietary needs   _____ _____

    - Health care services, including ability to respond to an emergency situation   _____ _____

Finances

2. What are the terms of occupancy? Do you buy an ownership interest or rent as a tenant?   _____ _____

3. If a deposit is required, what are the conditions for obtaining a refund if your parents' circumstances or decisions change?   _____ _____

4. What has been the resale value of ownership interest in the facility?   _____ _____

5. Do your parents have the right to sell, assign, or lease their unit?

6. What fees or charges must be paid?
   - base rate
   - extra services

7. Are rates tied to an inflation index or may they be raised at will? What has been the history of rate increases? Is one due to occur soon?

8. Will your parents' unit be held for them if they require hospitalization or a nursing home stay?

Restrictions

9. What restrictions (e.g. no smoking, no pets, no overnight visits) apply?

Management and Staffing

10. What are the experience and background of the management team?

11. What staff does the facility employ?

12. Is the level of staff turnover reasonable?

13. What is the staff-to-resident ratio?

PART III—CONDITIONS TO LOOK FOR DURING A VISIT

Facilities

1. A favorable first impression? _____ _____

2. Neighborhood is convenient, pleasant, and attractive? _____ _____

3. Facility appears well maintained? _____ _____

4. Facility appears well designed: e.g. adequate parking, elevators, ventilation, lighting? _____ _____

5. Adequate safety features: railings, curb cuts, etc.? _____ _____

6. Food service, if provided, appears clean, appetizing, and well run? _____ _____

Atmosphere and Attitudes

7. Staff attitudes are positive and professional? _____ _____

8. Other residents are friendly? _____ _____

Form 8.1
Checklist for Older Drivers

This checklist covers safety considerations for older drivers. Part I lists points seniors should review when considering continued driving. Part II covers points seniors should evaluate when considering reduced driving.

PART I—CHECKPOINTS FOR CONTINUED DRIVING

	Yes	No	n/a
1. Drivers license current?	☐	☐	☐
2. Insurance coverage adequate?	☐	☐	☐
3. Insurance premiums paid?	☐	☐	☐
4. Car(s) properly licensed?	☐	☐	☐
5. Car(s) in good working order?	☐	☐	☐
a. brakes	☐	☐	☐
b. engine idle	☐	☐	☐
c. accelerator linkage	☐	☐	☐
d. seatbelts	☐	☐	☐
e. tires	☐	☐	☐
f. brake pedal, accelerator pedal, and floormats	☐	☐	☐
6. Mirrors properly adjusted?	☐	☐	☐
7. Additional safety devices:			
a. center-mounted brake light	☐	☐	☐
b. backup warning buzzer	☐	☐	☐
c. emergency kit	☐	☐	☐

	Yes	No	n/a
8. Vision and corrective lenses adequate for driving, including night driving?	☐	☐	☐
9. Hearing adequate?	☐	☐	☐
10. Senior safe driver course completed within prior 24 months?	☐	☐	☐
11. Automobile club membership?	☐	☐	☐

PART II—CHECKPOINTS FOR REDUCED USE OF CAR

	Yes	No	n/a
1. Driver comfort—do physical limitations make driving uncomfortable or unsafe?	☐	☐	☐
2. Driver stress—does the driver become particularly anxious or confused while driving?	☐	☐	☐
3. Driver performance—any recent moving violations or accidents?	☐	☐	☐
4. Car costs—do total automobile expenses (insurance, license, upkeep, gas, parking) exceed costs of other alternatives?	☐	☐	☐
5. Possible driving modifications:			
a. no night driving	☐	☐	☐
b. no rush hour driving	☐	☐	☐
c. no freeway driving	☐	☐	☐
d. no driving in snow or dangerous conditions	☐	☐	☐

e. combined use of car and bus
   (park-and-ride)   ☐   ☐   ☐

f. ride sharing   ☐   ☐   ☐

6. Alternatives to continued driving:

a. senior transit pass   ☐   ☐   ☐

b. community vans   ☐   ☐   ☐

c. taxi coupons   ☐   ☐   ☐

d. home delivered products—
   groceries, prescriptions, etc. ☐   ☐   ☐

e. increased use of telephone   ☐   ☐   ☐

f. use of chore service workers
   for errands   ☐   ☐   ☐

Form 9.1
Senior Travel Planner

This form can be used to help plan and coordinate senior travel arrangements.

Part I — My (our) goals

✔ What do I (we) hope to get out of this trip:

_____

_____

_____

_____

Part II — When, and where to

✔ Preferred departure date:_____

✔ Preferred return date:_____

✔ Major destinations:_____

_____

_____

✔ Preliminary itinerary:_____

_____

_____

_____

_____

_____

_____

Part III — How much will it cost?

✔ Transportation expense,
including air, train, bus,
boat, or other $ _____

✔ Lodging costs at all
destinations $ _____

✔ Local travel, including bus,
taxi, rental car, hotel
transfers $ _____

✔ Meals including tips and
beverages $ _____

✔ Admissions/tickets $ _____

✔ Local tours/sightseeing $ _____

✔ Entertainment/activities,
including nightlife, green
fees, side trips $ _____

✔ Gifts $ _____

✔ Spending money $ _____

✔ Other incidentals $ _____

✔ **Total** $ _____

Part IV — Before I (we) leave

_____ Travel discounts checked out

_____ Special assistance arranged (if needed)

 _____ boarding assistance

 _____ special meals

 _____ wheelchair access

 _____ other personal or medical needs

_____ Adequate supply of
medications available

_____ Medical history and record of
current medications requirements
available.

_____ List of emergency contacts to carry

_____ Itinerary left with a close family
member or friend

_____ Personal identification

 _____ passport

 _____ driver's license

 _____ Medicare number

 _____ other health insurer name
and policy number

Part V—Other notes:

_____
_____
_____
_____
_____
_____
_____
_____
_____
_____
_____
_____
_____
_____
_____
_____
_____
_____
_____
_____
_____
_____
_____
_____
_____
_____
_____
_____
_____
_____
_____
_____

Form 14.1
Checklist for Selecting and Evaluating a Home Health Care Provider

Part I of this form may be used to organize information gathered in selecting a home health agency or independent home health professional. Part II is a checklist of factors to use in evaluating the quality of health care services provided in the home. Part III is for your additional notes.

PART I—QUESTIONS TO ASK BEFORE SELECTING A HOME HEALTH PROVIDER

Agency Name:

1. *License and accreditation.* Is the agency licensed and accredited? Is the professional currently licensed as a registered nurse or other health care specialist?

2. *Mix of skills and services.* Will the professional or agency be able to provide the particular skills and services your parent needs?

3. *Emergency coverage.* Is the provider able to offer 24-hour coverage? If not, what arrangements can be made for emergency situations?

   _____ _____

4. *Recommendations.* Is the agency or professional recommended by your parent's doctor or other health care provider?

   _____ _____

5. *Fees.* How will services be billed? If the agency has a base or standard charge, what is included in that charge, and what will be the costs of extra services?

   _____ _____

6. *Family involvement.* What is the agency's or professional's attitude toward involving family members in the caregiving team?

   _____ _____

7. *Supervision.* Will a supervisor from the agency visit your parent's home and discuss with your parent and family members any concerns that arise?

   _____ _____

8. *Questions and complaints.* What is the agency's approach to answering questions and resolving complaints?

   _____ _____

PART II—PERFORMANCE EVALUATION CRITERIA

Agency name:

_____ _____

1. *Demeanor.* Are all services provided in a punctual and courteous way?

   _____ _____

2. *Clarity.* Are care instructions given clearly both orally and in writing?

   _____ _____

3. *Teamwork.* Does the agency or professional make family members feel included in the caregiving team?

   _____ _____

4. *Progress notes.* Does the provider give the physician, your parent, and appropriate family members regular progress reports?

   _____ _____

5. *Quality assurance.* Has the agency reviewed its own performance? Has a supervisor contacted the patient or visited the home?

   _____ _____

6. *Professionalism.* Does the agency or professional respect your parent's privacy and confidentiality? Are your parents and family treated with respect?

   _____ _____

PART III—OTHER NOTES

Form 15.1
Nursing Home Selection Checklist

This form will help you compare important characteristics of two or more nursing homes. This information is organized into four parts: Part I, factors to consider before visiting a facility; Part II, conditions to observe during a facility visit; Part III, questions to ask before making a final selection; and Part IV, your other notes.

PART I—GENERAL CONSIDERATIONS BEFORE VISITING A FACILITY

Facility Name:

Reputation

Is the facility well regarded by your parent's physician or other health care professional?

Location

Does your parent's doctor regularly see patients at the facility?

Is the facility convenient for visits by family and friends?

PART II—CONDITIONS TO LOOK FOR DURING A VISIT

First Impressions

Does the facility appear and smell clean and well maintained? _____ _____

Do the residents appear comfortable and well cared for? _____ _____

Are residents neatly and appropriately dressed? Do they have clean hands, trimmed fingernails, and neatly fixed hair? Are men clean-shaven? _____ _____

Building and Grounds

Are the building and grounds well maintained? _____ _____

Are there walkways or a courtyard for outdoor visits in good weather? _____ _____

Are there safety rails in the hallways? _____ _____

Resident Rooms

Are the residents' rooms clean and comfortable, with adequate lighting, decor, and furniture? _____ _____

Are bathrooms and bathing rooms conveniently located and equipped with handrails and grab bars? _____ _____

How many persons share a room? Are privacy curtains used? _____ _____

Dining Room

Are menus posted? Do they seem varied and appealing? _____ _____

Are the kitchen and dining room areas clean and well maintained? _____ _____

Does there seem to be enough time for residents to take their meals without being rushed? _____ _____

How does the food taste? It is important to eat a meal there when checking out a facility. _____ _____

Social Programs

Is there a listing of upcoming events in the facility? Does it include activities that will interest your parent? _____ _____

Are residents in their rooms and in hallways, or are they involved in various activities? _____ _____

Does the facility try to keep residents informed on the world around? Are there calendars, posters, large print books available? _____ _____

Employee Attitudes and Appearance

Do the staff seem personally involved in the care and well-being of residents? Do they know residents by name? Are they friendly and courteous? Clean and well groomed?

    _____ _____

PART III—QUESTIONS TO ASK

Staffing and Services

How many registered and licensed practical nurses are on duty during each shift? What is the staff-to-resident ratio?

    _____ _____

Does the facility offer occupational therapy, physical therapy, social services, chaplaincy, speech therapy, dental care?

    _____ _____

Is there a social worker on staff?

    _____ _____

Financial

Which services are covered in the monthly base rate? What charges are made for other services?

    _____ _____

Are you or other family members being asked to guarantee payment?

Does the facility have Medicare and Medicaid contracts?

Is the facility willing to hold a patient's bed during a period of hospitalization?

Medical Care

How does the facility meet residents' medical care needs?

May residents retain their own doctor, or is there a "house physician?"

Family Involvement

How does the facility relate to families? Are families involved in team conferences?

Is there a support group a family member may join if desired?

Special Needs and Preferences

What is the facility's policy concerning:

Television in shared rooms?

Telephone service in patient rooms?

Smoking/no smoking?

Inspection Results

Is the facility's latest state
survey available for
inspection? Have problems
cited there been corrected?   _____ _____

Contractual Arrangements

What agreements will a new
patient and patient family be
asked to sign on admission?   _____ _____

PART IV—OTHER NOTES

_____

_____

_____

_____

_____

_____

_____

_____

_____

_____

_____

_____

_____

_____

_____

_____

_____

Form 17.1
List of Current Medications

PRESCRIPTION MEDICATIONS I AM TAKING REGULARLY OR AS NEEDED

Name of Medicine and Dose	Prescribing Physician, if any	Date Usage Began

OVER-THE-COUNTER MEDICATIONS I AM TAKING REGULARLY OR AS NEEDED

Name of Medicine and Dose	Prescribing Physician, if any	Date Usage Began

Form 17.2
Medication Check-off List

Week of: _____

Medication	Amount	Time	✔ each day a dose is taken						
			Sun	Mon	Tues	Wed	Thur	Fri	Sat
Morning									
Noon/Afternoon									

Form 17.2, continued

Week of: _____

Medication	Amount	Time	✔ each day a dose is taken						
			Sun	Mon	Tues	Wed	Thur	Fri	Sat
Evening/Dinnertime									
Bedtime/Night									

Form 19.1
Living Will

This is an example of a "Living Will," an expression of preferences and statement of instruction to physicians concerning the withholding and withdrawing of life sustaining procedures in the event of a terminal illness. *State laws vary on this subject; ask your health care provider, lawyer, or Senior Information and Referral concerning state requirements as they apply to you.* In most states, the maker of a Living Will may tailor its provisions according to his or her personal wishes, as long as those wishes are within the overall scope and intent of the law.

Directive to Physicians

I, _____ , being of sound mind, wilfully and voluntarily make known my desire that my life shall not be artificially prolonged under the circumstances set forth below, and do hereby declare that:

a. If at any time I should have an incurable injury, disease, or illness certified to be in a terminal condition by two physicians, and where the application of life-sustaining procedures would serve only to artificially prolong the moment of my death and where my physician determines that my death is imminent whether or not life-sustaining procedures are utilized, I direct that such procedures be withheld or withdrawn, and that I be permitted to die naturally.

b. In the absence of my ability to give directions regarding the use of such life-sustaining procedures, it is my intention that this directive shall be honored by my family and physician(s) as the final expression of my legal right to refuse medical or surgical treatment, and I accept the consequences from such refusal.

c. If I have been diagnosed as pregnant and that diagnosis is known to my physician, this directive shall have no force or effect during the course of my pregnancy.

d. I understand the full import of this directive, and I am emotionally and mentally competent to make this directive.

_____

Signature   Date

The person who signed this directive did so in my presence. I am personally acquainted with this person and believe him or her to be of sound mind. I am not related by blood or marriage to the person. I am not now entitled to receive any portion of his or her estate, either by will or by operation of law, nor do I have any claim against the person which could be asserted against the estate upon his or her decease. I am not the person's attending physician, nor am I an employee of that physician or of a health facility in which the person is a patient or resident.

_____   _____
Witness   Witness

_____   _____
Address   Address

Source: Revised Code of Washington, Section 70.122.030.

Form 22.1
Net Worth Statement

ASSETS	Cost (if known)	Estimated Value
Cash *Checking & savings accounts*	$	$
Short-term investments *Treasury Bills, certificates of deposit, money market funds*		
Stocks, bonds, and other securities		
Cash value of life insurance		
House		
Other real estate		
Retirement funds *IRAs, Keoghs, vested plans*		
Cars, boats, furnishings, etc.		
Other assests: *Art, jewelry, antiques, partnerships, etc.*		
Total Assets	$	$

LIABILITIES

Amount

Mortgages on personal residence $ _____

Mortgages on real estate investments   _____

Borrowings on life insurance   _____

Installment debts   _____

Personal loans   _____

Other obligations:

_____   _____

_____   _____

_____   _____

Total Liabilities $ _____

Net Worth
Total Estimated Value of Assets minus Total Liabilities $ _____

Form 22.2
Household Budget

INCOME	Annual Amount	
	in 19__	in 19__
Salary or wages	$	$
Social Security		
Retirement benefits:		
Pension payments		
IRA		
Keogh		
Profit sharing plans		
Deferred compensation plan		
Investment income:		
Interest and dividends—taxable		
Interest—non-taxable		
Net rental income:		
Other cash sources:		
Total Income	$	$

EXPENSES

Annual Amount
in 19___   in 19___

Housing:

    Rent or mortgage $ _____ $ _____

    Insurance

    Maintenance

    Taxes

Utilities
Electric, gas, water, etc.

Food

Clothing

Transportation
Gas, maintenance, payments, bus fare

Entertainment and recreation

Personal care

Medical and dental

Taxes

Other insurance

Gifts and contributions

Other costs:

_____

_____

Total Expenses $ _____ $ _____

Inflation adjustment factor
Select factor from Table A

Adjusted total expenses
*Total Expenses multiplied by inflation
adjustment factor* $ _____ $ _____

Net Income
Total Income minus Total Expenses $ _____ $ _____

Table A
INFLATION ADJUSTMENT FACTORS

Number of Years in the Future	Inflation Rate	
	4%	8%
1	1.04	1.08
2	1.08	1.17
3	1.12	1.26
4	1.17	1.36
5	1.27	1.47
6	1.27	1.59
7	1.32	1.71
8	1.37	1.85
9	1.42	2.00
10	1.48	2.16

Table B
LIFE EXPECTANCY TABLE*

Current Age	Expected Life	
	Male	Female
66	13.39	16.57
68	12.14	15.10
70	10.96	13.67
72	9.84	12.28
74	8.79	10.95
76	7.84	9.71
78	6.97	8.55
80	6.18	7.48
82	5.44	6.49
84	4.77	5.59
86	4.18	4.80

*Commissioners 1980 Standard Ordinary Table (1970-1975)

Form 23.1
Medical Bill Payment Record

This form should be used to keep track of medical bills and the amounts Medicare and private insurance will pay against them.

Name of provider	Date of service	Amount of bill	Medicare approved amount	Amount paid by medicare	Amount paid by supplemental insurance	Balance due	Date paid and check number

Form 23.1, continued

Name of provider	Date of service	Amount of bill	Medicare approved amount	Amount paid by medicare	Amount paid by supplemental insurance	Balance due	Date paid and check number

Form 25.1
Checklist for Purchasing Private Insurance

This form covers important considerations in purchasing and evaluating private insurance coverage. Part I lists factors to review before cancelling any existing coverage; Part II lists questions to ask in selecting Medicare supplement insurance coverage; Part III lists factors in choosing long-term care coverage.

PART I—BEFORE CANCELLING ANY EXISTING INSURANCE COVERAGE

1. Are there any major drawbacks to giving up existing coverage?

   - New limits for pre-existing conditions?

   - Start over with new deductible for this year?

   - Limits on renewability?

   - Other?

2. How does the existing coverage compare with the proposed new coverage in cost and scope of benefits? (Consider both short and long-terms!)

PART II—COMPARING MEDICARE SUPPLEMENT COVERAGE

	Policy #1	Policy #2
Company:		
Agent:		
Policy name:		

	Policy #1	Policy #2
	Yes No	Yes No

1. Will the policy pay some or all of the annual Medicare Part A deductible for hospitalization? How much?

   Policy #1: Yes ☐ No ☐ Policy #2: Yes ☐ No ☐

   _____ _____

2. Medicare limits lifetime psychiatric hospital care to 190 days. Does this policy provide benefits for psychiatric hospitalization? How much?

   Policy #1: Yes ☐ No ☐ Policy #2: Yes ☐ No ☐

   _____ _____

3. Will this policy pay some or all of the co-payment for the first eight days per year of the care in a Medicare certified skilled nursing facility?

   Policy #1: Yes ☐ No ☐ Policy #2: Yes ☐ No ☐

   _____ _____

4. Does this policy cover charges in excess of the Medicare approved charge for nursing homes, physicians, and other health care providers?

   Policy #1: Yes ☐ No ☐ Policy #2: Yes ☐ No ☐

   _____ _____

5. Will this policy cover care in a skilled nursing facility beyond the 100 day Medicare limit? How extensive?

   Policy #1: Yes ☐ No ☐ Policy #2: Yes ☐ No ☐

   _____ _____

6. For Medicare Part B services, will this policy pay the 20% co-payment? Are there any limitations?

   Policy #1: Yes ☐ No ☐ Policy #2: Yes ☐ No ☐

   _____ _____

7. Medicare will only cover $400 per year of out patient physical therapy. Does this policy extend that coverage?

   Policy #1: Yes ☐ No ☐ Policy #2: Yes ☐ No ☐

   _____ _____

PART III—CHOOSING LONG-TERM CARE COVERAGE

	Policy #1	Policy #2
Company:	_____	_____
Agent:	_____	_____
Policy name:	_____	_____

	Policy #1	Policy #2

1. Scope of coverage?

   - Skilled nursing facility _____ _____

   - Intermediate care nursing care facility _____ _____

   - Custodial care facility _____ _____

   - Home care services _____ _____

   - Case management services _____ _____

   - Other care services _____ _____

2. What are the limits of coverage?

   - Maximum life-time benefit for nursing home. _____ _____

   - Maximum life-time benefit for home health care services. _____ _____

   - Maximum length of stay in a nursing home. _____ _____

   - Maximum duration of home care service. _____ _____

   - Waiting period for pre-existing conditions. _____ _____

   - Coverage of Alzheimer's Disease. _____ _____

	Policy #1	Policy #2
• Waiting period before benefits start.	_____	_____
3. Does the policy allow purchase of additional coverage to offset inflation?	_____	_____
4. What conditions must be met before benefits begin?	_____	_____
• Physician certification of need.	_____	_____
• Prior hospitalization.	_____	_____
• Other: _____	_____	_____
5. Is the policy subject to cancellation?	_____	_____
If so, for what reasons?	_____	_____
6. How much does this coverage cost?		
• Monthly	_____	_____
• Quarterly	_____	_____
• Semi-annually	_____	_____
• Annually	_____	_____

Other notes: _____

_____

_____

_____

_____

_____

Form 27.1
Questions to Ask a Hospice Program

This form contains questions to ask in selecting a hospice care provider.

PART I—LICENSES AND AFFILIATIONS

Program:

1. Some states license hospice agencies. Is this agency fully licensed?

2. Does this agency belong to the National Hospice Organization?

PART II—PAYMENT

3. Is this agency approved to accept the Medicare Hospice Benefit?

4. If not accepting the Medicare Hospice Benefit, for what services will your parent be charged? On what basis are charges made?

5. Many hospice services are covered by Medicare or other insurance. What are the covered services? What help can the agency offer in processing claims?

6. Does the agency provide care to those who are uninsured or unable to pay? On what basis? _____ _____

PART III—SERVICES OFFERED

7. Does this agency offer 24-hour, seven day a week nursing coverage? If not, what coverage arrangements are available? _____ _____

8. Will the same care providers generally stay with the patient and family throughout the course of care? _____ _____

9. Does this agency provide hospital in-patient care as well as home care services? If not, what transfer arrangements will be made if needed? _____ _____

10. What family support services does this agency provide?

11. Does this agency provide respite care for primary caregivers when necessary? If not, is the agency able to help the family arrange for respite care from another source? _____ _____

Other notes: _____

_____

_____

_____

Form 28.1
Planning a Funeral
or Memorial Service

This form will help in planning a funeral or memorial service.

TYPE OF SERVICE PREFERRED

- ☐ Funeral—open casket
- ☐ Funeral—closed casket
- ☐ Memorial service
- ☐ Other: _____

- ☐ Religious
- ☐ Non religious
- ☐ Family only
- ☐ Open

LOGISTICAL ARRANGEMENTS

Location of service: _____

Time of service: _____

Person(s) officiating: _____

Do you wish to hold visiting hours before the service?

  When? _____ Where? _____

Do you wish to have a reception after the service? _____
  When? _____ Where? _____

CONTENT OF SERVICE

☐ Organ or other instrumental music
☐ Soloist
☐ Hymns or songs for congregational singing

Musical selections: _____

_____

_____

_____

Scripture readings/other readings: _____

_____

Eulogies/personal statements or recollections: _____

_____

Other important elements: _____

_____

PARTICIPANTS

Person(s) officiating: _____

_____

Musicians: _____

_____

Speaker(s): _____

_____

Pallbearers/honorary pallbearers: _____

_____

Ushers: _____

_____

Other notes: _____

_____

_____

_____

Index

Contributors

Mary Liz Chaffee

Mary Liz Chaffee, a registered nurse who received her Bachelor of Science in Nursing from the University of Washington, has specialized in eldercare for over 17 years. She works with Second Family, a consultation service in Seattle, Washington, providing families and older adults with assessment of needs, advice on options, care planning, recommendations for housing and other services, and on-going care monitoring of older adults.

Dixie Cole

Dixie Cole is an administrator and service planner with her Bachelor of Science in Psychology and Masters of Public Health in Health Services Administration and Planning. For six years she was Director of Community Services, Visiting Nurse Services, Seattle, Washington, and later was Director of Sacred Heart Home Health, Eugene, Oregon. For five years she was Special Assistant for Policy Development, U.S. Public Health Service.

Beverly J. Crump

Beverly Crump earned her Masters in Education and a Certificate of Study in Aging from the Institute on Aging at the University of Washington. She has 15 years experience in the field of aging, with special emphasis on teaching caregiving skills to the families of older adults. She has prepared several manuals on caregiving, including a training manual for the Family Support Project, University of Washington.

Karan Dawson

Karan Dawson is a registered pharmacist and lecturer, Department of Pharmacy Practice, School of Pharmacy, University of Washington. She is affiliated with The Northwest Geriatric Education Center and is a frequent speaker and writer on the subject of medications and the elderly.

Barbara A. Isenhour

Barbara Isenhour, a staff attorney with Evergreen Legal Services for over 17 years, received her law degree from the University of Washington. She specializes in senior law and has written and spoken extensively on Medicaid and Medicare.

Dennis E. Kenny

Dennis Kenny established CAREsource Program Development, Inc., in 1989 after practicing law for 16 years in both the public and private sectors. As a lawyer, he specialized in health care, focusing on ethical, physician/patient, and provider reimbursement issues. At CAREsource, he has been responsible for design and development of various health care and aging-related publications, videotapes, and software products.

Diane Dray Kenny

Diane Kenny is Vice President, CAREsource Program Development, Inc., where she has managed the design, completion, and distribution of numerous aging resource guides and related publications. She received her law degree from the University of Washington and practiced for 13 years in both public and private sectors, with emphasis on hospital law.

Joan R. Lewis

Joan Lewis, who earned her degree in counseling from the State University of New York, is a Senior Information Program Representative for the Washington State Insurance Commisioner's Office. She has directed a variety of human services programs and now concentrates on financial services for older adults and their families.

Julie Anderson Miller

Julie Miller, a counselor-case manager, Case Management Program, Seattle/King County Division on Aging, earned her Masters of Social Work at the University of Southern California. She is responsible for developing care plans and coordinating services for elderly individuals with complex problems such as chronic illness, substance abuse, homelessness, mental illness, and vulnerability due to abuse or exploitation. For two years she was a geriatric mental health specialist, providing mental health services to older adults.

Ellen A. Minotti

Ellen Minotti is a program analyst, King County Mental Health Program, with her Masters of Social Work from the University of Washington. For three years she was an administrative manager, Mental Health and Social Services Division, Community Home Health Care, Seattle, Washington, where she contributed to a program to serve isolated elderly residents of public housing and connect them to needed services in the community.

Kathleen Hughes Moore

Kathleen Moore received her law degree from Northwestern Law School, Lewis and Clark College. In her law practice, she concentrates on representation of older adults and their families, especially in connection with guardianships.

Elizabeth N. Oettinger

Elizabeth Oettinger is an Associate Minister at Plymouth Congregational Church in Seattle, Washington, with her Master of Divinity from Yale University Divinity School. In eleven years as an ordained minister, her pastoral work has included extensive bereavement and crisis counseling for individuals and families. Before becoming a minister, she was a member of the Board of Editors, *American Heritage* Magazine. She currently serves as a member of the Community Advisory Board, Hospice of Seattle.

Betty L. Pesznecker

Betty Pesznecker is an Associate Professor in the Community Health Care Systems Department, School of Nursing, University of Washington. She was Co-Principal Investigator on the Elderly Homecare Project funded by the Fred Meyer Charitable Trust from 1986 through 1989. A major focus of this grant was to facilitate self-care of elderly adults living at home.

Marty Richards

Marty Richards is a consultant on aging, with her Masters of Social Work from the University of Washington. She regularly advises nursing homes and provides counseling services to older adults and their families. She has published and taught extensively on aging issues, with emphasis on long-term care facilities and the social aspects of aging.

William C. Severson

William Severson is a lawyer with both personal and professional experience in dealing with the legal and financial issues involved in helping aging parents. He received his law degree from the University of Washington.

Thomas J. Tubbesing, M.D.

Thomas Tubbesing, M.D., is a graduate of the University of Iowa Medical School. He completed his ophthamology residency at Washington University, St. Louis, and is now a member of the medical staff of Group Health Cooperative of Puget Sound, Seattle.